Journey
Into the
MIRACULOUS

Experiencing the Touch of the Supernatural God

TODD BENTLEY

DESTINY IMAGE® PUBLISHERS, INC.
P.O. Box 310, Shippensburg, PA 17257-0310

"Speaking to the Purposes of God for this Generation and for the Generations to Come."

This book and all other Destiny Image, Revival Press, Mercy Place, Fresh Bread, Destiny Image Fiction, and Treasure House books are available at Christian bookstores and distributors worldwide.

For a U.S. bookstore nearest you, call **1-800-722-6774**.
For more information on foreign distributors, call **717-532-3040**.
Or reach us on the Internet: **www.destinyimage.com.**

ISBN 10: 0-7684-2606-5
ISBN 13: 978-0-7684-2606-9

For Worldwide Distribution, Printed in the U.S.A.

2 3 4 5 6 7 8 9 10 11 / 09 08

DEDICATION

I dedicate this book to my wife, Shonnah, and to my three wonderful children—Lauralee, Esther, and Elijah—who lovingly sacrifice me to the world. This is their story too. My family helps Jesus to shine through me.

ACKNOWLEDGMENTS

I want to thank the following people for sowing into my life:

- The Holy Spirit for incredible seasons of visitation.

- My mom and dad—what a joy that God has turned the heart of the father to the heart of his son. Henry and Erica Schmidt—you were my first real pastors. You looked beyond my biker exterior. Cliff Robertson, who helped lay Fresh Fire's foundation. Thanks for your love too, bro. My prophetic mentors—Bobby Connor, Patricia King, Bob Jones, Wesley and Stacey Campbell, and Paul Keith Davis. How could I avoid success with input from such godly, anointed friends?

- Thank goodness for Bonnie Jaggard, the intercessors, and their prayer. They are the true secret of my success. My hardworking, awesome office staff who keep things functioning when I'm on the road. The many anointed speakers I've had the privilege to work with. The Body of Christ, God's wonderful people.

- To the people who contributed reports or photos for this book: Greg Babish, Daniel Brennan, Greg Dennison, Ken Greter, Brian Hill, Dave Mercer, Cliff Pash, BB Rail, Ivan Roman, Steve Schultz, Jeff Vosgien, and Claudia Wintoch.

- Finally, to the editors of the premier edition of this book, Jackie Macgirvin, Kevin Paterson for the hours of editing and proofreading, and Darcia Bentley who took care of all of the many publishing details. Also, to my writer, Shae Cooke for her edit of this new edition.

ENDORSEMENTS

The Holy Spirit spoke to me a few years ago and said He was raising up a new, young champion named Todd. God would have who He would have—a raw young man with fresh faith, anointing, power, fire and zeal—the full-blown package. It's there. It's there.

—James W. Goll
Leading prophetic voice, author,
founder of Ministry to the Nations
Franklin, Tennessee

I've known Todd for a number of years and he is the most radical, faith-filled young man I've known in the whole wide world. He's just out there going for it. He's true blue to the Word, the Spirit of God, and to the Body of Christ. I'm excited about Todd and Fresh Fire and about global outreach to mobilize the Body of Christ. I encourage you to read this book, stand with this ministry, and be partners in the harvest.

—Patricia King
Extreme Prophetic Ministries, Cofounder of the War Room,
and Christian Services Association
Kelowna, B.C., Canada

Todd is the real deal. This book will inspire and build your faith to do the work of the ministry.

—Dr. Che Ahn
Senior Pastor, Harvest Rock Church
Pasadena, California
Author of *Into the Fire*

Todd Bentley's life story will inspire faith and courage. What an amazing story of God's mercy and power. Read it and then give it to a friend. Todd has ministered in several of our conferences in Kansas City. I have seen the Holy Spirit move powerfully through him as we have witnessed a number of dramatic healings. The Lord has graciously released an unusual anointing for healing in his ministry. I enjoy Todd and support his ministry. I know you will be blessed by his story and ministry.

—Mike Bickle
Best-selling author, Director of the
International House of Prayer
Kansas City, Missouri

I love Todd Bentley's ministry and everything about it. Rarely have I seen such a gift of faith in operation almost all the time. His faith is so contagious. When you're under Todd's ministry, you feel like you can go anywhere and do anything. No problem or obstacle is too big. He's so inclusive. He wants everyone to go with him all the time. To me, that's how Jesus would be. I encourage you to read this book, be inspired, laugh, cry, and then go out and do something about it!

Cofounder of New Life Church,
Praying the Bible International,
and Revival Now Ministries
Kelowna, B.C., Canada

There are few people who believe you can live in the supernatural on a daily level. We have this earthly life—there are bills to pay, people to contend with, and thorns in the flesh. The thing I love about Todd is that he talks about living in the supernatural on a daily basis. That's what I love and live for too—the supernatural every day—and I think God has clearly identified that in Todd. He has the revelation, that, since we are great in God's eyes already, we don't need to prove it to man…just walk simply in the revelation of the greater One in us, as so few have ever done. Then let's go and preach the Gospel.

—Kevin Prosch
Worship leader, Christian recording artist
Amarillo, Texas

It has been my delight to serve on the board of Todd Bentley's ministry advisors. I've been able to watch this young man from the early days of his ministry. God has placed an awesome anointing upon Todd's life. I believe he is a forerunner of a new breed that God is now raising up—part of a breed of believers with great grace and anointing. Your faith will be expanded as you read about how God is moving through this outstanding young man.

—Bobby Connor
Founder of Demonstration of God's Power Ministries
Moravian Falls, North Carolina

I love this book. *Journey Into the Miraculous* is a moving story about the extravagant grace of God. While Todd Bentley is a wonderful man with an unusual gift, this book is more than a story about his life. It's a prophetic declaration of God's intent for an entire generation. It invites those who are hungry and desperate for God to abandon themselves for the treasure of His presence. This book will ignite a holy passion for a holy God!

—*Bill Johnson*
Author, *When Heaven Invades Earth*
Senior Pastor, Bethel Church
Redding, California

Todd Bentley is a prophetic signpost of how, in this end time hour, God is supernaturally raising up men and women who will literally change the course of history. Todd is not only a sovereign vessel, but he lives in a sovereign time. The supernatural grace and the amazing acceleration that marks his life are not only available to him, but also to you—if only you will grab hold of all that God desires to give you! This book is a must—it is an insider's guide into how God can give us beauty for ashes, take the "Saul" in us and make us into a Paul, and defy all logic through His transforming love. Todd pulls back the curtains and lets us peer into the personal molding and making of one who lives with eternity set in his heart. His story disproves old paradigms, obliterates old wineskins, and is nothing less than one miracle after another. How amazing God's grace is in the life of this modern day hero of faith. Absolutely nothing is impossible when we ask for 100% of God and give Him nothing less than 100% in return.

—*Jill Austin*
Author, *Master Potter*
Founder, Master Potter Ministries
Kansas City, Missouri

Todd Bentley is a genuine Ephesians 4 gift to the Church and the nations. He carries a powerful anointing of healing and miracles that's touching the globe. Todd shares this gift in a unique manner with compassion and humor. I know Todd personally. His own story is a powerful testimony of the awesome transforming power of the risen Christ. This book is for all those hungry to see more of God's power in their lives. Get this book; digest it. You will be refreshed and inspired.

—*Dr. Mahesh Chavda*
Evangelist, author, founder of the Watch of the Lord
and All Nation's Church
Ft. Mill, South Carolina

TABLE OF CONTENTS

FOREWORD

We need to realize that God is moving on the earth today like never before. More people have been saved in the last decade of the second millennium than at any other time in history. In just ten years, over one-third of all conversions since the days of Jesus have taken place. At this present rate of salvation, soon there will be more Christians on plant earth than there are in heaven! But we need workers for the harvest field. So you must read Todd Bentley's book, not as theory or as an entertaining story about one person, but read it as a manual that will teach you how you also can do what Todd is doing.

In the late 1980s, we experienced a mini-revival that was to change us forever. God moved unexpectedly and within months, scores of conservative Evangelicals and Baptists were propelled by the word of the Lord to prayer, the poor, and the next generation. God prophesied to us over and over again about *"The*

Children." He told us about a coming generation that would do greater signs and wonders than anything we had ever seen. During the same time period that God was speaking to us at our church, He was also revealing the coming revival to many others in different locations. Ironically, at the very time we were receiving promises regarding "the children," Todd Bentley was only 12 years old and well on his way to becoming a criminal, an alcoholic, and a drug addict. In this book, you will read about what the blood of Christ can do in a life like that. We believe that Todd is a "first fruits" of what God has been planning for decades, and that an unprecedented wave of the power of God is about to hit the Church. We believe that Todd is a prototype of young revivalists—male and female who are being called out of the depths of darkness to move in a power that hitherto we had only hoped to see.

However, more than anything, Todd's story is a story about God. It is a story of the faith of God, who chooses a wild, broken, young man—one whom no one would have believed in—to become a vessel of healing for the multitudes. It is the story of the mercy of God that transcends all social, economic, racial, and religious barriers, and heals even the most incurable of diseases. It is the story of an invisible God who makes Himself visible through miraculous signs and wonders.

But it is also a story about a man co-laboring together with God. In fact, Todd's life provides us with a graphic example of what happens when a man pushes in for the revival experience that many in history have received. His testimony vividly shows the cooperation between God and man. Where would Todd be if he hadn't exercised tenacious faith? Even with sovereign callings (see Ephesians 2:10), many people don't walk them out. All the just live by *faith* and Todd looked at what others had done in God and determined that, if God had done it for someone else, then God could do it for him.

From our close friendship with Todd, we have seen the uniqueness of how God touches a man. God literally imparted to him supernatural intelligence, extra dimensions of personality and business acumen. In other words, God equipped Todd to do the job He gave him to do. No one today could imagine Todd Bentley as an introvert, but that is what he used to be. He cooperated with God to receive what most people never receive. And now the world is a better place for it. I would that we had millions more like him—millions who activated *their* faith and touched the power of God.

What most people don't realize is that Todd also has a passion for the poor. He is preaching an apostolic Gospel, complete with signs, wonders, and care for the poor. As we near the end of the age and the billion-soul harvest, we know conclusively that it will not take place without reaching the poor of the earth—especially women and children. The masses of humanity that are being exploited throughout the earth will have to be reached with a holistic message that gives them salvation, counteracts the powers of darkness, and elevates their physical well-being through healing, mercy, social justice, and micro-enterprise. In effect, this powerful message will have to totally transform communities. Todd is a new breed of revivalist who carries this transforming message. We encourage you to read this book, be inspired, laugh, cry, and then go out and do something about it!

Read this story for two reasons. First, although Jesus said, "Blessed are those who have not seen and yet believed," this book will give you the benefit of "seeing and believing." Beyond a shadow of a doubt, you will increase in faith as you read about real miracle after real miracle. In addition, you will learn that what God has done through Todd Bentley, He is also doing through many others around Todd. This young revivalist freely gives away what God has given to him and, as a result, there is a multiplication of the anointing. When you see what is possible in God *today*, you will gain faith to pray for a whole generation of believers to do the greater works that Jesus said His followers would do. As you read, cry out that the wave of power that has begun will turn into a *tsunami* and turn the hearts of people in every nation back to God. Pray for Todd Bentley to continue to minister in, and multiply, the miraculous anointing that God has given him. And pray for yourself, that you too will see miracles in your own sphere of influence. Then God will receive even more of the glory He deserves.

Wesley and Stacey Campbell
Founders, New Life Church, Praying the Bible International,
and Revival Now Ministries in Kelowna, B.C., Canada
September 2003

CHAPTER 1

THE END-TIME
HEALING REVIVAL

I was born on January 10, 1976 and born again between Christmas 1993 and the first week of January 1994. Looking back it is amazing to me how much sin I packed into those first eighteen years of my life. Nevertheless, even more amazing is that God sovereignly plucked me from the kingdom of darkness and translated me into the Kingdom of His wonderful Son, and He did this while I was His enemy, "While we were yet sinners, Christ died for us" (Romans 5:8). Praise the Lord!

FORERUNNER OF FIRE

For 20 years, the prophets have foretold about a youthful generation that will rise up, do holy exploits, and usher in a healing revival. In 1973, the Lord showed Prophet Bob Jones this coming anointing that would fall on God's people. Bob told me that I was part of the "first fruits" wave of a billion people whom God would light on fire.

My life is a message, a prophetic signpost of what God wants to do with millions of others. I am a forerunner and one of many who will carry the healing anointing to the nations. God has led me to put this book together not just to tell about my personal journey into the miraculous, but also to help people understand what God is doing in our time, and encourage readers to take steps of faith in areas where they may have been holding back.

If not you—whom will God use? If not now, when? We have an awesome, powerful God, and we are living in amazing times. It's time to walk in the miraculous!

JOEL'S ARMY

For a few decades, Prophet Paul Cain[1] had recurring visions concerning what many saints believe to be the approaching end times. One particular last day's revelation, which has come to be known as the "Joel's Army Vision," apparently appeared to Paul more than a hundred times.[2] In the vision, sports stadiums all over the U.S. fill and thousands upon thousands of people are miraculously healed in Jesus' name. Multitudes come to the Lord, the entire nation burns with revival fires, and it seems as though people in every nation are turning to Christ. Reports come through major newscasts about revival, the signs, wonders, and miracles. In his vision, Paul sees people on the platform minister without stopping for food, drink, or a change of clothes for three days, because supernatural strength sustains them.[2]

Then, Paul had a vision of a giant billboard that pointed to the church and read, "Joel's Army in Training," which was a strategic training of people who already knew their calling, but who were being honed and refined in the use of their gifts and talents, trained to walk in obedience to Jesus Christ.[3] They'd learn patient endurance, how to demonstrate the power of God, and, having learned all, stand against the enemy. As Christian soldiers, they'd have the mind of Christ, and "partake of the heavenly calling, and be a new breed, God's dread champions." As Heaven's champions, these believers would be filled with such passion for Jesus and power of the Spirit, that the host of darkness would dread their impact.

Cain also said that in the midst of the Laodicean church age of lethargy and apathy, that God was preparing in hiddenness an army to pull down enemy strongholds, and go forth in the power of God and have pure and undefiled religion. He's going to do this with people who have stripped themselves and separated themselves from the world, the flesh, and the devil. They will realize the end time is here and that things are in a mess and things at the end time are different. Just as it required total sacrifice on the part of the disciples to begin this thing, it will require an equal commitment from us to complete the task in the end times. Joel's mighty army, as described in Joel chapter 2 is the army of God— not a wicked army (as some have thought).

> "They are the ones with 'feet of iron not mixed with clay', with the wisdom of God alone, not imitators of other men of God. Some of the superstars of the church will fall. The Lord will have an army of holy anointed vessels to usher in His Kingdom so that no one man can take credit for it. It will be to the glory of God alone."[4]

Here is what Paul Cain and other leaders have said about this time:

- "No prophet or apostle who ever lived, equaled the power of these individuals in this great army of the Lord in these last days. No one ever had it, not even Elijah or Peter or Paul. No-one else enjoyed the power that is going to rest on this great army."[5]

23

- "The Lord said this, 'This is where my people will rise up as an army and bring millions into the Kingdom of God.'"[6]

- "This army is unique," says Jack Deere. "When this army comes, it's large and mighty. It's so mighty that there has never been anything like it before. What's going to happen now will transcend what Paul did, what David did and what Moses did."

- According to Rick Joyner, "What is about to come upon the earth is not just a revival, or another awakening; it is a veritable revolution. The vision was given in order to begin to awaken those who are destined to radically change the course, and even the very definition, of Christianity. The dismantling of organizations and disbanding of some works will be a positive and exhilarating experience for the Lord's faithful servants...the Lord will raise up a great company of prophets, teachers, pastors and apostles that will be of the spirit of Phinehas...this 'ministry of Phinehas' will save congregations, and at times, even whole nations. Nations will tremble at the mention of their name...."[7]

- Paul Cain says, "I believe one day soon Joel's Army will be in training...until it graduates into the stadium...but a right understanding of the plan of God for this generation brings this tremendous inclusion.... God's offering to you, this present generation, a greater privilege than was ever offered any generation at any time from Adam clear down through the millennium."

- "God's raising up a new standard, a new banner, if you will, that's going to radically change the expression, the understanding of Christianity in our generation.... God has invited us to have a role in establishing a new order of Christianity... God is offering to this generation something He has never offered to any other generation...beware lest old-order brethren rob you and steal this hope from you."[8]

- Benny Hinn agrees: "The day is coming, I tell you this, I know it like I know my name, the day is coming when there will not be one sick saint in the Body of Christ. No one will be raptured out of a hospital bed. You're all gonna be healed before the rapture."[9] (Benny Hinn, *Praise the Lord*, August 8, 1996).

- "You better be ready, church," Benny Hinn says about a last day's revival. "They're going to walk up to you at K-Mart and Albertson's. They're going to walk up in the mall and say, 'Hey, I know you're a Christian. There's something funny about you. I'm not sure I understand it...I've seen something in you and I've got to have it right now. I don't know whether it's called God or Jesus, but I've got to have it right now.'" (Blaisdell Arena, Honolulu, January 21, 1999).

- As Paul Cain says, these days will be marked by miracles: "All the sick are gonna be healed, the dead are gonna be raised and nations are gonna turn to God in a day." (Bob Jones and Paul Cain, *Selections from the Kansas City Prophets*, audiotape from discernment newsletter).

- "In the near future we will not be looking back at the early church with envy because of the great exploits of those days, but all will be saying that He certainly did save the best wine for last. The most glorious times in all of history have not come upon us. You, who have dreamed of one day being able to talk with Peter, John and Paul, are going to be surprised to find that they have all been waiting to talk to you" (Rick Joyner, *The Harvest*, Morning Star Publishing, 9, 1990).

MARKS OF THE HEALING REVIVAL

This is what I believe will happen in this healing revival:

Last Days' Anointing of Power

I have seen a glimpse of this anointing. We think the manifestations of the Holy Spirit in the early Church (Book of Acts) were glorious, however Scripture reveals that the glory of the latter house will transcend the glory of the former (see Haggai 2:9). We're going out with a bigger bang than what we entered with.

Massive Healings

There will be a renewed focus on the message of repentance because sickness and disease started with sin. As a revival of repentance and righteousness sweeps through the Church, we will see a mighty healing revival. During times of repentance, healings will happen supernaturally without the laying on of hands.

Saint's Revival

God is going to do away with a clergy/layman mentality and raise up the Body of Christ to do the work of the ministry. It has always been God's plan that every believer becomes involved in the ministry of Jesus, for Jesus said most assuredly, that "He who believes in Me, the works that I do he will do also; and greater works than these he will do, because I go to My Father" (John 14:12).

Children's Ministry

We know that the Kingdom isn't in word only, but also in power. I have seen a great move of healings and miracles at the hands of children as young as eleven and twelve years old. Today, God is using children to grow limbs and work creative miracles as they speak words of faith. Increasingly, children are going to move in the power of the Kingdom, driving out spirits and healing the sick because the Kingdom truly is theirs. Jesus said, "'Let the little children come to Me, and do not forbid them; for of such is the kingdom of heaven" (Matt. 19:14).

THE WARRIOR KING RALLIES HIS TROOPS

Just prior to my launch into the ministry, the Holy Spirit took me into a vision—an interactive trance where my senses fully operated. I found myself on the face of a mountain I knew to be Mt. Zion. I felt the chill of the wind as it blew through my hair. In the distance, I saw a small stream that flowed from the base of the mountain to the desert. There were groups comprised of two or three men, each clad in shining, brilliant armour and mounted on white horses. They approached from four directions to follow the stream to the base of the mountain. I knew in my spirit that they were being called to a secret council of the Lord.

A fascinating aspect of the vision was that each individual thought he was the only one called, not able to see or aware of each other, and hidden from the enemy. There were, in fact, thousands of warriors traveling to the council.

As I climbed to the mountaintop, I encountered Jesus as King of Kings and Lord of Lords. His face was stern and set as chiseled stone, His grizzly beard and His hair, were silver-white, as wool, and He had eyes of fire.

Upon His breastplate was the imprint of a golden eagle. He was so muscular, that the breastplate took on the ripples of His mighty chest! His biceps were enormous, the size of my head, and He had massive forearms and huge hands. There was Jesus, the mighty warrior God! He towered over me three to four times my height, so tall, He would have to bend down to communicate with me. Jesus' sword and shield lay at His side, and without a single word actually spoken, I suddenly received the following revelation:

"This is the council of the Lord. I have called you as one of many to be part of a last days' army and a last days' generation. My trumpet call has gone forth. There will be men and women who will be driving to work one day and the next day I will call them into the harvest."

All around the mountain, a canopy of dark clouds spewed thunder and lightning. I recalled how God would come down and visit Moses in the stormy tempest (see Exod. 19:16-25). I saw men and women resting and refreshing themselves around campfires. They anointed their shields and swords for battle. The Lord said,

"I have a hidden, secret army around the earth that I will enlist and uncover at My time. They are hidden away in the secret prayer closets—a generation of nameless, faceless nobodies. In My time, even in a day, I will uncover a new breed of apostles, pastors, prophets, and teachers; a new breed of ministry. You are one of many first fruits of an entire army that I am equipping in these days."

THE LAST DAYS' ELIJAH ANOINTING

I believe that the end-time anointing on the last days' Church is the Elijah anointing. Scripture tells us that John the Baptist walked in it.

He will also go before Him in the spirit and power of Elijah, 'to turn the hearts of the fathers to the children,' and the disobedient to the wisdom of the just, to make ready a people prepared for the Lord (Luke 1:17).

The Bible promises through the prophet Malachi (see Mal. 4:5) that God would send Elijah the prophet before the coming of the great and dreadful day of the Lord. "And he will turn the hearts of the fathers to the children, and the hearts of the children to their fathers, lest I come and strike the earth with a curse" (Mal. 4:6).

The Elijah anointing turns the hearts of children and nations to God as it did when the nation of Israel turned back to God in First Kings 18. Elijah called down fire from heaven to defeat the 450 prophets of Baal on Mt. Carmel. Hundreds of years later, when John the Baptist entered into ministry, many thought him to be Elijah, the man. However, it was actually the Elijah anointing resting upon John.

The Jews were aware of the promise about Elijah being the forerunner of the Messiah, when Christ proclaimed Himself as Messiah. In fact, in Matthew 17, the disciples asked Jesus, "Why then do the scribes say that Elijah must come first?" (v. 10). And Jesus answered them, "Indeed, Elijah is coming first and will restore all things" (v. 11). Then Jesus revealed to the disciples that Elijah had already come (v. 12), and they understood that Jesus spoke of John the Baptist (v. 13).

In the end, I believe that it won't be one man with the Elijah anointing but the spirit and anointing of Elijah on the Church operating in miracles and signs as Elijah functioned. In Matthew 17 on the Mount of Transfiguration, the Father sent Moses and Elijah as a prophetic fulfilment and sign of the Law and the prophets, and to show that Jesus was who He said He was. It was here that the Father announced: "This is My beloved Son, in whom I am well pleased. Hear Him!" (Matt. 17:5).

In this mountaintop experience, Moses represented the Old Covenant to the Jews, while Elijah represented the ushering in of the New Covenant and the coming power, which would rest on John the Baptist. The Book of Revelation references the two witnesses who clearly demonstrate the same miracles that Moses and Elijah demonstrated when they were on earth:

Then I was given a reed like a measuring rod. And the angel stood, saying, 'Rise and measure the temple of God, the altar, and those who worship there. But leave out the court, which is outside the temple, and do not measure it, for it has been given to the Gentiles. And they will tread the holy city underfoot for forty-two months. And I will give power to my two witnesses, and they will prophesy one thousand two hundred and sixty days, clothed in sackcloth.' These are the two olive trees and the two lampstands standing before the God of the earth. And if anyone wants to harm them, fire proceeds from their mouth and devours their enemies. And if anyone wants to harm them, he must be killed in this manner. These have power to shut heaven, so that no rain falls in the days of their prophecy; and they have power over waters to turn them to blood, and to strike the earth with all plagues, as often as they desire (Revelation 11:1-6).

This is a picture of the last days' anointing. God will give power to His two witnesses (Messianic Jews and Gentile believers). The above-referenced Scripture describes the last days' anointing of power, signs, and wonders as in the days of Moses and Elijah. Powerful miracles and healings will be released to bring in the great harvest. I believe it describes, not just two people anointed as "super evangelists," but the end-time Church, Messianic Jewish and Gentile believers operating in the spirit and power of Elijah and Moses.

Moses represents authority and Elijah represents power. Moses also speaks of the Old Covenant and Elijah speaks of both Old and New Covenants. How does Elijah represent the new? John the Baptist was the promised forerunner of the first coming. He came to prepare the way of the Lord and tell God's people to get ready for His coming! John was born in the anointing of Elijah (Luke 1:17). God has promised the spirit and power of

Elijah in these last days we live in, before the coming of the great and dreadful day of the Lord (the Second Coming).

THE LAST DAYS' HEALING REVIVAL

With the coming of the spirit and power of Elijah, we also have a promised healing revival (see Mal. 4:2). I believe that the key to the release of Elijah power and the great healing revival will be the great prayer movement. Remember in Revelation chapter 11, that before the power is given to the Church (v. 3), John is given a measuring rod. The angel instructs John to measure three things: the temple of God, the altar, and those who worship there. The temple can represent the believer's life or the Church—local, city-wide, or national. When worship, prayer, and intercession in the Church rise to a certain level, God will release His end-time power and the promise of the spirit of Elijah. God is checking the levels of intercession, worship, and prayer in the lives of believers, and in cities, and nations. Only when the bowls of Revelation chapter 8 are full can God release His power to the two witnesses: the Church, both Jew and Gentile. These two groups are called to represent the Old and New Covenants, to demonstrate the level of authority and power that Moses and Elijah walked in.

In Revelation chapter 11, the power was given to the two "lampstands"—Elijah and Moses (Rev. 11:2-6). Recall that Jesus walked in the midst of the seven lampstands (representing the Church), so in these last days, the Church will operate in the same power—signs, wonders, miracles, that Moses and Elijah walked in.

As on that mountain, I'm convinced that as we near the Second Coming of Christ, God will again confirm the Church as His beloved and His voice in the land. The Father will speak to the nations by bringing the spirit and power of Moses and Elijah upon His end-time army. Then He will release the

31

forerunners to prepare the way of the Lord and get a nation ready for God. It will be a movement of prophetic revelation, of power evangelism, and of healing that will turn nations to God, some in only a day!

THE COST OF THE ANOINTING

God said to me once, "I can give you any anointing that I have ever given to anyone else, if you can do what they did to get it." Friends, the anointing will cost you everything.

Someone once shared a vision he had of a man looking across a large, open plain, and seeing rolled-up mantles laying everywhere, (a mantle represents the anointing, the authority, the power, and ministry over another). He said that the man saw the mantles of great men and women of God—the mantles of Smith Wigglesworth, Kathryn Kuhlman, and Aimee Semple McPherson. He also saw the mantle of Elisha, of Elijah, and all of the greats who have gone before us. Then the Holy Spirit spoke to the man, and said, "Take any mantle you want! Which one do you want? Pick it up, take it...any one of them!"

The man replied, "Oh, I want Elijah's! Oh, I want to be like Smith Wigglesworth and have great faith! The mantle of John G. Lake! Oh my! The mantle of Elisha...think of that anointing! I could pick Kathryn Kuhlman's, and move in great miracles! Perhaps I should choose Martin Luther's and be a part of a great reformation."

Then suddenly, the man saw a bright glow appear from the ground, where another mantle lay, and it (the mantle) spoke to him: "Enoch walked with God so intimately that he was not." After seeing the life and the anointing of Enoch, he made his decision and said, "Before all the power mantles, I'd rather have the presence of the Lord." Then he picked up Enoch's mantle.

I believe that God is re-digging the ancient well and that He will use a last-days' army to usher in Isaiah 61:4, "And they shall rebuild the old ruins, they shall raise up the former desolations, and they shall repair the ruined cities." God is going to restore the desolations of many generations. He's going to take what's been lost in past revivals; the destinies that men and women didn't fulfill, and the mantles long since past, and He will restore and place those mantles on people as He pours out His Spirit in power again. There won't be 40, 50, or 60 years between great and mighty moves of God! The Bible lists great heroes of faith and their exploits, and they are just the foundation of the Kingdom that we'll build upon. God is offering us the opportunity to dare to believe Him to do in us, what He has done in the lives of these greats. Their experiences shouldn't be the ceiling, either; rather, the starting point for our upward journey of faith!

THE HALL OF FAITH

The Lord once took me by the Spirit to a place where I saw a hallway that went further than my eye could see. I call it the *Hall of Faith*. The walls were golden and shimmering with the light of His glory. It was not unlike being in a museum, and I felt it was a place in the Spirit where history had happened! A red carpet led me down a hallway, and as I walked the corridor, I saw portraits of the men and women that God had used, like Elijah, Elisha, Peter, Paul, Martin Luther, John G. Lake, Alexander Dowie, Aimee Semple McPherson, Jack Coe, A.A. Allen—people He used throughout history to shake nations and turn cities upside down!

Each portrait chronicled the achievement of a man or woman; how the Lord had used them, and the mantles that were on their lives. The entire corridor was like a memorial to great history makers. I've decided that I also want to do all the works that God has preordained for me and I want a huge portrait in the Hall of Faith!

In the vision, I knew this Hall of Faith was a place in the Spirit called "the great cloud of witnesses." I knew I was in the

Hall of Faith referred to in Hebrews 11, but the cloud of great witnesses mentioned in the next chapter of Hebrews surrounded me.

> *Therefore we also, since we are surrounded by so great a cloud of witnesses, let us lay aside every weight, and the sin which so easily ensnares us, and let us run with endurance the race that is set before us, looking unto Jesus, the author and finisher of our faith, who for the joy that was set before Him endured the cross, despising the shame, and has sat down at the right hand of the throne of God* (Hebrews 12:1-2).

During the experience I said, "God you're re-digging the ancient wells. It's time for a last days' army to receive Your power, apostolic authority, and healing. Bring it to the Church again—revival, reckless faith, and the anointing of authority that was on great men and women. It's time for the Church to see Your power. God, You're releasing the mantles of old. Bring the mighty anointing of the great women and men. Release new mantles and anointings, promises, and commissions—an anointing that will come upon a generation we've never yet seen! Oh Lord, release the purposes that were never fulfilled."

At the end of the hallway, I found myself standing behind the throne, but soon ushered before King Jesus on His throne. In the same way, God wants to commission all of us. I believe that we are living in God's end-time chosen generation. Who is going to be the Charles Finney, Maria Woodworth-Etter, Smith Wigglesworth, or Jonathan Edwards of today? These great men and women, these saints of old are gone. As we read the history of God's past moves, we need to lift our standard of expectation so that we can receive the great commissions He wants to give today. If God can do it for them, He can do it for us. Remember, the Bible says, "Elijah was a man just like us." (See James 5:17—NIV.)

Yes, God wants to do it again and in even *greater* measure. Recall that the glory of the latter house will be *greater* than the glory of the former house. That's a promise. The power of the early Church that we read about in Acts is an example of the *normal* Christian life—the way it should be, and that's the blueprint for us, and our lives, too, but the new dimension of this Christian life will be even greater!

Have faith in the God who does miracles! I pray that this book will be an encouragement for new Christians and those who were Christians long before I was even born. This book is a testimony of what God has done with one man, a forerunner. I pray that God will use my testimony to lift the bar of expectancy of how much of God we can receive and manifest now.

I want to challenge you to go hard after God. I pray, as David did, that God would "teach us to number our days, that we may gain a heart of wisdom" (Psalm 90:12). Then when our brief lives are over, yes, when I'm dog-paddling around the celestial sea in front of the throne, you can come and find me and say, "Todd, they just put my picture up in the Hall of Faith and it's even bigger than yours!"

ENDNOTES

1. Paul Cain Ministries, www.paulcain.org.

2. *Grace City Report Special Prophetic Edition*, Fall 1989.

3. Paul Cain, Mike Bickle, *Stadium Vision*, Kansas City Fellowship/Tape 6.

4. *Grace City Report Special Prophetic Edition*, Fall 1989.

5. Bob Jones and Paul Cain. Selections from the *Kansas City Prophets*, audiotape tape: 155C.

6. Benny Hinn, Honolulu, Blaisdell, January 21, 1999.

7. Rick Joyner, *The Harvest* (Charlotte: Morning Star Publishing, 1990), 9.

8. Paul Cain, *You Can Become the Word!*, Vineyard Prophetic Conference, 1989.

9. Benny Hinn, *Praise the Lord*, August 8, 1996.

CHAPTER 2

MY CHILDHOOD

My dad said it wouldn't be proper to have a child out of wedlock, so he married my mother. They moved from Ontario to the Sunshine Coast on a peninsula near Vancouver, British Columbia, Canada. They lived in a small apartment in the same building as my uncle who actually found my dad a job working in a mill. My father was only 19 when I was born, my mother, 29.

Within a year of my birth, my mother lost her hearing, the result of working on an assembly line in a factory making washers and dryers—the loud machinery eventually causing the deafness. I can't remember a time when she could hear. My father was very frustrated over her hearing loss, as it made it very difficult for them to communicate.

SATAN'S PLANS TO KILL ME

Satan had plans to take me out early in life, in fact, only days after my birth, on the ride home from hospital. Anxious to get me home, my dad hurriedly backed the car onto the road we'd travel home on. He didn't see the dumpster truck coming, and our car went between the front and back wheels of the huge truck, tearing the roof off. Thankfully, I was in my infant carrier on the back seat. I believe the devil tried to take my life, but God preserved me. Satan always attempts to kill a move of God in its infancy. Moses and Jesus are examples of that. Mark chapter 4 tells of the sower sowing the seed and the birds of the air immediately snatching the seed away. The enemy knew that God had a plan and purpose for me, even when I was a newborn. I'm confident that the devil and God were the only ones who knew, though. I know that as I grew older, I certainly never thought God would use me.

Five years later, I almost died in another bizarre accident. Dad and I were hanging out with one of his friends. I don't know why, but Dad's friend, Joe, threw me off a pier into the water and I almost drowned. My dad fished me out just in time to save my life. Looking back, I now believe that a spirit of death pursued me throughout my growing up years. Even though that spirit didn't get me, it did sometimes succeed in killing those I loved.

My earliest memory, during the time my parents were still together, was of my dog Goldie, a golden retriever—I loved this dog. She was my best friend. Dad came home one night and said the dog was killing the neighbor's sheep and it was important that we keep him in the pen or on a leash. I didn't really understand what that meant. The dog continued killing sheep and eventually had to be put down.

I had another narrow escape one day while accompanying my dad and his best friend on a bear hunting expedition. We were stalking a bear that had been coming onto a neighbor's property, attacking the sheep, and rummaging through the garbage. I told my dad that I needed to go to the bathroom, and, even though we were aware that the bear might be close by, he sent me around the corner of a shed by myself. Suddenly, about 14 feet away, there was the bear! It looked at me and rose on its hind legs. I tell you, you have no idea how big a bear looks on its hind legs to a little boy! My father shot it, but later joked that I had been "bear bait." He skinned the bear that night, and cooked it on an open fire. I still remember the smell and gamey taste of that meat. Not everything tastes like chicken!

I became very afraid of bears after that! Even though I loved nature and camping, the woods scared me.

DIVORCE AND BROKEN PROMISES

I was about four when Dad left. Really, my mom kicked him out because they fought and argued all of the time. He also struggled with drugs and alcohol—as many did in the hippie generation of the late '60s and early '70s, known as the era of free love, peace, and sex.

Dad lived in a hotel for a couple of weeks and then moved into a basement suite where he lived below a woman by the name of Darcia. Her boyfriend would buy drugs from Dad. Within a few short months, though, Dad was involved with Darcia and filed for divorce from my mom.

As a young boy, I struggled with the huge loss of my father, the pain of rejection due to the divorce, and the frustration of not being able to communicate with my mother. I regarded Darcia as the wicked stepmother of the east, and always hoped and dreamed for my parents to get back together. I viewed Darcia as the only thing preventing that from happening. Sadly, I even felt that she never accepted me as her son, because she had two children, daughters, of her own. Technically, they were my stepsisters, but I never felt we were a family even though we did things together. In my mind, her children were more important to her than I was, and that Dad had put Darcia first, caring more for her than for me. Anger consumed me, but I've come to realize that it's a part of the pain children experience because of divorce.

On the other side of the divorce equation, my mother and her family constantly bad-mouthed and berated Dad, who only had a sixth grade education, and left home at 16 to work. They referred to him as a "deadbeat," a "bum," and a drug addict who wouldn't "go anywhere." They weren't too fond of him, and this was difficult for me.

Living with my mother, things were tight. We'd have to line up for the food pantry, use food stamps, and I always wore second-hand clothes. Mom received a small check once a month for her disability, and then we could eat out. For a few days, there'd be good food in the refrigerator, and my favorite cereal in the cupboard.

But those years were filled with broken promises and betrayals from my father. Promised money and gifts often seemed to get "lost in the mail." I remember the tremendous disappointment when those eagerly anticipated gifts didn't arrive, especially around the winter holidays—that was a double whammy since my birthday fell shortly after Christmas, in January. Seldom did he follow through on sending gifts for either occasion. I'd talk to him on the phone and say, "I didn't get the Christmas present or the money you said you sent me," and he'd almost always reply with, "Son, I sent it—the post office must have lost it. I'll call them and see what's happened, because I really sent it."

I'd overhear my mother tell people about how Dad never sent child support, and she'd even say to me, "I'm not surprised that the parcel didn't show up, because he doesn't even send support for your food, clothing, or allowance." I wondered why my father didn't take care of me, and I blamed it on Darcia. I'd think, *"He must want to—but she won't let him."* Rejection and

dejection mounted, yet, no matter how often he lied and promised me that he'd sent whatever, no matter how often he'd say,
"Son, believe me, the post office lost it," I still considered him the
good guy—he couldn't do any wrong. I looked up to him. I still
idolized him. I wanted all the bad stuff to be a lie—and in some
ways, it was, in other ways, not so, as I later realized.

Sometimes I'd see my dad for summer vacation, and he'd
visit once or twice a year. He usually wouldn't call unless it was
Christmas or my birthday; I always had to initiate the call. I
wondered, therefore, what was wrong with me, and why he
didn't want to be with me. I eventually closed my heart to him,
because I thought he'd closed his to me.

ADVENTURES ON THE FARM

When I was about six, Dad and Darcia married and moved to
a farm in Alberta. One summer I visited him for five or six
weeks. I really enjoyed it as it was so different from what I was
used to. I fed pigs and climbed in the hayloft. I loved the farm,
except for those dumb chickens that for some reason terrified
me. In an effort to help me over this fear, one day, my father took
me to the chicken coop and instructed me to gather the eggs.

"How do I get them," I asked, "because they're all sitting on
them!"

"Just reach under their tails," he'd say, but I couldn't. Instead,
I'd "shoo" them away. The thought of eating those warm eggs dis-
gusted me too—so much different from cool, store-bought ones.

One day that same summer, Dad stopped in to see one of his
friends. He left me in the back seat of the car with instructions to
"stay put." His friend's son came out and while we were playing
in the car, I decided to show him how I could drive. I put the car
in neutral—it rolled forward, hitting the house, and causing
some damage to both.

Other than some of the pleasant adventures of that summer at the farm, there aren't many good childhood memories because I was forced to grow up too soon and take on adult responsibilities after Dad left, and it's no wonder that I became a very mixed up and angry kid.

I didn't know much about God or religion while I was growing up. Mom had been raised in the Salvation Army Church in Newfoundland but backslid at 18. She didn't want anything to do with God anymore because of her strict religious upbringing; a religious spirit had ruined her. She made me attend Sunday school for a few weeks. That experience was enough to teach me that there was a God we should serve, but I wasn't interested in spiritual things at the time.

DESCENT INTO DARKNESS

By the time I was eight, I remember having an interest in the occult. The devil was pulling me into his Kingdom using heavy metal music as bait. I was filled with a deepening anger and growing rage and took comfort in the music of AC/DC, Iron Maiden, Motley Crüe, and Metallica. Some of my favorite songs were *Highway to Hell* by AC/DC, *666 The Number of the Beast* by Iron Maiden and *Bark at the Moon* by Ozzy Osbourne. Then I moved on to a fascination with death-metal and bands that I knew were satanists, and actually idolized some of the bands and singers.

My anger drove me to violence against my own body. As I listened to this music, I'd cut my arm with a knife until it bled, and I'd lick the blood off. Once, while on a bus, I broke out a window by ramming it with my head. I'd throw tantrums, punching holes in walls, and slamming doors—blatant, random acts of anger. I believe the music started the whole process; it fed and fueled the hatred in me. This music made me feel strong and immortal—it seemed to calm my fears, insecurities, and feelings of rejection, giving me a false sense of security. Untouchable, I could take on the world!

At nine, I got involved in pornography. My father had a trunk full of pornographic magazines and movies, and I'd steal them when I visited. Soon, my addiction became unmanageable, especially since a friend who had access to his own storehouse of pornographic material supplied me as well. As a result, before my twelfth birthday, I'd already had several sexual encounters

My downward spiral continued at 12 and I also started drinking and smoking. I remember my first cigarette that I took from my mother and smoked behind a bush. It made me so dizzy I could barely stand, and I wanted to barf. I wondered, *How can anyone smoke this stuff?* Later, when I felt better, I found I actually liked the dizzy feeling I got, so I'd smoke again for the head rush, and then again and again, because it looked "cool," and was the "in" thing to do, especially in high school.

My first sip of alcohol was more out of curiosity. I wondered why people, like my mom and her family and friends liked it so much. I mixed my first drink, rum with Coca Cola, and I still remember the taste and the warm feeling, the buzz it gave me. Soon I'd sneak into Mom's alcohol cupboard to sip the gin, rum, and vodka. Christmas Eve was a highlight for me, because she always stocked it well for family and friends. They'd sit around and drink, and I'd get a little eggnog with a hint of rum. However, as soon as everyone left, I'd sneak into the cupboard and get my fill. You can guess how I'd usher in Christmas morning!

Stealing also was a part of my life as a youngster. I'd steal money from my mother to spend at the arcade, and once I stole a bunch of heavy metal music cassettes from a store. My uncle who lived upstairs discovered my "crime" and made me return everything to the store manager. However, this humbling experience wasn't enough to set me straight, and my behavior worsened.

DEEPER STILL...

I longed to be with my father and I enjoyed the times we were together, but they were usually destructive as we drank a lot together. One evening at only 11 years old, I was drunk and playing darts with him. Impaired coordination and sharp objects are not a good combination. Darts flew everywhere, narrowly missing Dad's pet canary in its cage—fortunately for the bird it didn't become a shish kabob.

At 12, Dad told me that if I ever wanted to do drugs, not to do them with my friends. He said, "If you want to smoke a joint, smoke it with me." I thought, *Wow...Dad does dope, and it's OK...he's inviting me to do dope with him!* That was a seed and it birthed a desire in my heart for drugs. I started with marijuana— one here, one there, only socially, with friends once in a while, but as with everything in my life, I became addicted to the high. Soon I lived from one high to the next—never mind moderation—I was too extreme! That's my DNA...to do something with everything in me, or not at all. As a Christian today, this trait has been redeemed—I still do things with gusto—all or nothing, because I want to be a radical, totally abandoned disciple who will take up the cross, deny myself, and follow Him (Luke 9:23).

Back in those dark days, the last high was never enough, and before long, plain joints didn't cut it—they had to be laced with opium, or cocaine, and eventually, PCP. My quest for a high led me to hashish and "hot knifing," and then to magic mushrooms, acid, and speed. Never satisfied, I always searched for more—it didn't matter the drug—codeine, Tylenol, even sniffing gas—I'd do anything for the ultimate high.

I wasn't a satanist, but dabbled in many areas of the occult, hoping to fill my spiritual hunger, but I did fill it with the dark side. Because of my drugs and growing communication with evil spirits, there was a high level of demonic activity in my home. Once, while getting a glass of water, something violently, physically shook my mother—even though she was alone. Remember my dad's friend who tossed me off the pier? A relative of his, George, held garage sales every Sunday in a big old house. When he died, a spirit posing as his ghost grabbed me and awoke me at night. Even after I left home, my mother continued to have weird demonic encounters, because I'd opened the door to that realm.

I would communicate with spirits from the grave and ask different ones to visit and empower me. While high, a familiar spirit that I believed to be the presence of Jim Morrison, would visit me. Though I never actually saw the spirit, I'd feel its presence. It would fill me with mystic feelings, and I actually believed that when I died, I'd spend eternity in bliss with Jim. How's that for screwed-up theology?

I'd also, for a time, get high on speed or acid, and listen to his group, *The Doors* for six-hour stretches, and also watch his movie repeatedly. I loved and worshiped the guy! That's not just a figure of speech—I literally felt that way toward him.

One day, I met a girl who also liked *The Doors*. Together, we'd get high on acid, and on one of our "trips," we acted out one of the scenes from the movie, although we were completely unaware we were even doing it. We weren't even talking with our own voices and freaked everyone out so badly, they didn't want us around anymore!

My quest for the ultimate high and sexual ecstasy propelled my involvement with the occult, and I'd make deals in my heart with the devil for those reasons. I thought about giving myself to him if he could increase my pleasure. Although I never did make an actual covenant, I did make that deal in my heart by calling on different sexual demons.

I was so hungry for the spirit world and so fascinated by ghosts, demons, and horror movies, that I'd go and get high and drunk in cemeteries. What I was really hungry for, though, was God, but I didn't know Him, or know how to find Him.

Today, people ask me if my involvement with the occult and my hunger for the dark side had anything to do with how quickly I eventually grew in the anointing. I believe that those demonic experiences did help me become more sensitive to the spirit realm. God is amazing—He can redeem anything!

CHAPTER 3

Chapter 3

ADOLESCENT CHOICES

I grew up with few restraints and little discipline. My mom always warned that my uncle would spank me when he got home but he never did. By age 13, I was smoking in my own home in front of Mom. She complained a little but really had no control over me. I was hate-filled and very violent to the point of physically abusing her. Once she chased me down the hallway with the belt when, to my shame, I grabbed it and slapped it across her face instead. I used violence to intimidate her to get my way. A simple gesture with my hand or a single glance of my eye struck fear in her.

I also liked to light fires as a teen. Once a friend and I broke into an excavator and stole a lighter and matches. I lit some grass on fire in the ditch outside of a home and it nearly spread to the neighbor's garage. You can imagine how my mom felt when the fire department arrived. After the fire incident, I received a small spanking and was grounded for a day or so. I found out that, since I was a juvenile, the police couldn't charge me. "Are you kidding?" I exclaimed, "What a great law!" From then on, I really took advantage of that loophole, constantly lighting fires in the bush outside our house.

Scary but true, I used to have fantasies about blowing up a grenade at school or random acts of violence. I actually talked about how many people I thought I could kill in one day, how many murders I could get away with, and how I would commit them. If somebody hurt me, I would dream about revenge.

I went to school through eighth grade before dropping out due to conflicts with other students as well as my own battles with criminal activity and court appearances. When I did attend school, I struggled with being able to apply myself and even grasp some of the simplest concepts. I remember being the class clown, and being picked last for sports teams.

In most classes, I usually got F's and D's but once I got a B— in French. No, it wasn't my great love for the beauty of the French language; it was because I sat beside a student more gifted in French and made a deal with her. I wouldn't snap her bra strap as long as she gave me the answers. What can I say? A scholar I'm not. If the teacher wanted us to read a book, I would ask if it was available as a movie.

My best school memories are of my eighth grade year when we would arrive at school an hour early every day just to have a frozen drink at the nearby gas station.

SMALL-TOWN LIFE, PARTIES, AND GANGS

Gibsons, the town where I lived growing up, boasted a population of about 5,000 people. It was in the boonies—the middle of nowhere and a 40-minute ferry ride just to get to the small peninsula where we lived.

Thus, there wasn't much to do in this small, secluded town. However, I got to know some people who lived in the same apartment building as Mom and I. Often, I'd play cribbage with a sixty-year-old woman who lived below us but the rest of my social circle comprised my aunt and uncle upstairs and a few neighborhood children whom I'd play hide-and-seek or kick-the-can with.

Later, as a teen, there wasn't that much more to do on a Friday night than to go to the cinema (and it featured one movie for several week runs), or hang out on the street or at the skateboard park. Sometimes as many as 200 young people would congregate in front of the grocery store or at the small mall. It was "cool" to cut classes, hang out at different locations, and smoke cigarettes.

Life in Gibsons was similar to what is portrayed in the movie *Footloose*. The school dance was the big event. There were only two high schools in town and they always competed against each other.

Even though the town was small, gang life was alive and well. In fact, there was what I call, a membership of "wanna-be gangsters" with some members actually affiliated with the infamous "Los Diablo's." Most of the "gangsters" however, were more like your local thugs—small-town troublemakers, who hung out in front of the local pizzeria.

The Hell's Angels fascinated me, though, and I aspired to be a member (who ever said I didn't have ambition, or goals?). I knew my father rode sometimes as a friend of a different biker gang, and I always enjoyed the parties he took me to—at a place called, *Angel's Acres*. Terror spread over town whenever this gang rode through for their three days of drugs, heavy metal music, women, and whatever else they found to amuse themselves.

I usually hung out with people older than I, and I didn't associate myself entirely with one gang, because I wanted everyone to like me, and keep the peace. Really, I preferred to be the go-between guy—but that position often caused trouble because I was never initiated into any one group. However, gang involvement wasn't good to many of my old friends. Today, some are dead, some are in jail, some are still involved with gangs, and some have even committed suicide. One of my best childhood friends, hooked on cocaine, and other drugs, shot himself with a shotgun. Considering where I could have ended up, I'm so thankful that God kept me through it all.

I could get anyone to do what I wanted just because I knew how to "talk the talk" and make deals I could never deliver. I used gang connections and threw around names to protect me in the street. If it was time for a fight, everyone would fight for me until they realized what was happening. "Hey wait a minute, why are we fighting your battles?" they would say, "You started this mess."

I was a loud mouth, a talk-bigger-than-I-was kind of guy. When my mess would finally catch up with me, (bad relationships, drug debt, theft or just too much "heat") I would just sneak away, tell no one, and head for the next town, sometimes after just a few months of living where I was. I burned many bridges, made countless enemies, ended up on the wrong side of gang members, received death threats, and just hurt and lied to many people. I always lived with a false identity because I never wanted anyone to know who I really was. I was afraid of rejection. Since I never changed my behavior from town to town, it usually took me about six months before I had to flee again. That scenario repeated itself at least three times in my life in about a two-year time span from 16 to 18 years of age.

A NEW CREATION IN CHRIST

At times when I've shared my testimony I've said, "There are events and activities in my past I don't speak about because I'm ashamed of them. My testimony is about who I am and what I am doing now, not who I was."

Testimony is a powerful tool. "And they overcame him by the blood of the Lamb and by the word of their testimony" (Rev. 12:11). I have shared my story hundreds of times, briefly generalizing the highlights of my past without going into any specific detail about what actually put me in prison. I've always felt that the story of who I am today and what God is doing is powerful enough testimony of His transforming power.

However, in recent years, several stories appeared about me in a political magazine bent upon and focused on critiquing religious and political issues, and on digging up dirt about frontline leaders. Yes, there were many inaccuracies in the articles, however, I must admit that my naïveté and lack of wisdom in dealing with the press also fed the fire of controversy. Today, I want to be sure that in the future no one can say I hid things or misled people about my past.

I am going to share some things here that you won't hear from the pulpit. Especially now, as our ministry has grown, God has favored us with spotlights in Christian and secular media, TV, radio, magazines, and more. With increased positive publicity, we can expect that the accuser of the brethren will be right there to stir up controversy.

They say old news is no news, but I want to be sure that I don't conceal any past details that could damage my ministry in the future. As I've recounted so far in this chapter, as a hate-filled, messed up youth, my lifestyle continued its descent into darkness until, eventually, I found myself involved in criminal activity and charged with sexual assault. Before I was saved, and as a minor, I hurt many people and spent time in prison because of it.

I haven't spoken in detail about all areas of my childhood—many of those early events were very painful, like when I was sexually abused at eight years old, or when I was aware that my childhood friend was abused by his stepfather. Then I watched my friend abuse his stepsister and continue the destructive cycle.

He became a drug addict, reached a place of despair, and committed suicide.

I was forced into my first sexual encounter with a woman at age eleven. I thank God for the Blood of Jesus! The world system says once an alcoholic, always an alcoholic; once an addict, always an addict, but I know that "if the Son makes you free, you shall indeed be free!" (John 8:36). God can restore purity to the prostitute, set the rapist and sex offender free, and save the worst murderer, like Saul, and make him into Paul, the greatest apostle. There is hope for everyone lost in sin. The Bible says that "if anyone is in Christ, he is a new creation; old things have passed away; behold, all things have become new" (2 Corinthians 5:17).

Although these areas of my past are very ugly, the Blood of Jesus has washed away every stain. "If we confess our sins, He is faithful and just to forgive us our sins and to cleanse us from all unrighteousness" (1 John 1:9).

For centuries people have asked this one question—"Is the Blood of Jesus enough?" In my own ministry, this issue has been raised repeatedly, especially by the media. I have been challenged by the mistakes of my past, and I've wrestled with whether the blood is enough. In the future, the accuser of the brethren will continue to challenge the wonder-working power of the blood of Jesus and the salvation experience of the Cross. Yet, no assault of the enemy can overcome Christ's power, in my life and in others, to save and transform.

The devil has many in the church today living under guilt, condemnation, and shame. His plan is to keep us in a prison of regret, constantly challenging the authenticity of the blood. When the devil keeps bringing up our past, he is saying that you are forever guilty of your past actions and sin even though your repentance is genuine. Yet we know the devil is a liar!

For years I knew God's love and forgiveness but still felt the sting of shame and guilt. When man, circumstances, media, or the devil brought up my past, I would relive the pain, defeat, regret, and hopelessness of sin. Remembrance of sin separates us from God's love and creates a feeling of unworthiness before God.

Even though I knew God's forgiveness and unconditional love, I was challenged with this thought: "Does forgiveness mean forgetting?" The Cross, the message of grace, and the power of the blood of Jesus has been, and will be, challenged in my life and the life of all believers. I felt it necessary to exalt the blood of the Lamb in this part of my testimony and to revel in its power to cleanse the conscience, forgive the sinner, and overcome the accuser. The blood of the Lamb is our greatest weapon of spiritual warfare! When I was saved I did a lot of repenting and reconciling, trying to make relationships right. Later, I'll explain about the process that God took me through to get out from under the constant condemnation of the devil.

DESTINATION...PRISON

After the courts sentenced me to prison, I remember being escorted, with my hands and feet shackled, to a small aircraft, which I was convinced, would crash. Although I was going to a juvenile facility, I definitely didn't find myself at a country club or a minimum-security institution. At times, they incarcerated me with murderers and sex offenders, where inmates were raped and stabbed. What an environment for a young teen. I spent time in five different prisons, but for just one sentence. It was typical to be moved around a lot in those days because each facility emphasized different rehabilitation programs.

First I went to a mental evaluation facility for fourteen days. Most young people arrived there for assessment and placement. I wasn't crazy or anything, at least not then (that didn't happen until I got into the ministry, ha ha!). I was in "lock down" most days when they weren't conducting stress and other psychological testing on me.

The first night in youth prison, I was afraid because I had heard many stories about what happens to the "new guy." One story described a "blanket party" initiation. Four or five guys would wrap a person in a blanket and hold him down. Then they would place a bar of soap in a sock. A bar of soap in a sweat sock is a dangerous weapon—it can do a lot of damage. I was so scared. I lay awake worrying almost all night. However, the initiation never happened to me, but it sure did to the other guys.

My first day in another facility, one of the inmates wanted to test me. He approached me out of nowhere, shook my hand, and greeted me. Then he punched me in the face and took off running. I didn't follow. It was a "what-will-this-guy-do-and-who-is-he?" moment of testing. He wanted to know if I would rat him out or run in fear. Eventually, we became friends, and thankfully, the whole time I was incarcerated, that was the only time that I got "hit." Older inmates protected me because I was a first-rate manipulator and could get people on my side.

While I was in the third prison, several Christians tried to share with me about Jesus. Every Wednesday I attended a Bible study because the woman who led it was pretty, and because I always had a God hunger down deep inside (I just wanted to do what I wanted to do and worry about God later.) Those meetings also helped fill time and answered many of my questions. I would stay behind after the session, asking all about God and the universe and about what I thought were contradictions in the Bible. Once, the leader showed a video on the discovery of Noah's ark from an archaeological dig. The documentary showed physical and scientific evidence that the ark rested on Mount Ararat. That gripped me!

Sometimes I attended church on Sunday morning with the chaplain because it got me out of prison for a change. I thought it was tough and cool to walk into church in my prison garb and have everyone stare at me. Hey…the women would admire me because I was a macho, bad boy from prison, wouldn't they? I figured that most of the girls were probably forced by their parents to attend church in the first place, and really didn't want to be there. I knew that I needed God, but always thought I would get serious about Him when I was older.

Several times in the correctional facility or on the street, a preacher would come up to me, give me his business card, and say, "If you ever want to have a coffee, give me a call." I remembered that. There was a man in the youth detention center who took an interest in me and in the music that I liked. He reviewed the lyrics and asked why I listened to that kind of music. He said that I could get music with the same kind of beat but with different words and a different spirit. He tried to explain to me why there was power in music.

Then, he bought me a Christian metal tape by a group called *Holy Soldier*. They were a screaming, metal-head band. This impressed and interested me, especially since the guy went out of his way to select it for me. I remember that when I finally got out of prison, I'd carry my ghetto blaster on my shoulder and blast out my favorite song from the cassette, *Virtue and Vice*. It was Christian music, but nobody recognized it as such. Years later, when I became a Christian, I found this man, explained what had happened, and it really blessed him.

In prison, another young man always wanted to talk with me. He took the time and interest to probe and to ask me about my life: my father, what it was like growing up, how I felt about things—his friendship touched me deeply. I knew that both he and the other man were Christians, and were praying for me.

I was released a little early for good behavior, serving fourteen months of an eighteen month sentence. As a ward of the court, the authorities placed me in the foster care system for two main reasons. The first being that my mother and I didn't get along, and the second because the town where my mother lived prohibited me from returning because of my criminal background, and because the manager of my mother's apartment building had lodged so many complaints about the fighting, screaming, and swearing arguments.

THE FIRST OF MANY FOSTER HOMES

The first foster home was temporary until they could find a permanent place for me. It was in Cloverdale, British Columbia, and I was there for only a few weeks. But that was where the Lord started working on my heart for what was to come. At this home, I met Shane, another foster kid who had lived there for a couple of years. His past was similar to mine—gangs, prison, drugs, and so on, but he had become a Christian. One day, he invited me to church to see him be baptized. Two other foster kids there also were Christians, and attended an on-fire youth group at Christian Life Assembly in Langley, British Columbia. The foster parents were Christian too, and I believe God appointed them to help prepare my heart!

Although they never shared the Gospel with me outright, they took me to church to watch Shane's water baptism. The church happened to be the same one that the correctional facility had taken me to for a Christmas play! I watched as Shane and about 30 other young people shared their testimonies and then were baptized. I wondered, *Could this happen to me?* The sense of family amazed me, and I nearly cried when these young people shared how the love of Jesus had changed them. I almost accepted Christ as my personal Lord and Savior that night, but I didn't. Nevertheless, I recall silently asking God, *God, have you been trying to speak to me over these past eight months?* First the ministry in prison, and now my first foster care home.

I really wanted to stay in that family and to know what it was like to belong. What I really sought was my heavenly Father's love but before long, the courts shipped me off to another foster home in Maple Ridge, B.C. I still remember the two tiny, white, Maltese dogs I playfully and endlessly tormented for fun. How I loved those little dogs, especially Jeepers. I'd wrestle with them and body slam them until they'd become so wound up, they'd want to eat the couch! Then they just wouldn't calm down.

These foster parents tried hard to include me as a part of their family, and went out of their way to mother and father me. We'd even have meals together, and I felt they genuinely cared about me and my future. During my stay, an eighteen-year-old foster sister and two other foster kids arrived and left.

However, in this home, I continued to use drugs, and with some of my younger foster brothers. But still, God had plans for me. I recall one day someone driving by and rolling down his window yelling, "Jesus loves you!" It was what I call a "drive-by evangelistic effort!" I remember arriving home that night thinking, *Did he say that because God told him to, or did he say it because he's weird...maybe God's thinking about me...did God tell him to say that?* It made me start to think about God, and to recall those instances where people took time to demonstrate His love to me, like in prison, or at the first foster home. My heart softened in the knowledge of people praying for me.

Even so, my sinful lifestyle continued. At sixteen, I started breaking into vehicles to hopefully find drugs, or something I could sell to purchase them. One night I broke into twenty-four cars!

There was also another time when a friend and I got drunk, and he said, "Hey, it would be great if we stole a car." And I asked, "How are we going to do that?"

He told me about a car in an underground garage he knew of, where the people he babysat for parked their car.

"Where are we going to get the keys?" I asked. He pulled out an "extra set" of keys from his pocket and told me that he'd taken them while babysitting for the people. "It will be easy—you get the car in the parking garage, and drive it out, and then I'll drive us to downtown Vancouver for a joyride. I remember thinking, *I can't even drive! How will I get the car out of the garage?*

It was 2 A.M., and I got into the car, but to my dismay, I discovered that it was a stick shift. *Just my luck*, I thought. I didn't know how to drive an automatic, let alone a stick. (The last time I'd tried my hand at the wheel, was while drunk, and I'd plowed the car right through the wall of my Dad's buddy's house.)

I started the vehicle, and it jerked and stalled as I tried to drive it out of the garage. Finally, after I'd pulled it out about ten feet, my friend yelled, "Hurry up! Hurry up!" and I said, "I can't…I can't …" and scrambled out of it, leaving it right there in the middle of the garage. I took off running. Later, I was so embarrassed that I couldn't steal it, but my friend and I were able to laugh about it later.

My addiction to drugs escalated while I lived in Maple Ridge. This, too, is where I got into major trouble with gangs, especially because of my bad temper. Several times in a 6-month span, I'd get myself into dangerous situations and serious fights. There was one particular one that still stands out. I'd been interested in a particular girl—for more than a physical relationship, and a particular fellow had been badmouthing her, and describing the awful things he wanted to do to her. We argued, and one night, while I walked back to my foster home, on the dark street, he snuck up from behind and attempted to butterfly kick me in the head. I stuck my switchblade to his throat and would have killed him, but he called out to some people in a nearby house.

Sadly, about halfway through my stay with the Maple Ridge family, things went downhill for me at alarming speed because of my growing addiction. A girl I liked broke up with me. Although it shouldn't have been a big deal, it was because of my emotional state and the delusion that drugs gave me. This deeply affected me, and I couldn't decide whether I wanted to live or die—I wasn't rational. One day, I planned to "scare" the group that I'd been hanging out with—especially the girl who'd dumped me. So, deciding that dying was better than living anyhow, I stole a bottle of extra strength Tylenol from a store at the mall, and downed 40 pills.

After roaming the mall for a little while, I suddenly got scared, and realized that my life was slipping away (this isn't what 'shop till you drop' really means!). One of my drug friends saw me, and I told what I'd done. The mall had a leisure center outside with a pool, so my friend ran for the lifeguards, and they sent me to hospital. The doctor pumped my stomach and hooked up IV's. Unfortunately, though, I was allergic to the drug overdose treatments, and broke into red hives, and then thrashed around uncontrollably and wildly, doing the "funky chicken." I truly thought I was dying, and it terrified me. When my foster mom arrived, I screamed, "I don't want to die…I don't want to die!" She cried with me, and stayed close while they pumped my stomach, however, as scared as I was, this was only the first of three drug overdoses I'd take in eighteen months.

Even though many other foster kids went through their doors, this family wanted to keep me. However, my out-of-control lifestyle prohibited that because I violated most of the rules—my anger and hurt inside, and the dark outside forces compelled me to pursue my destructive lifestyle. How often I'd been fetched out of ditches and hauled home drunk by the police! This drug overdose wasn't enough to make me quit drugs or alcohol. One day a drug dealer even knocked on the door at my home to tell them I owed him money. I'd also sneak women into my room to do drugs and party together. Some of the rooms in the house were "off limits," and I'd break into them. Imagine—for those "minor" infractions, they kicked me out! Hello? That's what I thought—but I know that this foster family did all that they could to love me and include me—but I just couldn't receive their love—frankly, I didn't know how to receive it. Sadly, one day, they finally said, "Todd, we can't keep you."

The courts moved me to a third foster home, which was more like a holding tank while they searched for a drug rehabilitation program that would take me in. Even though I saw a drug counselor weekly, I didn't sincerely desire freedom from my addictions—I still got high and drunk regularly. However, before my acceptance into the program, ironically called, "Exodus," I was kicked out of the whole foster care system because of my drinking and drug use. At 17, I wasn't yet ready to give it all up.

I NEED HELP, DAD

I had nowhere to go, so I phoned Dad, hoping to go back to school and get a job. He hadn't heard from me for over two years. I had assumed that because we only talked once when I was in prison, that I had shamed him so much that he just went on with his own life. Through all of my rejection and fear, I never kept up contact with family. According to my dad, I shut him off and didn't want a relationship with him.

But when I called I said, "I need help, Dad. I've got no place to live. I'm a drug addict, and I can't go back to Mom's."

He said, "Come to Qualicum Beach (a small tourist/retirement town on Vancouver Island, much smaller than Gibsons). You can't stay with me and Darcia, but I'll find a place for you."

In the off-season, the hotels rented their spare rooms at very low rates. Dad rented me a furnished apartment on the beach at a place called the "Captain's Inn." Located only two blocks from their place, I'd walk over for dinner four or five times a week. Dad and I were about the same size, so he also gave me some of his clothes and his black Dayton biker boots. He and Darcia tried their best to help me rebuild my life.

Dad also helped me find a job as a dishwasher at a hotel, even though I was receiving monthly government assistance. I didn't report this extra income to the government, but rather squandered all of it to feed my addictions and parties (later though, I reported and repaid the government fully). Six months later, the hotel fired me because I'd stolen my employer's booze, arrived late or stoned, and sometimes simply didn't show up. I also started back to school (grade ten because I was 17), but they expelled me within the first month because I refused to do homework, missed many days, and attended high on drugs.

Dad got me another job at a gas station working the night shift, but I soon quit in favor of partying. In spite of his best efforts to help me, nothing worked. I couldn't stay away from the drugs and alcohol. It didn't help that we'd drink together, just as we did when I was eleven. We also smoked pot and hash together. I was just like a cat at the sound of a can opener when drugs and alcohol were around. If I couldn't find drugs, Dad would "sell" me some, or I'd do something for him to get a hit, like cleaning out the garage, or walking the dogs, or washing his car. Sometimes though, he'd just give them to me.

When the peak tourist season arrived, I had to find another place to live. I moved out of the Captain's Inn and into a large room in a house that belonged to a single mother. To use the bathroom, I'd have to go into her part of the home, not good, especially when I was drunk or stoned and barging through her room in the middle of the night to be sick in the bathroom. Honestly, I never remembered how I ever got there or arrived back to my own bed.

OVERDOSE AGAIN

It was in her home that I overdosed a second time, this time a bad trip on LSD, which, unbeknownst to me, was laced with strychnine (rat poison). I ran to her crying and screaming, "I'm dead. I've died and the demons are coming to get me right now!" Then I raced back and forth across her lawn, convinced I was dead and going to hell.

When the ambulance arrived, I yelled at the paramedics, "I don't want to die, I don't want to die!" They put me into a straight jacket and sent me off to the hospital where I really started to hallucinate. I thought I was in a tropical jungle with big, colorful birds, like the Fruit Loops cereal toucan. Everything was colorful and I felt the heat from the Amazon sun. I even asked the nurses, "Do you know that we're on a safari?"

When I awoke the next day, I couldn't remember a thing. The nurses told me about the poison and the safari, and when I asked where my shoes were so I could go home, they told me I hadn't been wearing any. There and then I made a decision to never do drugs again. "I'm done with them," I said to myself, although I knew I had another hit waiting for me at home.

The hospital was located thirty minutes away, and I wondered how I'd get home, especially with no shoes and no money. I didn't want my father to know what happened, but by now, the whole town knew. There was a Hispanic man sitting the lobby, he stared at me, and I stared back, but before long, he said, "I'll give you a ride…where are you going?"

"Back to Qualicum Beach," I replied. We got into his car and drove for about ten minutes, and during that time, I'd been thinking seriously about quitting drugs for good. Just then, the man said, "Hey buddy, open up that glove box." Inside was a big bag of dope. I don't know how, but I attracted drug dealers like manure draws flies. It was as though the devil himself was there to meet me.

"Roll one up."

"How big?" I asked.

"Make it as big as you want …"

Free dope! This had to be satan! I rolled one up the size of a cigar and got high right there in the car. Five minutes after my arrival home, I popped the rest of the acid I had there. Then the woman evicted me. Fortunately, the tourist off-season had rolled around again, and I moved back into the Captain's Inn.

Sex, drugs, and rock and roll were my life. Every day, for years, I got high—I had to just to keep the 'buzz' going. I smoked dope like cigarettes—and regularly downed whiskey, speed, and LSD.

MY THIRD OVERDOSE

A friend and I went out to farms to pick mushrooms. We'd dig through the dung until we'd each filled our bag. He wanted to sell his mushrooms, but I just wanted to eat mine—I remembered the mushroom highs I got with my Dad, especially when he baked magic mushroom cookies. Back at my apartment, I wasn't quite sure how many mushrooms I should put into the cookies, but after careful consideration, decided to use them all. I ate nearly an entire bread bag full of cookies, and then stuffed the teapot full and drank mushroom tea. Within a few hours, my head spun. I vomited, and the walls closed in. Sick and hallucinating, paranoia set in, and I obsessively kept peering out of the window, thinking that every car that stopped and every person out there, hundreds, were meeting to conspire against me. Imagine those old movies where the villagers storm the castle carrying torches and pitchforks, shouting, "Let's skin him alive!" I thought the whole town was in on the plot. It was dark when I ran out into the street—behind every headlight was a driver about to get me. Sick for days and days afterward, it took me months to overcome my paranoia.

Things never improved—I continued to get into trouble with the police, and still I refused to change my ways. Once, I hid a seventeen-year-old woman who had escaped from juvenile prison with me. We got high together in my hotel for days. However, eventually, the Captain's Inn evicted me for good, because I didn't pay my rent. It wasn't until some time later that my father found out about the eviction, and the loss of both of my jobs.

Sometimes he would come by and wake me up in the mornings so I'd make it to work on time. One day I didn't answer the door, so he used his key to enter. He was shocked to find that the all of the furniture he'd bought was gone, including an antique seventy-year-old trunk that he'd given me for my clothes that had belonged to my grandfather. Everything I had I'd sold for drugs, including this family heirloom. Anything I hadn't sold was taken by drug friends or traded for money. I was totally gone.

CHAPTER 4

THE HOUND OF HEAVEN
ON MY TRAIL

I awoke that last morning and realized I was on the street with no place to go, having lost everything, and with no sense of direction. Afraid to turn once again to my Dad for help, I finally broke into a trailer, and slept there for a night.

The next morning, I admitted to myself that I'd hit rock bottom, and decided to hitchhike back to Mom's. I called my Aunt Bell and asked her if Mom would have me back home, and I knew by the excitement in her voice, that at least somebody would be glad to see me. It would be good to have familiar family and old friends around me again. I'd lost a lot of weight, and wasn't in good health, plus, I was almost eighteen. It had been four years since I'd left my Mom, and I hadn't kept in touch much, primarily because of her deafness, and the fact that I didn't like to write. Because I moved around so much, she often didn't even know how to contact me. For good reason, she was still scared of me—I was still angry, out of control, and violent. The demons still influenced me, as did my addictions. She never knew what I would do next, but other than these "minor" flaws, I was the "model" son!

MY OLD FRIEND AARON

When I arrived home, I discovered that Aaron, one of my best friends from grade school, was now a drug dealer with access to everything. He and I went back a long way—I remember sleeping over at his house and phoning girls I had a crush on. He'd pretend I wasn't there, and then ask them questions about me while I listened on an extension.

Now that Aaron was a drug addict and dealer, what an excellent opportunity to get my drugs for the next few months. Our relationship became that of supply and demand—he supplied me and I demanded everything that he could get his hands on. Because he was such a good friend, I could pay him later, or sometimes not at all.

Aaron had had frequent demonic visitations since he was a young child. He said that a demon named "Raven" rode with him on the back of his bicycle. We would sit at Mom's apartment and talk about ghosts and demons, Ouija boards and more. Aaron and I would "hot box" my small room. We'd close the door and smoke enough marijuana to fill the room with smoke. After Mom went to bed I would hot-knife hash on her stove, drink her alcohol till 4:00 A.M. and then sleep until noon everyday.

My drug habits escalated. So much so, that I'd do a mix of coke, LSD, and speed three to four times per week, and also lace my joints with PCP (angel dust), opium, or methamphetamines (speed or crank). If I was desperate for a high (I needed highs to function), I'd resort to sniffing gas or popping whatever pills I could find. When I rolled out of bed, I'd reach for a joint or a beer—I couldn't function even socially without them. My life had to be a fantasy world, and it was rooted in anger, fear, rejection, and self-hatred. But that was all about to change…

AARON, BORN AGAIN?

One day I went looking for Aaron to get a fix, but to my shock, he refused to sell or supply me anything. Hello? He said that a few days previously, while in his trailer and walking from the living room to the kitchen, that the heavens opened up and God Himself came down. He said that he fell to the floor, had a revelation of Jesus, and was born again. *"Born Again"*…I was beginning to hate that term.

A few weeks later I was having coffee in a restaurant with about six of my friends when this boisterous guy named Wally came in. He was about 6' 4", 240 pounds and had a big beard. Wally had a reputation in our community; no one messed with him. He'd been to prison and was an alcoholic. At one time, he made his living as an enforcer for the mob—they had a loan shark operation and if anyone was behind in a payment Wally found him, roughed him up, and broke his legs. Interestingly, Wally was instrumental in bringing me to the Lord, because he had at one time worked for Doug, the man who first discipled me (together they used to break legs for the Mafia).

Wally carried in a large, white, Catholic family Bible, slammed it down on our table, and said, "Do you know where I got this Bible?"

Of course, I thought, *No…and I don't really care!*

But he didn't wait for an answer. Instead, he explained about how he had become saved, and then went on with his story:

He explained how determined he was afterward to get himself a Bible, so he went to a Catholic bookstore to buy one. "I saw this Bible, and looked at the price tag written on the shelf below. It was more money than I had in my pocket, so I just asked God for the money I needed, put the Bible back on the shelf, and turned to go. I heard a thud, and turned back around. The Bible had fallen off of the shelf, and opened up. In red ink in the corner of the inside cover, was the sale price, and it was the exact amount of money I had. So I got me a Bible ..."

Wow—that was the second supernatural testimony I'd heard. *Oh no,* I thought, *another one like Aaron?* Yet, even though it perplexed me, it did cause me to question. *What's happening? I'd always believed in God, and figured I would come to Him "sometime," but not now...*Along the way, many had taken the time to share with me about the Lord, but I'd turned them all down. Here was God, setting up divine encounters, yet I didn't want anything to do with Him. Nevertheless, God had planted all of those seeds— and little did I know that my grandmother and grandfather were regularly watering them in prayer.

EVANGELISM—WALLY STYLE

A few weeks later, while visiting with Aaron in his trailer, I badgered and begged him to get me one more "doobie." He finally caved in. While I got high in his bathroom, though, someone outside of the trailer banged at the door. "This is the police with a search warrant!" yelled the intruder. I said, "Oh...no!" I believed that it was indeed the police or someone out to get us. Aaron and I were both always paranoid—living scared because of our lifestyle and involvement with the drug world. Everyone seemingly conspired against us. As a result, Aaron kept guns, baseball bats, and crowbars all over the trailer. We could always pull a knife out from under the sofa in an "emergency."

Aaron grabbed a baseball bat, and peeked behind the curtain. It was Wally, and his big, white Bible! By now, he wasn't knocking on the door normally, but almost kicking down the door to get in. Aaron opened it for him, and Wally barged in, grabbed a chair, sat right down in front of me, and started to preach. Never mind the kind approach—he didn't even use the "Four Spiritual Laws"…instead, he was in my face with "hell fire and brimstone!"

He crammed that big white bible down my throat. I'm talking Bible thumping big time. He said, "Todd, you're going to have to get saved."

"I don't want to listen to you, stop preaching at me."

But he kept on. "You better repent or you're going to burn."

"Stop preaching at me. I don't want to listen."

Wally wouldn't quit and I became irate and yelled, "Stop preaching at me—I don't want to listen!"

Wally said, "If you'll do one thing, I won't talk to you about Jesus anymore."

Relieved, I asked him what he wanted me to do, and he said, "Take this Bible, and put it on your lap. Close your eyes, open it up to any place you want to, and put your finger on the page, then, look down, and read aloud the first words that you see."

If only to get him off of my back, I thought, but I knew that he spoke truth, but I wasn't ready…I'd give my life to Christ later. Frankly though, I also wondered if God really would speak to me. So, after he placed the Bible in my lap, I opened it, raised my finger in the air, and brought it down on a page. Then I peered down to the words that rested just above my finger—not in the general area, but right above my finger, and I read the following words:

"Listen now"

They rolled out of my mouth like thunder and lightning. In that moment, the fear of God, accompanied with great urgency, came pouring into that trailer. I cried out for Jesus to save me. I wasn't playing around any more. I prayed the sinner's prayer and I gave Him my heart and life. I'd prayed this prayer before, but that night I really meant it. (By the way, I don't recommend Bible roulette as a good way to get direction, but God was gracious and used it on that occasion.)

A JESUS HIGH

I was born again in that trailer and for the first time in my life, I felt free. The paranoia and burdens fell off. I felt as light as a feather. I thought that if I jumped in the air I would float away. I was on a super high. There's no high like the Most High, and believe me, I've experienced them all. God immediately delivered me from drugs and alcohol. I never had a single craving or withdrawal symptom. Three weeks later, I quit cigarettes. What drug and alcohol programs couldn't do, Jesus did.

I ran out of the trailer—I wanted to tell everyone! First I found a phone booth and called my aunt. She was a good Catholic, and I thought she would be excited. Still jumping with excitement in the phone booth, her response was laughter. "Maybe someone else, but not Todd Bentley!"

When I hung up, several elderly women were assembled, waiting to use the phone, what did they think of my ranting and raving? I didn't care—from that day forward, I was as bold for God as I was for unrighteousness. Right there, I started to witness, and I haven't stopped. I've never been ashamed of the Gospel, how could I be in light of my experience with the Living God who is as real a person as any I know, and my Friend.

THE LAST BAD TRIP

Two days later I was at Mom's house and I saw a joint—the last one. I knew that I was free from my addiction but I wondered what would happen if I smoked it. I had two small puffs and suddenly I was higher than I'd ever been—my senses dramatically heightened.

I knew that it was a bad supernatural trip because although I was used to constant paranoia—this was paranoia times ten. I dashed around the apartment from one window to the next to see who was coming for me, and my mind raced as I collapsed on the sofa. Darkness invaded the room and evil beings gnashed out at me so close, I could almost feel their breath, and in the spirit, I heard shrieks.

God let me feel separation from Him. It was a taste of hell. The moment I realized what was happening, I cried out to God, and immediately joy and the Spirit of the fear of the Lord came. This experience contributed greatly to my desire to see people snatched out of the fire spoken of in Jude 1:23.

SATANIC ATTACKS

The enemy didn't give up easily. The number 999 (666 upside down) appeared on my cupboard within two hours of my being in Mom's house and leaving. It seemed as though the paint had been removed in that one area only; the rest of the surface remained untouched. As soon as I saw that number on my cupboard, I felt a demonic presence and I knew that something had been in the house and had left a mark just to say, "Todd, we know you. We know where you live." It was an attack from the enemy to plant fear in me. I didn't know what to do except pray and rebuke it.

That was the beginning of a renewed satanic assault on my life, though now as a recently born-again believer. I often heard demons growl and scrape on the walls of my home. For several days in a row, in the early morning hours of 1 or 2 A.M., I'd hear a commotion from my mother's bedroom; voices, banging, crashing, and clanging, as well as "people" fighting and hitting each other. However, when I'd run into her room, it would all stop, and Mom would be soundly sleeping. Strangely, her body would be turned 90 degrees so that she lay horizontally along the headboard, her legs on the bedside table. She'd startle when I awoke her, but have no idea what had transpired.

One evening, I discovered her in the middle of the floor, her wrist broken. At the hospital, when medical personnel asked her what happened, she told them it was just a bad dream. However, at home later, she confided to me that she protected me, because she thought that I had done it, considering my past history of abuse.

After those experiences, and over many months, the Lord orchestrated several deliverance sessions for me. Although I was radically saved and serving Jesus, the Lord needed to set me free from the demonic influences I had allowed into my life through my past ungodly lifestyle. During the deliverance sessions, I spoke in different voices and demonstrated supernatural strength. It would take four or five men to hold me down. At one session, twenty-five demons were cast out. No pigs were safe that day! Praise God for His cleansing, healing, and delivering power!

The reason I've recounted here my past is certainly not to glorify sin; I'm ashamed of the lifestyle I lived. I retell these parts of my story to emphasize the fact that I'm ordinary. God didn't choose to use me because my mother dedicated me to the Lord and sent me off to live my early life cloistered away in a monastery studying "the disciplines" each day.

In following pages, I'll share some of the extraordinary encounters I had with the Lord. I hope now, by the foundation that I've laid, that you understand that God didn't pre-qualify me— that I'm as real and ordinary as the next guy. God can take ordinary people and do extraordinary things through them. We see this from Genesis to Revelation. As God said to the apostle Paul, "My grace is sufficient for you, for My strength is made perfect in weakness" (2 Cor. 12:9).

CHAPTER 5

FIRST VISITATION—THE OUTPOURING

Immediately after my salvation, I got into the Bible. I was so hungry I would read the four Gospels in one setting. As I digested Scripture, I could feel wind blow up and down my arms. The windows weren't open, so I knew God was near. I remember the excitement of those first months and the hunger that I could never satisfy for His presence and the Word.

I'd stay up all night Saturday reading the Bible, praying, and watching Christian broadcasts. I so hungered for God! In my mind, there was not enough time in a day and I was even concerned that I'd oversleep and miss church on Sunday. Remember, it was my habit to sleep in until 1 o'clock in the afternoon!

COME HOLY SPIRIT

As a new Christian, I hung out with men who were part of the Full Gospel Business Men's Fellowship. These believers taught me about the baptism of the Holy Spirit. They discipled me, and graced me with the opportunity to share a 10-minute testimony at their retreats. On Mondays, I hung out with the charismatic Catholics—their meetings had a really laid-back atmosphere where people learned to move in the gifts.

I began to learn about the kingdom of Heaven and Jesus through the Holy Spirit. My second real encounter with the Holy Spirit was born out of hunger to know Him. I did word studies on the Holy Spirit in a Catholic concordance that I'd purchased at the Catholic bookstore (Wally and I were their best customers!). At the time, I didn't know there was a difference between Catholic and Protestant concordances.

Two months after my salvation, I had an overwhelming desire for the Holy Spirit. Never satisfied, I kept thinking that there must be more. In my research and studies, I read and took notes on countless biblical references to the Holy Spirit. Then I said to my brothers at the Full Gospel Businessmen's fellowship, "I want more! I'm a new Christian. I'm reading Scripture four to five hours a day, but there's still a hunger burning in my soul!"

"We've got to get you then, filled with the Spirit!" they replied. And so, they prayed over me for the baptism of the Holy Spirit. In an attempt to "jump start" me in the prayer language, they asked me to repeat, "Abba, Abba, Abba," over and over, and then said, that I'd received "tongues," even though I couldn't speak another language.

This is ridiculous, I thought, *I don't feel a 'spring' springing up...I don't feel living water flowing from my belly*....What I sought was the baptism in fire—as in the book of Acts. I wanted something supernatural like a spontaneous burst of uncontrollable joy and tongues, so that I knew that I was filled with the Spirit, and not just making something up.

As God would have it, a short while later, I visited the city of Kelowna, a great eagle's nest today for many prophets and prophetic people. This is where I would receive my wonderful prayer language. It was around midnight, three days into my stay, and I felt overwhelmed by the presence of God. As I stepped onto the shore of Okanagan Lake, my heart felt as though it was bursting. My heart said, "Yes…this is tongues." But my mind said, "No," as it tried to figure out what was happening in the deeper parts of my spirit.

DOVE FROM HEAVEN

I said, "Holy Spirit, give me a sign." Then in an instant, the dark midnight sky illuminated with heavenly glory. The heavens opened with a bright flash and a white dove materialized out of thin air and flew across the lake to a nearby tree. Although it was a single dove, it sounded as the flapping wings of ten thousand doves. The noise filled the sky and rumbled in my spirit; the sound of a ripping, rushing, and mighty wind filled my ears. I knew in my spirit that heaven had opened. When I turned toward the tree, the dove was gone. I thought, "OK, that works."

I had received not only tongues, but also an enduement of power from on high for miracles, signs, and wonders. I continued speaking in my new language until the wee hours of the morning. I still don't know if I really saw the dove in the natural, or if it was a vision. However, that was my first real experience with seeing in the spirit. To this day, I consistently constantly spend much time speaking in tongues. It's how I stir up the Spirit of wisdom, empty myself, receive revelation, and get into the mind of Christ.

MORE OF THE HOLY SPIRIT

After that experience, I hungered for even more of God and the Word. Every time I opened my Bible, the words leapt off the page and it was like taking a drink to quench my incredible thirst for knowledge of Him.

With excitement, I asked my mentors at Full Gospel, "What's next?"

"That's it. You're baptized in the Holy Ghost, speaking in tongues and you have the gift of prophecy." Then, someone gave me a book by Benny Hinn titled, *Good Morning, Holy Spirit.* Up until that time, I'd never heard of Benny, or of revival. It was just what I needed and I thought, *That's what I want—more of the Holy Spirit!*

After I finished the book, I realized that I also needed what Benny had—intimacy with God's Spirit. I now understood that God wanted me to have a deeper relationship with His Spirit. God is not partial but He favors those who diligently seek Him; He favors those who hunger and thirst after Him.

I didn't know what to do except to pray simple prayers, so I prayed, "I want to know you, Holy Spirit, just like Benny knows you and just like this woman, Kathryn that he talks about. I'm asking You to come into my bedroom as a person in the same way You did for Benny. I want to have a conversation with You wonderful, Holy Spirit. I want to feel electricity and weep uncontrollably. I want so much of Your presence that I can't get up off my bed. I want you to be more real to me."

He answered my cry. I had a visitation of the person of the Holy Spirit. My body shook and I felt electricity. Once while I was under a heavy anointing my friend stopped by and yelled to me, "Come on, let's go." It was all I could do to shout back, "I'm in my room." When he opened the door to my room and saw me, he said, "Why are you shaking?"

"I don't know. I think it's the Holy Spirit."

"Why would the Holy Spirit make you shake?"

"I don't know but He's been doing it for about three hours."

"Get up off your bed."

"I can't. I can't move. My whole body is numb, and I'm sinking into the mattress."

"This is a demon possessing you. You can't even do what you want to do. That's not the Lord."

"I don't know, but it feels good." I said as my friend tried to pull me from the bed.

HOLY SPIRIT, I LOVE YOU

Despite my friend's views about my experience, I knew it was from God, and every day I couldn't wait to get home from my job cleaning gutters and washing vinyl siding to be in His presence. I'd race into my bedroom and be hit with what felt like an electrical force field. The Holy Spirit was waiting for me and I believe He was just as excited about being with me as I was about being with Him! When we were together, it was similar to that emotional high that two six-year-old children would have together on Christmas morning.

I'd close the bedroom door and weep, standing for three hours and telling Him how much I loved Him, and I'd feel tangible love back. This incredible intimacy lasted from four to twelve hours every day for almost three months. The Spirit of God breathed on the pages of the Bible. This wasn't the baptism of the Holy Ghost—it wasn't speaking in tongues, it was a Person in my home, who today is as real to me as the Father and the Son.

Within three months of my salvation, I'd discovered that the Holy Spirit isn't limited to convicting people, to slaying them in the power, or to manifesting gifts and miracles through them. The Holy Spirit is a Person whom I can converse with. I can say, "Holy Spirit, I love You, and I'm glad that we are partners. Together we can bring Jesus to the world. You inspired people to write this

Bible—help me understand it. Place Scripture in my heart so they are not just words. I can't even say, 'Jesus is Lord' without You!"

Then I'd open my Bible and feel Him hover over me. When we conversed, time flew by.

God is sovereign and He'll do whatever He wants, but I volunteered to let Him work through me. I said, "I want You to open this Bible to me and I'm going to take this message all over the world. I ask You for wisdom and revelation. I'm going to talk to You from this day forward. I want You to be my best friend. I want to know Your presence and Your person in this place. I ask You to come."

I loved, welcomed, and yielded to the Holy Spirit daily. God revealed Himself to me as I hungered for Him. It was almost like dating—the freshness of a new love. To this day, the Holy Spirit is as real to me as any person is. He constantly speaks to me through the inner audible voice of God.

I've been in such communion with the Holy Spirit, where His presence was so real, that when I stepped out of my room, I would feel Him move with me to the elevator. When I got in my car, I would feel a person slip into the seat next to me. When people visited me at home, they'd get zapped by an invisible, electrical force field in whatever room I was in, and then bounce back. I'd say, "Hey, what happened?" and they'd say that something "zapped" them. There were also times people couldn't even get close to me without falling. Years later, Shonnah, my wife, while washing dishes while a friend was visiting, suddenly went down under the power as I walked into the kitchen. Her friend screamed, "Your face is glowing!"

The Holy Spirit would move with me like a cloud. I recall a time when, as I got into a friend's car, he just wept. Another time I spoke at a Christian school, and as I shared about the Holy Spirit, and openly loved and honored Him, many of the youth fell out under the power in holy laughter. I was like, "Hey, what's happening here?" (I didn't yet know how to move in the "flow"). They'd reply, "There's fire coming off you," though I didn't feel anything. Nevertheless, I remembered reading about some of these manifestations in Benny's book, and with excitement, I knew that it was happening to me, too.

In those wonderful days of growing intimacy with the Holy Spirit, I had nothing to do *but* pursue Him, though no one understood what was happening in my life.

A GEOGRAPHICAL CHANGE

Within this three-month period, I heard God's audible voice clearly for the first time. "I want you to move to Abbotsford, British Columbia," He said.

"God, there's no Abbotsford, B.C. I've never heard of it…" I replied (boy, did I have a lot to learn). "…besides, my church has sponsored me to go to Bible school—I've been accepted. They are even going to pay for it. I'm going to get a suit and tie, cut my hair, look like the rest of the preachers and meet my wife. Even if there's an Abbotsford, I can't just tell my friends at church I'm leaving."

Yet God's audible command to me continued to ring and resonate through my being—it was as if my whole head filled with the idea of Abbotsford. I had heard God so clearly and I remember thinking to myself, *This must be how God speaks audibly.* Today, He still constantly speaks to me, and I can still hear Him whisper in my ear.

In those days, I didn't know a lot about Christianity, but I had learned that a prophetic word should be confirmed in the mouth of two witnesses. Therefore, I told God He would have to confirm my move to the "mythical" town of Abbotsford.

THE CHARISMATIC CATHOLICS

Around this time, I had been hanging out with the charismatic Catholics. They seemed to be the most alive church group in town. I attended their meetings once a week, and people were encouraged to practice prophecy and spiritual gifts. During worship time, I started to 'hear' simple words, like, "He loves you," or even passages of Scripture. I'd become so excited, even with a few words, and I'd tremble and shake before I spoke them. Once He told me, "I am here," and the strength of those words kept building and building, until finally I arose and yelled out, "Thus saith the Lord…'I am here'." Wow—people thought I was a great little fireball!

One night at the Catholic meeting the Lord spoke to me Hebrews 12:22, "You have come to Mount Zion and to the city of the living God…" I didn't know what to do with it. I went to the microphone, read the verse, sat down and everyone cheered. I didn't realize that the Scripture was for me. (I found out later that when we receive revelation we don't always know what to do with it. Sometimes revelation can be progressive and it can be months or years before we "get" the understanding.)

MISLED

Because I was hungry for the gifts of the Spirit, I hooked up with a man in the community called *Frenchie*. Frenchie had a reputation of receiving visitations and moving in extraordinary demonstrations of the Spirit. He lived on a boat at the marina where people brought the sick and they would get healed. He would cast demons out of people and lead them to Jesus. It was even rumored that he could tell people in detail what they had done that morning. The church called him an "independent, lone wolf" and, in many ways, he was. He was anointed, but he was rebellious and had issues with authority and leadership.

I was very interested in learning from him because he was moving in the Spirit in a stronger way than what I saw happening at the church. Frenchie usually didn't go to the church because he saw them as "too religious." Now when I look back, I understand that although He had a God-given gift, and a lot of charisma, he wasn't solid in issues of character. Nevertheless, I didn't understand those things—I was just hungry for the supernatural. I talked to my dad on the phone one day and when I went to see Frenchie on his little boat he told me about the conversation in such detail that I knew he had a true gift from God.

It wasn't until later that his character was revealed to me. Before I met him, he had married and divorced two or three women and had multiple affairs. He'd become angry and violent with the wharf manager and curse at him. He got his food from the dumpsters at the Safeway grocery store at night when the leftovers and outdated breads, meat and food were thrown out. It took me a few months to see his flaws. Frenchie did help me to move into the things of the Spirit. God used that experience to teach me. "Todd, I want to anoint you and use you," He said, "but I want you to be one who loves Me, knows Me, and wants to be like Me more than one who wants My gifts and My power. If you will always remember to dwell, rest, and soak in My presence, I will use you to shake the nations. But, remember, I am more concerned about what I can do in you than through you."

The Lord showed me through Frenchie's charisma, gifting, and lack of character, that it's possible to have His power but not be in right relationship with Him. I don't want to be like the foolish virgins or the ones who prophesied and cast out demons in His name. What did He say about them? "Depart from Me. I never knew you," or literally, "Depart from Me for I once knew you, but you have since not allowed yourself to be known" (Matthew 7:23). Although I was beginning to move in the gifts quickly, I pressed in even harder to the Lord.

GEOGRAPHICAL GUIDANCE

A few weeks later, Barry, my boss, and I were out in the woods, in the middle of nowhere. Recall where I lived on the Sunshine coast—to get to Gibsons required a 40-minute ferry ride. Barry and I were miles away from anywhere, therefore, in the bush, and sitting on a picnic table, when God sent me a messenger.

According to this fellow, the Lord had spoken to him and told him to bike across Canada, and for some reason (I have never learned), he decided to take the ferry ride to the island and pedal more than forty miles to exactly where we were in the forest. He didn't know we were there, and I'd never met him before. He pedaled up to us on his mountain bike, and recognized my boss.

"Barry," he exclaimed, "I can't believe it's you! When did *you* move here?" Then he said, "You're not going to believe what's happening...there's an outpouring of God in Abbotsford, B.C., you've got to come to Abbotsford!"

This had to be the voice of God. This fellow had no idea how God was using him. Barry turned and said, "Todd, do you want to go to Abbotsford? We can share an apartment."

"Praise God," I said, "I got a prophetic word about Abbotsford!"

That's how God moved me supernaturally from one community to the next. Barry and I did share an apartment in Abbotsford, and the next thing I needed was a church, no easy feat in what was known as Canada's Bible belt. With over a hundred churches to choose from, Barry suggested and recommended the church he used to attend—a tiny church with about fifty members.

I walked through the door a little late one Sunday, and stood in the back. "Friend," the pastor said as he opened the sermon, "You have come to Mount Zion and to the city of the living God." I fell out under the power right there in the back of the little church—this is exactly what the Lord had spoken to me through Scripture. The pastor hadn't even spoken specifically to me—but it was confirmation. This was destiny. I was in my city, and in my church. Someone had gotten hold of my life, and He was a whole lot bigger than I was. It appeared that He knew what I was doing even before I did it.

CHAPTER 6

HERE COMES THE
BRIDE—RELUCTANTLY

"Barry what's to do in this Abbotsford town?" I queried my friend one day. He suggested attending the citywide youth revival, *God Rock*, that was held on Friday nights in an old shopping mall. There they worshiped God with heavy rock-style music. This youth revival was birthed out of the Toronto outpouring as God moved in power on Generation X. Hundreds of young people in their teens and early twenties gathered, coming from every type of background and subculture—punks, metal heads, preps, Goths, and Kool-Aid kids with green or pink hair.

Since I didn't have a license or a car, I asked Barry to find a ride for me. He made a few phone calls and eventually contacted Shonnah, a girl from my new church. She agreed to drive me to God Rock. Later I found out that she had second thoughts and complained to her parents that she didn't want to pick me up. "I don't know this guy," she said, "Who is he and why can't Barry take him?" She even toyed with the idea of calling to cancel and tried to convince her best friend, Roswetta, to ride with her. Roswetta (pronounced *Rosevita*) was a tad conservative at the time and thought Shonnah was in a cult, as did Shonnah's parents, and even the pastor of our small church. When Roswetta wouldn't come along, Shonnah finally resigned herself to her fate, arrived at my basement apartment, and knocked on my door.

Shonnah had grown up Catholic. She got saved at 16 when the Lord healed her of bone cancer and a spot on her lungs. Several Christians, including some ministers, prayed for her over a period of several weeks and God blessed her with a miracle. The nurturing of the church impacted her immediate family and they all got saved too, including her dad who had been an alcoholic for over twenty years.

Shonnah, seven years older than I am, had been waiting and praying for a husband for ten years. She and I, however, were opposites. I was loud and outgoing, and she was quiet and conservative, especially when talking to guys. She had a job and a driver's license, had never touched drugs, dated, or even kissed a guy—a real Miss-Goody-Two-Shoes, the reserved Catholic girl; This was who came knocking at *my* door!

She was met, on the other hand, and on the other side of the door, by what looked like, a Hell's Angel's biker (that would be me) sporting a big goatee, long hair, earrings, bandana, and ripped jeans. I hadn't bothered to change my look since Dad and I had partied with them several years previously. In the natural, I was the last person you'd want your daughter to marry! We couldn't be more different, but oh, God does have a sense of humor!

I opened the door and sucked in a deep breath when I saw her. She was beautiful. I tried to regain my suave and debonair persona by blurting out, "Just a minute," and slamming the door in her face. I ran to Barry, ranting about her beauty and how I'd have no chance with a woman like that. She was a preppy and I was a hood. Well, I finally opened the door. I found out later that while on the 10-minute ride to God Rock, she silently prayed, "Oh God, help me…help me!" She was so scared that I think she might have thought I was going to mug her!

We walked into the meeting, already underway with loud music and dimmed lights—like a club. "Where do you want to sit?" I asked her.

"I don't know, just pick somewhere," she said.

I pointed to some chairs, and (I discovered later) we sat directly in front of Chris—a guy she'd had a crush on. In fact, she felt that the Lord had told her that they were going to marry. She said she was thinking, *Oh great…he's going to think Todd and I are together.…* Worse still, when the pastor told us to turn around to greet the person behind us, I immediately swung around and shook Chris's hand. To him it must have appeared as, "In your face buddy—she's mine now!" But all that time, I had no idea they were even friends.

A few minutes later Roswetta showed up at the meeting; she had decided to join us and help her friend. Roswetta, a conservative Mennonite girl, wasn't sure about these spiritual manifestations in the meeting: drunkenness in the Spirit, falling on the floor, shaking, groaning, laughing, and crying. Remember, this was in 1994 when the spiritual renewal movement, or the "Toronto blessing," was going all over the world. This meeting was the first time that I had even seen the manifestations of the Spirit outside of my apartment.

During the worship, there was a call for prayer and Shonnah went forward. I remember her bending backwards and forwards like a tree swaying in the wind. I thought to myself, "Why is she shaking and doing the Gumby?"

Suddenly, I felt an anger churn deep inside me. I tried to squelch it but it rose from inside with violent thoughts. Overcome by a demon, I threw myself at the chairs and knocked them flying. I screamed, cursed, and writhed on the floor like a snake. Then I rolled and screamed and tried to avoid the four or five guys who tried to restrain and deliver me. Fortunately, Shonnah was oblivious to what was happening, however, Roswetta had a front-row seat to my performance—it certainly did little to quell her fears of the meeting being a 'cult' thing, and certainly was not a great first impression. The good thing about this incident was that I received a powerful deliverance from some lingering demonic bondages.

THE PURSUIT

By meeting's end, I was infatuated with Shonnah, so I devised a plan. I observed whom she hung out with and discovered we had some mutual friends. "Coincidentally" within a few short weeks, we found ourselves with the same group of friends and in the same restaurants after the revival meetings.

A friend of mine, Gerard, was a friend of Earl and Val, Shonnah's parents. Gerard and I hung out a lot at his apartment doing "carpet time" together, as we enjoyed the presence of the Holy Spirit. However, after a few weeks, I confessed to him how I felt about Shonnah. Afterward, it was Shonnah this, and Shonnah that and Shonnah, Shonnah, Shonnah! It used to be, "Jesus, Jesus, and Jesus!" Gerard finally got fed up and said, "If you don't ask her out, I'll do it for you!" So the next time he saw Shonnah, he said, "The new guy, Todd, likes you and wants to go out with you."

"No thanks," Shonnah answered, "He's too wild. Please let him know that I am not interested, but please be nice about it."

Perplexed but not in despair, struck down but not destroyed, I continued to arrange meetings just to be near her, but acted as though I just wanted to be friends. She thought I'd lost interest, which was fine with her! She picked me up a few more times for God Rock, and we even did prayer ministry together. She loved to hang with me because she liked my fiery preaching, evangelism, and anointing. I was everything she wanted in a Christian, but nothing she wanted in a boyfriend. Sometimes we'd meet as early as 10 A.M. and hang out together until 3 A.M. praying and ministering with others.

On a previous occasion, the Lord had actually shown me an open vision of Shonnah. It was my first open-eyed vision. I was in my living room and my fireplace mantel opened up, kind of like a TV screen, and I saw us embracing in a wheat field that was ready for harvest. We were both weeping and I was wearing a tux and she wore a wedding dress. As the vision unfolded, her friend Roswetta (who was now my friend) was talking with me in the living room about Shonnah. I described the open vision to her as it happened. The presence of the Lord fell and we both wept. Roswetta said, "I can't see it but I can feel goose bumps." During this vision, I also received an anointing of creativity, poetry, and writing. In fact, I even received a three-page prophetic poem that I read at our wedding. I still write prophetic poems for my wife to this day.

A woman in our church, Helen, had a niece who was vexed with an evil spirit and was slowly dying. She asked me to pray for her, and I asked Shonnah to come along. Returning from the prayer time, and as Helen drove us home, I asked, "Helen, how do you know when you've found the right one?"

All three of us engaged in an enthusiastic conversation about marriage. Shonnah was really getting into it because she still felt like the Lord had told her she was going to marry Chris. She wondered why I asked all these questions. Then she remembered a conversation we'd had a few weeks earlier at a restaurant. Shonnah overheard me tell my friend Steve that the Lord had shown me who I'd marry. They badgered me at the table until I gave a description of the one the Lord showed me. Apparently, Shonnah was sitting there thinking, "I sure hope it's not me."

I interpreted Shonnah's enthusiasm for the marriage conversation as a hint to me that she had re-thought her decision and was now interested in me. I thought that perhaps the Lord had shown her our future marriage the same way He had shown me. I sensed that Shonnah, too, had brushed off her fears that I was still interested in her because I had "backed off" in recent weeks. Helen dropped us off at my apartment where Shonnah had parked her car. I forget where we had to go together after Helen left, but as we drove off, my misperception of her change of heart—those things I considered hints to move forward, gave me the courage to blurt out and say, "The Lord has shown me that you are going to be my wife."

This didn't go down too well—at least not as I thought it would as I had played that phrase over and over in my mind before I'd said it. Instead of a tearful embrace, enthusiastic laughter and the excitement I was looking for, Shonnah said, "No way— God has not spoken to me at all—I don't see it!" Ouch!

In the natural, I wasn't that great a catch. I didn't have a job or work skills, and I wasn't interested in those skills because I was "doing the work of the ministry." I saw it as living by faith while cashing my welfare checks and living off of everyone else, including my roommate. My pastor, Henry, who had been discipling me, tried to encourage me toward employment, but the message wasn't getting through. He and others recognized the evangelistic call on my life, but they knew it was in the future. I thought it was for "now." Besides my unemployed status, my wild background, lack of education, and my recent conversation were black marks against me. I didn't even have a driver's license, and still lived out of a backpack. Another very viable and legitimate concern was whether my zeal for the Lord would burn out, causing me to backslide and return to my previous lifestyle, because I'd been walking with the Lord for less than a year.

LETTING GO OF EXPECTATIONS

Shonnah had a list she'd made of the characteristics she wanted in a husband. She'd been praying over it for ten years and had women in the church praying for her future spouse. I exceeded all of the spiritual requirements, but she'd also been praying for a good-looking virgin and she didn't think I fit either of those criteria. I wasn't a virgin, for sure, but I was hoping I'd squeak by on the other qualification (this is known as denial and wishful thinking).

Shonnah's parents and my pastor knew that she was the one for me. One of the elders had a dream confirming it. Shonnah's brother knew it. I wondered why God wasn't telling the one person whose opinion *really* mattered. It did seem to be a bit of an obstacle.

Shonnah worked the graveyard shift at a bakery. With the help of her friends there, she came to realize that she talked about me all the time and that she missed me when we were apart. One of her friends at work said, "I don't believe you aren't interested. You like him; you're just not admitting it."

"No I don't." (This too is known as denial and wishful thinking!)

She kept getting hung up on her list of requirements. Then she read a book called *Passion and Purity* in which someone asked how important it was that her potential spouse is good looking. The reply was, "What if you are the tool God wants to use to bless someone else with what they want? Get your eyes off yourself."

The Lord led Shonnah to ask, "What if God wants to bless Todd with me?" She had been living in a fairytale world and her friends had to help her see her true feelings because she had an expectation of what "it" would look like.

The most important characteristics are love, devotion, and passion for God. Yes, beauty is in the eye of the beholder. Yet God can help us see the beauty in others. I believe it's important to have expectations regarding a mate but not to hold God to our unrealistic expectations if they aren't His requirements. I encourage single Christians to ask the Lord what their ideal husband or wife looks like for them. There are many single people who won't accept the spouse of God's choosing because of a physical flaw. Deciding on a life's partner needs to be by the Spirit, not by the flesh, natural attraction, or lust. The Lord isn't against dating, but God has a choice for each one.

Dear reader, if you're single, I want to encourage you to keep your eyes on Jesus and ask Him to help you make your list. If you're married and your original motives for saying "I do" were not right or from the Lord, don't misconstrue my previous comments as an endorsement for divorce. Invite Jesus and His principles into your life, and He will bless and honor your covenant as you do the same. The issue of divorce and remarriage is a whole topic in itself and I won't get into it right now. (Now, back to my story—sometimes I just can't help lapsing into a sermonette.)

FINALLY!

Shonnah finally believed that I was God's answer to her ten years of prayer. Since everyone else believed this too, we decided not to have a long engagement. I whole-heartedly embraced Paul's philosophy, "better to marry than to burn". Long engagements are fine but if both parties, pastoral leadership, and those you are in relationship with feel you're making a good decision, then why give room for the devil to attack? We decided to get married in five weeks, May 22, 1995.

We were so on fire in those days that even at my "bachelor party," we evangelized. First, at the restaurant, they dressed me in a white shirt imprinted with the words, *Prisoner of Love*, then they put a ball and chain on my ankle, and a toilet seat around my head, and instructed me to go to the grocery store to purchase toilet paper and chocolate sauce for the seat. Everyone accompanied me, but we were so passionate about reaching people that we all just stood out in front of the store for a while first to share with people about Jesus.

"What are you doing?" they'd ask.

"It's my bachelor's party and I want to tell you about Jesus," I'd say. (Even years later in my ministry as I travel doing big crusades, we still take people into the market to do prophetic evangelism.)

The night before my wedding, I barely slept. I had butterflies in my stomach. My friends stayed the night. In the morning my mother came over and, sure enough, we got into one of the biggest fights we'd had in years—and believe me, we'd had some doozies. In the midst of our fight that day I said, "Mom you're wrecking my wedding day. How can you make me feel like this? How can you be so selfish?" But by the time I was ready to leave for the church I fell on my knees and apologized for all the ways I'd hurt her then and in the past. We wept and prayed together. God wanted to expose some things in my life and be sure I was ready to "leave and cleave."

From that day forward, I had an open door to minister to her. She read my newsletters and began watching Billy Graham on TV. She read all of the Christian material I brought to her. She would even let Shonnah and I pray for her.

THE MOST BEAUTIFUL BRIDE IN THE WORLD

I arrived at the wedding hall, nervous and excited wondering what would happen when I saw her for the first time in her wedding gown. It's still so vivid—I remember the moment the music began to play and the door opened, I'll never forget her beauty as she stepped out into the aisle with her father. She took my breath away and I thought I'd pass out. "Are you okay," said my best man.

We had a beautiful reception. The church was like a family for us. They prepared the hall, and all of the details of a perfect wedding, and then pulled together a potluck reception. They even blessed us on our way by stuffing my Dayton boots with money (a collection from family and friends). That day we left for a short honeymoon to Qualicum Beach, and yet, today, the honeymoon continues. (It's worth the wait my single friend… God has a mate for you.)

CHAPTER 7

THE CLEANSING PROCESS

As in every believer's walk with Jesus, my conversion was only the beginning of the transformation. Next came the working out of my salvation with fear and trembling. One of the first things to go in my ongoing cleansing process was a poverty mindset, the idea that God probably didn't want me to have anything at all. My attitude was, "I won't presume on God, whatever He gives me is OK." I had a "crumbs-from-Your-table-are-good-enough" mentality. I was just thankful that I was saved and not going to hell but I really didn't expect much from God. I felt so unworthy of anything good and pure because I knew how many lives I had destroyed. I struggled daily with rejection .

God used my relationship with my wife to teach me about His unconditional love for me. Shonnah was sixteen when He healed her of cancer and she became born again. At that time I was ten and dabbling in the occult, but little did I know that my wife and the intercessors were already praying for me. I was overwhelmed that God would keep a woman pure 26 years for me. She never did drugs, drank, or smoked; she kept herself from men and was on fire for God. She was everything that I ever could have wanted in a woman and I felt completely unworthy. I struggled with thoughts like, "How could I have someone so pure? I'm going to corrupt her."

Once, when I was newly married, a woman in church said, "Todd Bentley, you are not for Shonnah but Shonnah is for you. God kept Shonnah all these years as a gift to give to you." She was a tangible evidence of His love for me. God used Shonnah's love, time and again, as I struggled with guilt, condemnation, unworthiness, and rejection. I'd mess up, come short of my expectations, hurt her, and feel terrible. It was like Paul's struggle—what I wanted to do I didn't and what I didn't want to do I did. At times, I'd be insensitive and she'd be right there to say, "I forgive you." Then I'd fall, sin against God, and feel such condemnation. She would say, "If I can forgive you every day, then why can't God?" Then I would think, *My wife loves me so much—surely His love is even greater!*

EMPLOYMENT

I'd always struggled to hold a job and be financially responsible. Most of my life I didn't even care about working. In the past, I worked and collected welfare at the same time. I saw the government as my enemy, and I was going to keep every dollar I could. I thought that God would call me into the ministry any second but others convinced me that I needed to work and support my family. It was a struggle—I'd get a job and then be laid off, then I'd get another job and the place would go bankrupt. I'd start my own business and it would go well—for a while—then the bottom would drop out. It really wasn't until I entered into ministry that I began to believe that God even wanted *me* to be blessed and to enjoy His goodness in my own life.

DELIVERANCE

In the first couple of years after I was born again, God dealt with me repeatedly, bringing deliverance, imparting a greater revelation of my acceptance, and pouring out His cleansing grace.

I recall that one such instance, before I moved to Abbotsford, where I'd been at the home of some Catholic friends. Right in the middle of Bible study, the Lord told me that I had a demon of fear.

"Oh God, what am I going to do?" I asked. He told me to talk to Frenchie. So I walked right up to him and said, "Frenchie, I have a demon of ..." and when I said, "fear," my whole body contorted, and I started flailing, screaming, and writhing as a snake. People jumped on me to subdue me, but I threw them across the room, and then started to rip at the furniture. It took five people sitting on me, and two hours of deliverance before I was free. This was the first deliverance session that the Lord had divinely arranged for me.

Another time, God touched my life during a Vineyard revival meeting. I was at the altar to get prayer ministry when churning emotions rose up inside me. Destructive thoughts overwhelmed me with thoughts like, *I just want to kill myself....* Anger, murder, death, suicide, and violence raged inside of me. I writhed and screamed on the floor. It was a spirit of death and it was connected to my fascination with Jim Morrison and my drug overdoses. I went through deliverance until one in the morning.

Once more, I was at my local church during a city prayer gathering. During the worship service, I started screaming at the top of my lungs for my father. Picture that, right in the middle of the service and I'm yelling, "Dad, daddy!" Here I was, Mr. *Cool*, still looking like a biker and believing that "big boys don't cry." This time it wasn't a demon, though, it was just the pain, the ache, the loneliness of not knowing the love and acceptance of my father. Everyone there, about thirty or so people, began to intercede for me. I became a lump of weeping mush on the floor, crying like a baby but dressed as a biker. I bawled for hours, totally overcome by the revelation of the Father's love for me. My friends had to carry me to a vehicle, and then drove me home and carried me into my house, because I couldn't walk I was so intoxicated with the Lord's love.

Outside of my own prayer life, I had many other tremendous encounters in which God set me free from bondages, brought me a revelation of His love, and dealt with my past. I believe the Holy Spirit was saying, "This is MY fish. I want to get him clean and get him on the market as soon as possible!" So, yes, God did a very quick work in my life!

CHILDREN

As in my wedding and cleansing process, most events in my life seemed to happen fast. Therefore, Shonnah and I asked, "Why not have kids right away too?" However, because of Shonnah's past fight with cancer, the doctor said she had a slim (one percent) chance of conceiving. After fourteen months, we were convinced he was right.

Shonnah received prayer one day from a prophet who had a word of knowledge for barrenness. The power of God went through her and seven days later, she conceived. I was so excited when we discovered she was pregnant. From then on, every day for me was like waiting for Christmas!

One day, while in the bathroom, and with Shonnah's due date still a few months away, I said to the Lord, "I just can't wait any longer for this child, can You bring the labor on early?" Everything else God had given me had come so fast, so I pled, "give me the baby—You can give it to me in half the time, and it can come out done!" Then I heard an audible voice say, "I'm even more excited and more passionate about your child than you are!"

I broke down and wept. "Look at you," He said, "Look how excited you are about having the baby! You can't wait. That's what I'm like! Every morning I'm just as excited about fellow-shipping with you! Would you come and be with Me?" His words wrecked my life.

The Lord also used Lauralee's birth to show me the love of the Father. When she was born, I would hold her while I paced the halls singing spontaneous love songs to her. The Lord said, "The way you see this child is how I see you. Is there anything she could ever do that would make you stop loving her?"

He used the emotions of how I felt toward my daughter and related it to His feelings for me. "That's how I sing over you...that's how I delight in you and rejoice over you with singing."

This powerful message freed me from the feeling that God was angry with me.

VISUALIZING THE FUTURE

My pastor, Henry Schmidt, continued to disciple me while I headed to the skateboard park or the street to evangelize. I still wore my hair long with a beard, leather jacket, and ripped pants for extra effect. Even so, I had this voracious appetite for God and as great a desire to share with others the treasures I had found in relationship with Jesus and the Holy Spirit.

I had lots of opportunity to share Christ as well as my testimony to youth groups, Christian schools, a coffee house, and the skateboard park. I set up a tract booth outside of the mall. I'd give a tract or magazine to everyone who was "foolish enough" to walk close enough by me. Often I was in the street for up to four hours. I made opportunities. I took teams into the street and even conducted open air crusades Saturday evenings in the park whether people wanted to listen to me or not. I was on fire. The world was my parish. I didn't wait to share until someone offered me a stadium. I soon came to understand that what you do in secret, the Lord rewards openly.

A desire for God to use me in the nations began to grow; I used to lie on my bed and have, what I call, Holy Ghost fantasies until midnight—even three in the morning. Sometimes the sun rose while I still dreamed about what I would do that day, imagining the day in my spirit. Although awake, I would imagine myself preaching in Africa and could picture stadiums filled with multitudes or see people healed and raised from the dead. It was like a sanctified daydream. Even King David, in Psalm 63:6-7, speaks of lying on his bed and meditating on the Lord in the night watch (which was 3 A.M. to 6 A.M.). I also believe that, during these night watches, David was reliving in his imagination all that God had done in the past—how God delivered him, guided his life, and provided for him. Here is David, in the early-morning hours, meditating on his destiny, dreaming about what it would be like to fulfill what God had said would happen in and through his life. I see David even recreating the scenario, in his mind, of what it would look like when God defeated his enemy.

When I was a newly saved Christian of only two months, I knew what the prophetic word over my life was and the promise of the Bible about my destiny. So I would lie on my bed and daydream that tens of thousands were streaming to the altars, asking Jesus to be their Savior. In my imagination, I'd picture myself praying for the deaf and I'd hear the crowds screaming. I would see the mother whose son was just healed of deafness say, "My son can hear" as tears rolled down her face. Day after day I'd have these big dreams from a big God about big stuff. I see now that I had a big, God-inspired imagination. Yet, back then I would say, "Lord forgive me for my pride. It is wrong for me to think of something this great." Then I'd think to myself, *Who am I that God would use me?* With these condemning thoughts came a sense of guilt about wanting God to fulfill my dreams and do great things in and through my life (I realized later that God was initiating my dreams and desires and that the devil was trying to discourage me from them). But the God-dreams became stronger—and the next day, there I was *again* in Africa and India holding crusades just like the spiritual greats, Reinhardt Bonnke and Benny Hinn.

Eventually, because of surrendering my sanctified imagination to God, I learned to release destiny by seeing myself preaching in stadiums or healing the sick. I believed in a big God and I had big dreams. Actually, according to Scripture, it was the calling forth of things that weren't as though they were (see Rom. 4:17). I was cultivating the promise of God that He had birthed in my heart; I knew I was called as an evangelist. This principle of, "calling things forth" (which is a kind of prophecy) became a major key in birthing my ministry. To understand this concept more fully let me share two biblical examples of this visualization process.

Even though Abraham and his wife were past childbearing years, God had a destiny for them. He told Abraham to look at the stars to illustrate how numerous his descendants would be (Gen. 15:5). Abraham had to visualize it to help get it in his spirit. We see the same principle demonstrated in Genesis 30:31–43. Jacob increases the flock of spotted goats by putting striped or speckled branches in the watering troughs so that the goats would see them when they came to drink and when they mated.

In the New Testament, the apostle Paul echoes this truth: "But we all, with unveiled face, beholding as in a mirror the glory of the Lord, are being transformed into the same image from glory to glory, just as by the Spirit of the Lord" (2 Cor. 3:18). As I like to say, "What you see, you be."

In the beginning, I didn't understand this principle and I'd repent after I "saw" myself preach in stadiums. "Lord, forgive my pride," I'd say, "I'm hungry for You, but I also want to be faithful to what You've called me to now." I'd walk down the street in Abbotsford preaching to the trees along the road, pretending they were people. Really, it wasn't my pride. It was the Holy Spirit putting destiny in me.

FORETASTE OF THINGS TO COME

On one occasion, I was invited to speak at a local Mennonite youth group. I gave my testimony and taught about the Holy Spirit and intimacy with Him. During the altar call, young people fell under the power of the Spirit—some shook, while others were touched in many other ways (all spiritual manifestations were foreign to this group of youth). Thus began a revival in that youth group and it grew from about 25 members to 100 in less than a year.

Some time later, I was introduced to Kevin Paterson and a group of local youth pastors who had been meeting for over a year for weekly prayer. They felt led to start an inter-church revival meeting called Fresh Fire. In 1997, they met in a storefront church with a small group of spiritually hungry young people. Their vision was to pray, worship, prophesy, hear God, and ignite a revival fire through youth of the city.

I shared once at Fresh Fire and they invited me to accompany them and a team of youth to minister at "The Street Church" in Vancouver. I spent about two eight-hour days in prayer, preparing for my evening message. Since I had no religious training, I didn't realize that, to many Christians, this would be considered excessive. That evening the youth ministered with drama, music, and testimonies. I got up to preach and the Holy Spirit fell. Halfway through my sermon, people rushed to the front, falling on their knees and calling out for the Lord. Many street people were saved and healed that night. After that experience, I preached more regularly at Fresh Fire meetings.

These two experiences, the one with the Mennonite youth group and the other at The Street Church, were some of the initial evidences of God's hand on my life for ministering in the supernatural. I believe God was giving me a foretaste of things to come.

CHAPTER 8

MARINATING AND PICKLING IN THE HOLY SPIRIT

Four years after my salvation, I still preached in the streets and had a daily prayer life where I regularly spent extended hours, days, months waiting in His presence, fasting, studying the Bible, and hungering even more for God. I wanted Him to use me, and I knew that one day, He would. I never doubted what someone had told me only two months after I accepted the Lord into my life, that I had the mantle of an evangelist, and was called to reach people.

However, I always struggled as to whether I needed to work a secular job because I knew that I was called to the ministry. I believed the call was "now" and that I should live by faith. I remember having to come to the place where I died to my vision of full-time ministry. I said, "God I want to thank You for my wife and children and I'm going to do what I have to do to be a mature Christian man, husband, and father.

I worked in a sawmill stacking lumber—this is what was known as the "green chain." The lumber came out of the saw cut to different sizes, then down a conveyer belt where I'd grab the lumber, haul it off the green chain, and stack it according to length. It was a good job with good pay—the best I'd ever had.

I learned that it wasn't so much about who I was in the pulpit as much as it was about who I was in the home and in the marketplace. I wanted to be a witness. I wanted to know Him and seek His face and not His hand. I had to let Him work character in me. Yet, I still couldn't shake the passion inside for doing Christian ministry. I was consumed with God and His call.

Every day I would go to the mill, but there was still a vision, a passion, a knowing that God was going to use me in the nations. I wanted to see thousands saved and be used by God in miracles and healings. The great evangelists throughout history inspired me. However, I had to die to these dreams regularly and say, "I'll love You and I'll serve You, Lord, whether or not You use me in 'full-time ministry.'"

Within months of giving my passion for ministry to Him, He resurrected it and gave it back. I felt as Abraham laying Isaac down on the altar. The test was, "Will you love Me more than you love the vision?"

MY SECOND SEASON OF VISITATION

It was shortly after the powerful experience at The Street Church, that I resolved to spend more time in prayer and in the presence of the Holy Spirit. With Fresh Fire asking me to preach more often at their youth meetings, they soon moved the meetings to the basement of the Anglican Church at the invitation of the youth pastor, Jean-Marc Russi. I desperately wanted God more and desired to see Him pour out His Spirit through me at these meetings.

I developed tendinitis at work and had to go on compensation for three months. I cried out to the Lord: "Oh God, please visit me in power again like You did in that first extended season of visitation when I was introduced to the Holy Spirit."

I purposed in my heart that I would pursue an encounter with God and committed that the time I normally spent working, I would spend with the Lord. I pressed in each day in desperation to sense His presence. I wanted to hear His voice and cried out for a life-changing encounter with His glory.

"If I draw near to You, You said You would draw near to me," I'd pray. Every day, I cried out for Him to fulfill His promises. "You said, 'If I search for You with all of my heart, then I would find You.'" I sensed moments of His presence, but inside, I was never satisfied—I wanted more! For almost two weeks I did everything I'd learned—praise, worship, speaking in tongues, interceding, and all I knew about prayer. There was a measure of routine to my prayer life that consisted of a half hour of speaking in tongues, a half hour of praise, and fifteen minutes of spontaneous prayer. "God I want to feel Your presence," was my cry—I knew there was more.

Then one day it happened. At home, in my living room, I desperately cried out for His presence. "Visit me Lord," I pleaded, "Come a little bit closer." In the midst of my desperate pursuit of a breakthrough, suddenly and without warning, a wind filled my lungs and I became supernaturally mute, just as Zechariah did in the temple. The atmosphere of my room changed and I became aware of a strong presence of the Lord. I saw the smoke of His glory moving toward me—like liquid honey, like a warm blanket it enveloped me. Electricity moved through my body and I was overwhelmed by the intense, weighty presence of God pressing on me. The apostle Paul talked about that "weight of glory" in Second Corinthians 4:17. The glory settled on my body and weighed me down. It was almost as if I was entering into sleep, and I fell off my chair onto the carpeted floor.

Again, I was powerless to regain my strength, and was reminded of when the glory fell in Solomon's temple and the priests couldn't stand to minister because of the cloud. Wave after wave of the Lord's presence and electricity moved through my body and it was only hours later, after I got up, that my voice returned. "Something's happened to me!" I cried.

"MORE LORD"

There was a new excitement in my spirit in prayer, a fiery passion in me to repeat the previous day's experience. Wrecked, I didn't want to do anything except spend time with the Lord. For four to twelve hours each day I would seek Him in my apartment. Most of my time with Him I simply lay in His presence, soaking and marinating in the glory, allowing the Holy Spirit to saturate me. I grew more intimately acquainted with the heart and voice of the Spirit as He visited me in sweet, loving ways and in dramatic encounters. Each day when I finished praying and soaking, I would eagerly anticipate what would happen the next time I prayed.

I distinctly remember day two of this visitation. "Shonnah," I said, "I'm going to take some time to enter into the Lord's presence." As I opened the door to my prayer room, stepped inside and closed the door, I became aware of not just the presence of Jesus, but the presence of the *person* Jesus! He stood in the center of the room, and I mumbled, "Thank You Jesus," several times, and then I just shook and wept. This time it took no effort to enter into the glory, because the glory waited for me!

The third day as I prepared to pray, I kept thinking, *What's going to happen today?* Thirsty, I went into the kitchen for a glass of juice before I commenced, and as I opened the refrigerator and then poured the juice into the glass, I became aware again of the presence of a person walking up behind me. "I know it's You, Jesus!" I called out, even though I could not see Him with my physical eyes. Then I fell to my knees, juice, jug, and all. On the floor in front of the open refrigerator door, I just knelt there and wept, and I knew I was weeping at His feet.

VISION OF GETHSEMANE

In a vision, Jesus took me to the garden of Gethsemane. I watched the crucifixion, the suffering, and the intensity of Jesus' emotions. Throughout the encounter, I was fully aware of all of my natural senses as I wept and felt the deep despair of the moment.

It was through that experience that I understood the intensity of the Father's love and desire for me. As I watched, Jesus asked if the cup could pass from Him and then said, "Nevertheless, not My will but Your will be done." With great intensity, the Father sternly said, "It is My will, drink the cup." It wasn't stern as in "angry," but stern as in "urgent," birthed out of passion. "Yes, take the cup," the Father seemed to be saying, "because I can't wait to get the world redeemed...I long to be with them, to have them back in intimacy with Me." He was feeling the agony of His one Son but wanted the others as His children too.

Jesus was sweating great drops of blood, wrestling back and forth, and anticipating the awful agony of taking the cup. It was so intense. The revelation began to sink in. Jesus abandoned His life because of the Father's great desire to delight in me. As the Father loved the Son, I realized, *He loves me with this same fiery passion that I was seeing.*

"May they be brought to complete unity to let the world know that You sent Me and have loved them even as You have loved Me" (John 17:23 NIV). This Scripture reinforced that love I saw in my visionary experience. John says that the Father loved me as He loves Jesus—Wow! Then I started to apply this incredible divine truth. If God hears the prayers of Jesus, then He must hear mine. The revelation came in great waves—even though I was desperately seeking intimacy with Him, His intense passion to be with me was even greater. This heart-level truth dealt a major blow to the enemy's hold on me concerning my past.

The experience left me numbed and with a deep conviction that I needed to completely abandon my life to Him. I felt an intimacy and a new oneness with the Lord, realizing that He would bleed and endure such agony and suffering for me. Day after day, I sat at His feet and enjoyed His presence—in this place, numerous encounters followed each one as powerful as these initial three visitations. There were times the encounters happened daily. God would visit with visions, trances, dreams, revelation, angelic visitations, and even His audible voice—things I'd read about in the Bible but now experiencing. Yes, the "God, who at various times and in various ways spoke" (Heb. 1:1) was now speaking to me in various ways too.

A supernatural God, I believe, wants the supernatural to be natural and common. Realize that when I speak of visions, trances, visitations, miracles, and visits to the third heaven, that really, I haven't known anything else since I was saved. All that I've known is the Gospel. It was only when I became involved with Christians that I found out how out of the ordinary it was for North American believers to experience God in that way. When you read the Bible you find out that all these experiences should be ordinary. This intense season of soaking in His presence and receiving revelation lasted three months.

CHAPTER 9

COUNTDOWN TO SPIRITUAL BLAST-OFF

During those three months the Lord dealt with me on five issues:

- Intimacy
- The prophetic
- Healing
- Evangelism
- Repentance

Since intimacy is such a huge part of my life, I do want to share some teaching on the subject, and therefore, I'm dedicating this entire chapter to intimacy, and will pick up the other four subjects in Chapter 10.

INTIMACY

For three months, I did carpet time. I purposed that I wouldn't ask the Lord for anything. I practiced just being and beholding the glory, in worship. I waited and listened more than anything else. The Lord taught me how to empty my mind, to sit at His feet like Mary, to gaze upon His beauty, and to soak and be still. He showed me Isaiah 30:15 "…in returning and rest you shall be saved; in quietness and confidence shall be your strength…'"

The Holy Spirit taught me that I didn't need to do all the talking, praying, and the "charismania" acts or the praying in tongues, devotions, and intense prayer to make Him come down. He wanted to be with me more than I wanted to be with Him. While all of these disciplines are important, during this particular season of soaking, God wanted me to come and just be in His presence without a list of needs or the sense of duty expected to accompany prayer. I remember thinking, "But if I stop talking, God's going to forget that I'm here wanting to be in His presence. Because the only time I'm with God is when I'm praying." I thought that the minute I stopped speaking in tongues, praising, worshiping, or reading the Word, the presence of the Lord was going to wane.

But the Holy Spirit wanted to teach me the place of resting. Later I would understand that the Spirit was preparing me to be part of the great contemplative prayer movement that He was raising up. The Lord began to teach me about resting through Scripture verses. He showed me that He "acts for the one who waits for Him" (Isaiah 64:4) and that "they that wait upon the Lord shall renew their strength; they shall mount up with wings as eagles; they shall run, and not be weary; and they shall walk, and not faint" (Isaiah 40:31). He also whispered to me: "Be still and know that I am God" (Psalm 46:10).

I was excited about growing in rest and intimacy with the Holy Spirit—I knew from experience that in that place, even without praying sometimes, God begins to give us the desires of our hearts. I walked in such intimacy with Jesus when I first got saved. I remember a time when I walked from my kitchen to my bedroom and thought, *Oh, I've got to have a peanut butter sandwich*, but I couldn't find any in the cupboard. *Oh, man! I really want peanut butter!* I kept thinking, but then I just went to bed. The next morning when Shonnah awoke, she opened the garage door and there was a jar of peanut butter sitting on the stairs.

POSITIONED IN QUIETNESS

During this season, I learned that soaking in His presence releases prophetic revelation into our lives. Just like Mary, who sat at Jesus' feet and listened to His teachings (see Luke 10:39), I was positioning myself in quietness and stillness before Him so I could hear His voice. Many believers don't hear God's voice because they don't practice quietness, stillness, or soaking in the Lord's glory.

First Samuel chapter 3 indicates/infers that the key to Samuel's hearing was that of positioning himself—lying down where the ark of God was:

> *"and before the lamp of God went out in the tabernacle of the LORD where the ark of God was, and while Samuel was lying down, that the LORD called Samuel. And he answered, "Here I am!"* (1 Samuel 3:3-4).

In those days, the Bible tells us, that the word of the Lord was rare and there was no widespread revelation. Yet the word of the Lord and the revelation of Jesus came to Samuel while he lay where the ark of God was. That's where God wants to bring us—to the place of His presence. Once, while I was lying on the floor I said,

"God, how I want You. You don't know how much I want You and Your presence."

"I want yours more," He clearly replied.

"Lord, You want me more than I want You?" I questioned. "Oh God, how many times have I withheld myself from You?"

The Genesis account of God's first relationship with man confirms this divine passion for relationship with His children.

Oh. how the Father loved to come down and walk in the cool of the day with Adam and Eve. The Father even went searching for them when that sweet relationship was broken. "Where are you, Adam? Where's our intimacy?" I can imagine God asking. "What happened to our times of just being together in the garden and talking? I miss it. I want your presence more than you want Mine."

DESPERATE FOR MORE

There was a time when the Holy Spirit fell on me with a spirit of holiness and desperation. I felt like I didn't know God; I felt as though God was a million miles away, even though I knew I had a relationship with the Holy Spirit. People around me said, "Todd, if I could only have half of what you've got, I'd be satisfied. Who are you to hunger for more?" In response I would say, "Compared to how deep I know I can go, I'm not really deep at all." Passion and holy desperation came over me as I walked into this valley of death, this wilderness. At the same time, I was still experiencing God's manifest glory on me. Yet, I knew I had only begun my journey of intimacy. "No, Lord, I know there's more."

So I spent a few days in prayer, never ceasing from the moment I awoke to bedtime, where I sought Him, and sought to draw ever nearer, crying out, "Oh, Lord, more, deeper…" I locked myself in that room and prayed in tongues, read the Word, played worship tapes, and worshiped Him. Drawing ever nearer to Him was my quest—I wasn't satisfied with where I was or where I'd been, I just searched for the next realm in Him—for that place of glory-to-glory!

Whatever got in my way was going to get out of the way because I didn't have a shovel in my hand—the hunger inside me had the force of a bulldozer. "Either You touch me God, or I'm going to Heaven. That's it!" I was so hungry I actually thought I'd die if God didn't visit me. It was an unquenchable thirst. Every day I'd rest in His presence on my floor—drinking in the wine of

His Spirit. I'd attend every revival meeting or conference I could get to, yet I still hungered for more. *I've got to go deeper...there's a well I haven't touched!* was my heart's cry, and then I'd stir myself up to take hold of Him, "God, I'm seeking You, I'm searching for You with all of my heart. You said I'd find You...You said if I'd draw near to You, You'd draw near to me...fall on me!"

This season of intimacy was so wonderful that sometimes when I awoke in the morning, I could still feel the lingering presence of the previous day's meeting with God, like dew resting on me.

STAY HOLY SPIRIT

During these times of visitation, I was afraid that the Lord's fellowship would leave and I would cry out, "Oh no, the Lord's leaving, fellowship is over." But one particular time I was so hungry that I jumped from the floor and yelled, "No! God, I'm going to take hold of You!" I wouldn't let Him go and chased Him. "God," I cried, with determination, "Draw near to me. Fall on me again. Who are You to make me hungry and not feed me? Who are You to make me thirsty and not give me to drink? You fall on me with this glory, and then You just take Yourself away? Forget it, God. I'm going to seek You until You fall on me again."

Then, I'd pray in tongues and seek the Lord for another hour. Wham!—sandwiched to the floor again for another four hours! Whenever the presence of the Lord lifted, I'd be like a wild animal going after its prey and I'd fly off the floor and say, "Lord, No!" chasing Him down, time and again and the cycle continued—wham and whoosh, on the floor again. Sometimes this cycle continued for as long as twelve hours.

The Holy Spirit emphasized over and over, "Todd, I'm trying to teach you how to receive. You don't have to strive. I know you're hungry, but I want to reveal Myself to you more than you want Me to reveal Myself. You've got to quiet yourself. You've got to become still. That's why I took the words out of your mouth. It's to get you positioned in quietness at My feet and in the place of stillness so I can speak to you."

I finally understood that it was as though two people were conversing, though both talking at the same time—one wouldn't hear the other, would they? There are times for talking, times for listening, and times for enjoying sweet fellowship! After this revelation, I went back into prayer and just said, "Come Lord. I just want to lie in Your glory, in Your river, and wham!—God's glory for four hours!

Even to this day when I soak I say, "Alright, Lord. You know I'm here. I don't have to tell You. You're not dumb. I'm just going to get on the floor." The Lord shows up with His glory presence.

SOAKING PARTY

We decided to hold "soaking" parties because people always asked if they could come over just to lay together on the carpet and soak with me. Often, Shonnah and I soaked with our friends. One day eight people plus my pastor arrived, and after a time of worship, the Lord's presence came and rested heavily upon us. It's hard to describe, but it was as though an electric honey blanket descended on the room and I knew in that moment that the Lord was about to take me into a "trance."

"Let's just be still in His presence," I instructed, but suddenly, the walls of my apartment seemed to disappear. His presence overwhelmed me and suddenly I saw grass.

"The grass..." I shouted, "the grass! Can you see it?" The grass moved and had life—the glory came off it and it was the greenest grass I'd ever seen. When I stepped in it, the Presence of the Lord tingled through my body—I felt it between my toes and under my feet. Whenever I looked at it, it would say things to me, though without conversation. It had life, as though God Himself was in it. At first, everyone thought I was crazy, but then they, too, experienced aspects of the vision.

My eyes panned the scene, and I saw a forest and trees that stretched farther than my eyes could see. The carpeting had become grass with river banks on both sides. Though I was fully conscious, all I saw was this paradise of God. Every time I looked, I'd be overwhelmed by another wave of glory, intoxicated with God's presence. My thoughts kept saying, *He gave showers of blessing and grass in the field for everyone...*

Some of the group received Scripture verses from the Lord every time I shared something. The vision became so real and vivid! And then, my eyes opened really wide as I watched water pour into the room from the kitchen and across the carpet, to about an inch deep. The carpet actually appeared wet, as though my wife had left the bathtub or the dishwasher had leaked.

"The river just came into my living room!" I screamed. No one knew what to do. The pastor jumped off the couch and threw himself onto the floor and into this revelatory river. I saw it rise a couple of feet and then it flowed over his back—a vibrant rushing flow. All the while I saw the grass and the trees— this was a full-on interactive prophetic experience! The more I shared details of the vision, and the more the others allowed themselves to be taken into what I saw, the more the vision grew. At that point, one of the fellows was on his back, under the power, and the others were having experiences too. Though they weren't "seeing" what I saw and experienced in my senses, they experienced the vision in a realm of emotions.

In the vision next, I suddenly saw an enormous tree, right in the middle of my apartment. The body of the tree resembled a mass of stalks intertwined to form its massive trunk. The stalks represented elements of the glory of God. Some were gold, some silver, some bronze, and some were amber. They shimmered with the golden light of His presence. The tree's branches were heavy and weighed down to within three feet from the ground with massive, ripe fruit, not unlike the types of fruit that Joshua and Caleb brought out of the Promised Land. This was the Tree of Life!

Some of us ate from that prophetic tree—we experienced its fruit! As I described some of the fruit that I saw, pastor, still swimming in the river, responded with delight when he tasted of it. Although he had not seen the tree, he still ate of the fruit. I heard his lips smack and then —"ummmm…ummm…yum!" As the others ate they exploded in outbursts of joy and laughter, as others groaned—simply overwhelmed by tastes of His glory.

All of a sudden, I said, "Shhhhh" and there was nothing but silence. In the midst of it, and from a different realm, I heard a sound like a bass note going off on the inside of my spirit man. So I asked, "Can you hear it?" No one did. The same thing happened on the road to Damascus. Paul's companions saw the light, but they couldn't hear the voice. Nevertheless, this sound was so real to me that I thought for sure the others could hear, too. Then, right then, I heard the sound of the Lord God walking in the garden, and then I realized I was in the Garden of Eden…in Paradise!

The vision changed then. It was as though we were playing hide-and-seek with the Lord—and He was searching for us. "Adam, where are you?" I knew this was an invitation to walk with God in the cool of the day. The Lord was inviting us to intimacy—to taste and see that He is good.

Another time, I had gathered with a few other prophetic people in the home of Patricia King, simply to bask in the Lord's presence and wait on Him, to see if He would speak with us. Suddenly, the room was filled with flashes of light followed by a lightning bolt. Patricia screamed, "Did you see that? What was it? I think it was lightning!"

Everyone present saw it too. We dimmed the lights and waited on the Lord by candlelight. The lightning flashed for some time and then a corporate wave of intercession fell upon us, and we all started speaking in Chinese tongues. Some actually "saw" themselves preaching in China.

ANGELS, ANGELS, ANGELS

Angels also started to appear during my soaking times. They'd come into my bedroom as pillars of shimmering light moving to and fro. Shonnah saw them too, and we'd both lay there, trembling and weeping.

Once, just before my commissioning into ministry, a huge angel appeared in my living room. He stood about twenty-feet tall and towered through the ceiling of the apartment above. His massive chest was level with my ceiling! It wouldn't be until several years later that I understood the significance of the visitation of this particular angel.

RESTING IN HIS PRESENCE

During this time, the Holy Spirit emphasized often the importance of resting in His presence. I learned that God never leaves. We only leave Him when our mind wanders or strays into worry and concern. But, did you know it is possible to live in God's glory? In his writings, *Practicing the Presence of God: The Best Rule of Holy Life*[1], Brother Lawrence describes how he learned to live in the presence of the Lord (I encourage you to read his writings—they have blessed me greatly.)

Another reason people can't get into God's presence, even when their mind is on God, is because they're too busy trying to find God when He's actually right there. Mike Bickle, director of the International House of Prayer of Kansas City, one of the most visible organizations of the 24-7 prayer movement, says: "It's like trying to get into a room you're already in."

When I prayed and told God that I was running after Him and searched for Him, He told me that He was right here, living inside of me. He said, "All My glory, the same Spirit that raised Jesus from the dead is inside of you."

Quiet yourself and think about entering into that glory that's in you. As born again believers, each of us is a New Testament "Ark of the Covenant" with God's presence living in us—the key is to be still and quiet.

Listening prayer became my greatest weapon. I wanted (and still want) Jesus more than anything. I spent more time in His presence than anywhere else. I exercised my spiritual senses by listening to the Spirit. I was dwelling in the Secret Place of the Most High, focusing on Jesus. Today, I have a grace now to call others into a "God hunger." This soaking season was in reality, a special time of personal revival.

THE SECRET PLACE

Resting in His presence equipped me for the work of the ministry. God used that three-month time to impart the anointings I carry in ministry now which are power, healings, and prophetic blessings. The thrust of our entire ministry is built on the foundation of this season of soaking.

As I cried out for more intimacy with the Holy Spirit, I entered into a place where I grew dramatically in the receiving of spiritual gifts. This is the Secret Place—it was living here that I received revelation. The Lord gave me prophetic insights into the Kingdom in that place.

I still remember one of the most revelatory messages I preached early on—it's still one of the most sought-after tape series, *The Secret Place*. During this time, in a matter of two minutes, I received a prophetic revelation, which I call *The Father's House*. The revelation is about nine rooms in a house that each correspond to nine levels of intimacy with the Father. Oddly, I was in the bathroom brushing my teeth when I went out in the spirit and the Lord gave me this revelation where I was taken into the Father's house and permitted access and entrance into these rooms.

CONTAGIOUS FIRE

For the first nine months of my personal revival, I preached on intimacy, God chasing, holy hunger, soaking, and Holy Ghost visitation. For the three-month season, I ministered every night at the Fresh Fire youth meetings, which was nondenominational. We had youth attend who were from Baptist, Mennonite, Pentecostal, Anglican, independent charismatic and various other churches. Every Friday evening I shared my experiences: my encounters and visitations, my worship and prayer times with the youth, and they as well as the youth pastors watched my life transform. The Lord's presence broke into our meetings with powerful manifestations. All I'd do is share my testimony of what God was doing, and when the youth saw the hunger and desperation I had for God, it became as a contagious fire! They clamored for intimacy with the Lord, too, and God used me to usher in His presence into those meetings to draw others into the same place of intimacy. In His presence, the Holy Spirit powerfully touched the young people, and they would fall under the power of the Spirit, drunk, shaking, laughing, joyful exuberation. These phenomena and visitations of the Holy Spirit occurred sovereignly, without hype or prompting by the leadership. Even more amazing, the majority of those attending were from conservative backgrounds and had never even heard of such outpourings, but they were learning about the precious Holy Spirit— big time.

I recall a profound outpouring at the youth meeting where at least thirty Mennonite youth ended up on the floor in travailing intercession or in fits of holy laughter, screaming for God to touch them. The meeting had gone late, and parents had begun to arrive to find their kids. Kevin Paterson ran around saying, "Pray for me guys...I have to talk to the parents and try to explain what God is doing here to their kids ...their parents don't believe in this...they're conservative and don't express themselves like this...try and get the kids 'sober!'."

Some of the youth had to be helped up the stairs to their parents. I remember thinking, "We'll get phone calls on this," but they never came. Although some kids didn't return, many more came, hungry to experience what they heard God was doing among their peers.

ENDNOTE

1. www.ccel.org/l/**lawrence**/practice/. These writings were compiled after the death of Brother Lawrence in 1691, and are public domain.

CHAPTER 10

SPIRITUAL BLAST-OFF
(Growing in the Prophetic, Healing, Evangelism, and Repentance)

PROPHECY

The season of intimacy eventually grew into another level of God's preparation in my life. During my hours in the Holy Spirit's presence each day, I cried out to Him for more prophetic insights. Once I had tasted the anointing for ministry, each day I prayed, "Lord I want to prophesy over someone today," because I wanted to give it away.

I prophesied to all the youth on Friday nights. Sometimes the Lord would give me specific words before I prophesied and other times I would just step out in faith, begin to prophesy, and hope the Lord would join me. "If [you have the gift of] prophecy, let us prophesy in proportion to our faith" (Romans 12:6).

I had become so full of God's presence; I had to give it away. I remember sitting with two youth pastors in the church office and the Spirit of prophecy fell on me. Literally, a mantle fell—Whap! "I'm going to prophesy," I said. I'd given little words here and there but this was like a torrent where I could feel the prophetic bubble up in my spirit. So, I prophesied over them and it became so intense that I swung open the door, raced down the hallway, and yelled, "Is there anyone out here whom I can prophesy over… it's flowing …where's the secretary?"

I looked for *targets* … I mean … *people*…everyone at the church…it kept flowing and people went out under the power—weeping and shaking. It was similar to Saul's experience (see 1 Sam. 10:10), when the Spirit of prophecy fell on him and he prophesied non-stop from morning 'til night.

When I prophesied over the Fresh Fire youth, I'd minister, pray, and prophesy into the early morning hours sometimes, and it would radically transform them as God spoke life and destiny into their lives. During this prophetic season, I was invited to speak to a group of youth who were holding a Saturday night prayer meeting at a Mennonite high school in town. While in worship time, the Lord gave me visions for the group as well as specific prophetic words for individuals. Most of the attendees had never heard about the prophetic word, but when I began to minister prophetically, leaders and youth were powerfully affected by the accurate words of the Lord. Consider that this was a Mennonite school, and yet here were young people falling under the power as we prayed and prophesied over them. This spawned a local youth revival and the Fresh Fire meetings grew as more young people sought to be transformed by the Spirit's power.

HEALING

The second clear season I entered into during my preparation for full-time ministry was a period of growth in faith for healing and miracles. Even before my soaking season started, I had a foretaste of the healing anointing the night we took the young people of Fresh Fire to The Street Church in downtown Vancouver. As I spoke of this church in a previous chapter, it was a ministry to the homeless, criminals, street kids, and prostitutes. It is significant that my ministry to these broken people was the springboard that launched me into my season of intimacy and the powerful things to follow (Scripture tells us that God has compassion on the broken and poor in spirit).

This meeting was my first real, crusade-type meeting. I still remember the smell of alcohol on people in the little storefront church. It was March. It was cold. People lined up on the street. Oh was I excited and I said "God, the food tonight is hot dogs. I love hot dogs!" I thought, *I'm going to share my testimony and ask God for the same kind of power we've seen on Friday to be here tonight.*

During my testimony, even before I gave the altar call, four men and a woman came forward and just stood at the altar. I signaled my youth team with a look that said, "What's going on...find out what they want," because I didn't know whether they were there to disrupt the meeting, or what. As I continued to preach, one of the team members yelled out, "They want to get saved...NOW!" Then the woman said, "I'm a prostitute, I'm a drug addict, and I have AIDS. I feel dirty, and I want to be clean!" After I led her to the Lord, she screamed, wept, and shook as a demon left her, and then she fell to the floor and vibrated under the power of the Holy Spirit! Whoa—what a change to her countenance after that! Shortly afterward, I opened the altar for everyone to come and be saved. As I walked to the bus after the meeting, all I could think of was, *"I want to do this for the rest of my life...I'm hungry for God's power!"* A few weeks later, I received a report that the woman had been totally healed and delivered also from her addictions.

Later on in my soaking season, God stirred an even greater desire in me to be used in healing and miracles. For days and days

JOURNEY INTO THE MIRACULOUS

I studied everything I could about healing and delved and poured through the Bible. The more I studied His word, the more revelation He gave me, and before long, just reading about or meditating on the truths about healing, or hearing the testimonies of others wasn't enough. I felt compelled to stretch my faith and actually pray for the sick and that's exactly what I did. Everywhere I went, whomever I met that needed the Lord's touch, I prayed for. I even visited the sick in hospitals so that I could activate the scriptural truths that I had learned.

A Grandfather is Healed!

On Friday nights, the fire of God fell and ignited the lives of youth who came from a kaleidoscope of denominations and backgrounds. One impossible night, as I preached about radical faith, the Holy Spirit said, "Todd, you've got to pray for that girl over there." Later in the evening, the fourteen year old girl, Julie, approached me and asked me to pray with her. Her grandfather in the United States had suffered a stroke that left him mute as well as paralyzed on his left side. "He doesn't know Jesus...please pray that he would be healed and know that Jesus was the one who did the miracle," she asked.

We agreed together and prayed, "Jesus, I ask You to heal Julie's grandfather ..." and just then, Jesus interrupted our prayer ...

"What are you doing, Todd?" the Lord asked.

"I'm praying!"

"You just preached on radical faith for the impossible ...what are you going to do about this?"

I knew in my heart that my prayer for the girl's grandfather was simply a courtesy prayer, but my faith changed right then as I prayed, and suddenly I was translated in the spirit to the man's hospital bed where he lay asleep and hooked up to IV's and a heart monitor. I laid hands on him and rebuked the effects of

stroke. The man rose out of his bed and ran down the hospital hallway, the IV still in his arm! Hours later, I learned that Julie received
a telephone call a few hours later after she'd returned home ...

"Praise Jesus, praise Jesus...I've been healed!" shouted her
grandfather. Then he shared how the power of God entered into
his body and how the Lord supernaturally healed every trace of
that stroke. As Julie recounted the story, I found it hard to believe. It took her three times to convince me because I thought
that I'd just visualized the scene in the hospital. But eventually, I
believed, even though I thought, *Wow...this is cool...but why me?*
That's a question I've asked often.

Often the healings and miracles I prayed for at those Friday
meetings started through a word of knowledge and prayer of
faith. Before each one, I'd wait on the Lord, and then I'd see pic-
tures and scenes in my mind of faces or of healings that would
happen. I'd see things in the spirit, like people bending over and
touching their toes, or taking a brace off a leg. At the actual
meeting, I'd simply recount what I'd seen earlier, or I'd suddenly
feel someone's infirmity in or on my own body.

There was a sixteen-year-old girl who suffered such a severe
case of scoliosis, that she couldn't stand straight. As the Lord
touched her, we heard a "cracking" sound, and her spine
straightened, her bones adjusted, and she was able to stand straight
and tall! She cried as she watched her leg become normal, it was
so awesome. We saw others healed of various pains like in the
shoulder, neck, or back. Weekly, the youth would press in and
hunger for more of the Spirit. The Holy Spirit would fall and it
was as though He supernaturally conducted the meetings! It was
an unbelievable atmosphere, where the youth would pray and cry
out for souls, worship passionately, dance to the Lord, or prophesy
over another. Yes, even the prophetic anointing was contagious.
The Spirit of prophecy would come, and youth would prophesy
spontaneously under my mantle, not at all unlike the story of Saul

(see 1 Sam. 10:10), prophesying when he came into contact with the prophets.

As these young people earnestly pursued the Lord and desired the spiritual gifts (according to First Corinthians 14:1), they also grew in the prophetic anointing. We were all amazed by God's powerful workings as He orchestrated our small meetings. So many young people were saved, transformed, and radically wrecked for Jesus as they received revelation of their prophetic destiny in the Lord.

Stretching My Faith

It was T.L. Osborn's book *Healing the Sick* that would further ignite and activate my passion to walk in God's power. As I read it, chapter by chapter, I'd preach it, and also pray the healing Scriptures provided in it aloud, proclaiming God's word by faith.

There really was no specific prophetic call on my life for healing; no vision or an angel saying, "Todd, I've called you to healing ministry." Rather, what I had was a holy hunger and desire. The Bible tells us to earnestly desire spiritual gifts, and I earnestly desired them! Fueled by stories of others whom God had used in the past, I said, "Healing is for me!" After all, Jesus clearly told us, "I say to you, he who believes in Me, the works that I do he will do also; and greater works than these he will do, because I go to My Father" (John 14:12). God also promised us that signs would follow those who believe:

> *In My name they will cast out demons; they will speak with new tongues; they will take up serpents; and if they drink anything deadly, it will by no means hurt them; they will lay hands on the sick, and they will recover* (Mark 16:17,18).

In James 5:15, I also saw that "the prayer of faith will save the sick, and the Lord will raise him up." I wondered why I couldn't pray the prayer of faith if healing was so clearly a powerful truth in

Scripture. It was like, *Why can't I preach healing like those other guys and pray in faith for the sick; why wouldn't God do for me what He did for them?*

In my journey into the ministry of healing, I continued to discover new truths. "God," I said, "there has to be a release of Your power that comes through fasting." I remember going on three-day fasts. I didn't pray a lot though. Rather, I read and reread every account of the healing ministry of Jesus recorded in the Gospels–every story about Jesus the Healer, and then I prayed that His stories would become real in my life. Over and over, day after day, I read and prayed pondered and questioned. What did the healing look like? What were His motives? Then I examined His language, the way He prayed, spoke, and did things.

Because I had learned this completely new dimension of expressing myself in prayer (soaking), I had become very receptive to the Holy Spirit. A day or two before most meetings, I'd wait in His presence and just say, "Lord, show me the things You want to do in the meeting tonight," and He always came through.

As I continued to step out in faith, using the Word and the teaching models of Osborne and the healing line model of laying on of hands, of evangelist Oral Roberts, I see more and more people healed, and the anointing increased. I discovered that the key to the healing ministry was to persist in prayer whether there were results or not. My motto was,

> *It's our job to do the praying, and*
> *God's job to do the healing ...*

As God began to release more and more healings, I experienced something I hadn't seen yet in my meetings. A woman received healing in her seat without the laying on of hands—just by sitting under the anointing she was healed of chronic wrist pain. "My wrist is healed!" she suddenly cried out.

As the healing and prophetic anointings increased at our meetings, I felt a strong urge and desire to take God's power outside of the church walls.

EVANGELISM

So, God stirred a greater passion for evangelism in my heart again. I longed especially to take this increased prophetic anointing to the streets!

"If it works in the church," the Holy Spirit said to me, "why can't it work in the marketplace?" Then He illuminated First Corinthians 14:24-25 to me:

> But if all prophesy, and an unbeliever or an uninformed person comes in, he is convinced by all, he is convicted by all. And thus the secrets of his heart are revealed; and so, falling down on his face, he will worship God and report that God is truly among you.

One Friday after the Fresh Fire service I asked, "Who wants to go out into the market to do prophetic evangelism?" Hands raised, and as a group we went out believing for a prophetic anointing to impact the lost. We fanned out, with some of us hitting a sandwich shop, and others a doughnut shop a few doors down.

At the sandwich shop, two employees, a young man and a young woman, overheard us talk about the healings and prophetic words of our meetings. One asked a question about psychics, and I answered, "Forget about psychics! Do you know that God speaks today?" Then I described some prophetic experiences, and asked if they wanted to hear from the Lord. "God created you," I explained, "and He has a plan and a purpose for your life. I'm going to ask Him for just one thought that He has about you!"

Four youth then entered the restaurant, and they asked, "What's going on here?"

"You know how psychics can sometimes tell you details about your life," I said. "well, I've got a gift like that from Jesus, and it's called the gift of prophecy. I'm just about to tell these two people here about their destiny. If you want to hear yours, get in line!"

The first employee volunteered right away, but the young woman was hesitant. The others looked on to see what would happen. I told the first employee about how hurtful it had been for him when his father left and his parents divorced. I also told him about what was going on in his life with drugs, and that he might go to prison. Tears welled up in this young man's eyes and he could barely compose himself.

The Lord also really touched the second employee, a young woman. As I laid hands on her, I was able to describe the inside of her bedroom right down to the last detail, including her stuffed animals. She was so afraid; she freaked out and ran back behind the counter. I wondered why the Lord "gave me" details of the most intimate room in her house, and became concerned that she might view me as a peeping tom, or even that I may have been stalking her. But the Lord told me that He wanted to bring her into the most intimate place.

Those watching were amazed, and lined right up to be next. The toughest of the group challenged me. "Do me!" he demanded. The Lord revealed to me that he was an avid athlete and a football player, and that he had broken up with a girlfriend many months before, but still deeply missed her.

He turned with wide-eyed amazement to his friends. "Did you hear that?" he asked them, and they all laughed, because they knew it to be true. Then came the softening word as I told him how he was tough on the outside, but soft on the inside and that no one knew that he would sometimes cry on his bed at night. This word deeply touched this young jock and his friends.

Everyone finally met back up in the parking lot, and the four unsaved kids that we'd ministered to, went to find their friends to see if "it" would work for them as well. "Do this guy," they said, and then "That one there!" The first employee that we'd ministered to accepted Jesus, and one of the youth as well, falling under the power. I invited everyone to church. This was our very first encounter with prophetic evangelism during my soaking season.

Weeks later, on Halloween night, one of the young men I'd prophesied over at the restaurant attended church with two friends, and asked me to prophesy over them. One came to the Lord, they all heard the Gospel, and they all experienced the reality of God—something they would never forget!

A WORD FOR THE WAITRESS

God continued to touch the lost through prophetic words. Shonnah, my friend Steve, and I were in a restaurant, and I was asking myself, "Why can't I, in faith, ask the Holy Spirit for a word for the waitress?" So I said to everyone seated with me, "Let's ask God to give each of us a piece of information for the waitress."

When I prayed, I felt an impression that she had grown up in a religious environment and that at 11 or 12 years of age, she'd suffered abuse. I sensed that she was angry with God and blamed Him for betraying her. I said, "The Lord tells me things about people from time to time," and then I shared with her what I felt. Taken aback and by surprise, she said, "Yes," but didn't know what else to say, and walked away.

She arrived back shortly afterward with our drinks, and I asked Steve, "Do you have a word for her?" but he indicated that he'd only had a picture in his mind.

"I saw a birdcage out on a balcony," he said, "with a bird in it."

We rolled our eyes at him. But the waitress suddenly said, "That's my apartment!" God used that picture to show her that He knew every detail of her life!

I jumped in and shared another word of knowledge. "The reason you don't want to give your life to the Lord is because the boyfriend whom you live with doesn't want anything to do with Christianity, and you're afraid you'll lose him."

Although she didn't give her life to Jesus that day, we prayed together that the boyfriend would give his life to God. By the time we left, she knew that the Lord had spoken to her, and that she had a call on her life!

THE CONVENIENCE STORE

Even before my soaking season, I had a heart for evangelism. One evening, quite late, I dropped by a convenience store for some junk food and chatted for a few moments with the clerk. He asked me what I had been up to that evening, and I said, "I just returned from a radical youth service called, *God Rock*."

"I don't believe in that God stuff," he said, "I'm an atheist."

I shared my testimony, and it seemed to go OK, so I ended the story with, "When you're alone sometime, ask Jesus to reveal Himself to you." *There*, I thought, *I've sowed the seed*...and I departed. Weeks later, after another God Rock service, Steve, Shonnah, Roswetta and I returned to the convenience store for some food, and I wanted to see how my seed had grown. Steve and I went in, while the women remained in the car. Steve headed to the sandwich bar in the rear of the store, and I waved "Hi," and walked toward the slush machine. Suddenly, "Oh look—it's the God fanatics," yelled the clerk sarcastically. Two of the clerk's friends were also in the store. They wore the 80's rocker garb—ripped jeans, jean jackets, long hair, AC/DC T-shirts, and trucker-type hats. Phew, they reeked of alcohol and marijuana. All three mocked and scoffed us.

"Come on over and tell them what you told me," the clerk motioned. But suddenly I felt something like a deep groan and cramp in my belly, as though something was going to erupt. I had heard about some meetings where people would roar like lions, and I thought it ridiculous, but my heart said, "Do it...do it!" and my mind said, "Don't!" But my heart won out, and all at once, it was as though a river came out of my mouth, and I fell to my knees and roared! I fell under the power, and then Steve did! His arm flew into the air, still holding the sandwich, the lettuce flying everywhere. Now picture Steve—the humble, soft-spoken-nice guy, who's hardly ever noticed, now turned old time, turn-or-burn revivalist! Even his voice gained an attention-getting edge, *"IF YOU DON'T CHANGE YOUR WAYS, YOU WILL GO TO HELL!"* he yelled at the top of his lungs. Well, the spirit of fear hit that place, I'll tell you. The clerk and his friends dove behind the counter, cowering. Finally, the clerk stood and pointed over the counter with one finger shaking and said, "Is...is that your God?"

No one mocked now! Just as we placed our purchases on the counter, the door opened, and an old, dirty bum walked in with a couple of pop bottles to exchange for a refund. He plunked them on the counter, and as the clerks gave him his money, he said right to them, "You better listen to what these two guys are telling you, because it's true!"

Then he turned and walked out. When we returned to the car, we asked Shonnah and Roswetta if they'd seen this "bum," and they told us that no one had entered since we had, nor had anyone left.

THROWN OUT OF THE DONUT SHOP

Wow, those were our radical evangelism days! We even scoured a doughnut shop for "prey." One day, Steve and another friend, Brian, and I visited a popular doughnut shop wanting to witness. We went from table to table, with no results. There was a little side room in those days for smokers, and it was full of customers. "Preach in there, Todd," they said, "You can stand on one of the tables to preach."

Well, it *was* midnight, so I entered the room and stood on a chair. "Do you believe in Jesus? I began. "I once was a drug addict, but now I'm a new creation. You can become a new creation too!"

People were like, "shut up!"

Although we were kicked out of the restaurant, we congratulated ourselves for our obedience to the Lord! Steve had so turned into an evangelistic fireball that it got to the point where no one dared go with him to a movie or a store if they had any kind of schedule they had to keep. Sometimes he'd be two or more hours late because he may have picked up a hitchhiker, for instance, that he'd led to Christ. Go to a restaurant with Steve, and he'd share Christ with everyone he passed as he made his way to the table, or he'd hand out tracts along the way!

REPENTANCE

God continued to pour out His Spirit of intimacy, stir up the prophetic, increase the healing anointing, and impart evangelistic zeal. Many of the Fresh Fire youth caught the fervor and accompanied me to witness and prophesy to the lost.

In addition to intimacy, the prophetic, healing, and evangelism, God took me into a fifth area that I refer to as the "Holy Spirit boot camp of deep repentance." The intimate times of soaking continued as the Lord gave me specific Scriptures that applied to the youth ministry and to my calling. During prayer one day, I had an open vision of one single red rose. Just as I wondered if I could touch it, the rose exploded into a ball of fire! *What did it mean?* The Holy Spirit revealed the meaning by saying, "The desert shall blossom as a rose." Then He brought to my remembrance Isaiah

35, and I knew that what that Scripture revealed, would be my ministry mandate. The three major themes of this passage are:

- The revival mandate to bring glory, refreshing, and wine in the wilderness so the deserts "shall rejoice and blossom." Everything was about the presence of the Lord.

- Then the miracles happened—"the eyes of the blind shall be opened and the tongue of the dumb sing."

- The "highway of holiness." Week after week I preached the conviction of sin, repentance, holiness, and the consecrated life. I realized that the highway of miracles and glory was the highway of holiness.

In the early days of my Christian life, the Holy Spirit sternly dealt with me about ungodly music, sexual purity, and a set-apart lifestyle. Now I began to see the lukewarmness in the Christian youth of the city—such as compromise, toleration of sin, unclean movies, and ungodly music. This time of refining was crucial for my future ministry And I began preaching fiery messages on repentance and on dying to self. Many youth repented and embraced set-apart lifestyles. Some even destroyed ungodly music, fetishes, and charms. There was a sincere passion in many youth to become extreme radical disciples, and to obey the Lord no matter the cost by asking, "What would Jesus do?"

Each week backsliders turned to the Lord. The Spirit warmed cold hearts. Young people lay prostrate before Him, weeping at the altars. I remember praying, "Oh God don't let me be a fiery, long-bony-fingered, John-the-Baptist-style, prophetic, repentance preacher for the rest of my life. Let me preach love and soaking." However, there was a desperate need for this message at the time. Today, we still need to see this kind of preaching in the church.

PREPARATION FOR THE NATIONS

My ministry involvement with the Fresh Fire youth group lasted about five months until I traveled regularly to take the fire of God on the road. Together, we had all grown and learned through those five main lessons the Holy Spirit taught me, those of intimacy, prophecy, healing, evangelism, and repentance. Revival broke out in that inter-church youth group and attendance grew substantially. Hundreds of hungry youth over the months arrived at that small Anglican church for a touch of God's fire. Sometimes the Spirit arrived with such intensity that it created a Holy Ghost (orderly) chaos! Whether it was an intense joy of the Lord, a shaking, a travailing for souls, healing, worshiping, dancing, prophesying, or falling under His power, the power of the Lord wrecked and transformed lives and imparted a hunger and thirst for Jesus.

My ministry thus far, (the revival ministry with the youth and my prophetic vision of the Isaiah 35 fiery rose,) confirmed that there would be three measures of my future ministry. Those measures were, first, revival (through intimacy and God's prophetic voice); then healing, and third, a strong preacher's anointing for holiness, repentance, and the abandoned life. From that Isaiah vision, I knew that one day the ministry that we had in that small church basement would become Fresh Fire Ministries International, but I didn't know when.

CHAPTER 11

LAUNCH INTO MINISTRY

Patricia King, a prophetess from British Columbia, heard about the experiences in my prayer closet and how it had spilled out in the youth meetings. It thrilled and excited her to learn how God had been moving through the youth. Though I had attended several of her conferences over the years, and had even worshiped in her home with a group, we didn't have a personal relationship. Patricia's mind-set was, "Great, the Gen-X revival generation—we've got another guy—one of thousands that God will raise up—and he's right here, in my area!"

In May of 1998, she asked me to share my testimony at a women's conference that upcoming Mother's Day, to encourage mothers whose sons might be backslidden or living a lifestyle similar to mine before I met Christ. She allotted me ten minutes to speak.

On Mother's Day morning, as I prepared for my time with the gathering, I sensed something new would happen. I was at the end of my three-month soaking season, still on compensation, but had planned to return to my job at the sawmill, even though it would be hard for me, since I'd been used to praying for four to eight hours in preparation for most of the ministry opportunities that came my way up until then. This particular morning though, I was in a state of expectation, almost like a kid on Christmas morning. I sensed that I was in for an intense visitation or something. "What's up God? What are You going to do?" I knew in my heart that He had something planned beyond anything I had yet to experience.

The Holy Spirit spoke to me and said, "Todd, I want you to pray in tongues," and suddenly I felt an incredible burden. Something hit my spirit, and it felt as though I was about to birth destiny, that I was loosing something and setting something in order—calling things that are not as though they were! It was as though I was pulling something out of the heavens. I felt purpose! I knew deep inside of me that what was happening would determine what was going to happen in my future. It was as though I was releasing a city whose builder and maker was God! I knew that I was setting things in place for my destiny—I was about to birth not one meeting, but a multitude of invitations to do meetings around the world. This time praying in the spirit was like no other—something was happening, right then, right there!

The sensation was new to me, and, therefore, confusing! I prayed mysteries while I paced back and forth in the living room. My mind kicked in, *Why are you doing this? You're not a minister and you've never been to Bible school!* Then my thoughts scolded me, *You're going back to work in the mill...no one knows who you are...you're in a church with fifty people. Why do you think you're building a ministry?*

On the one hand, I had a vision from the Lord. However, on the other hand, I thought, *I can't do this...the situation isn't right.*

This is foolishness; I'm only twenty-two years old. I'm invited to do one meeting, and only for ten minutes!

My entire body groaned, almost like contractions. I prayed in English, and decreed in the spirit the thoughts that broke in. "God, I call forth right now those whom You've called to be partners with the ministry. I birth them and I pray they will have the money they need." But my mind rebutted and said, *You don't even have a ministry, and you certainly don't have any partners!* I'd pray again, "God, I pray now that Your miracle healing power would come upon this service, and continue into other meetings." Then again, that brain of mine would say, *God, I don't have any meetings,* but the Holy Spirit said, "You're building a city whose builder and maker is God! You're doing it on the level of intercession. You're loosing it in the spirit now so it can come forth in the future, even though it may be ten years down the road."

I was confused, it was as though a spiritual battle had launched in my mind. I heard Shonnah awaken, and I went into the bedroom where she lay. Sleepily, she said, "I just had a dream, where I was walking very fast while praying in tongues, and someone said, "Why are you doing this?" and I answered, "I don't know, but I know it's the right thing to do." Then Shonnah rolled over and went back to sleep (although she claims she'd entered into the rest of the Lord!).

At the end of that visitation, after about four hours of praying in the spirit, I felt peace, heat, electricity, and a sense of someone looking over my shoulder. I realized then that the Lord Himself was visiting me. He wasn't in physical form, but I felt His wonderful presence behind me. I tried to see Him, but He stayed always behind me. Nevertheless, I knew it was Him, and I heard Him audibly say, "Watch and see!"

Something big was up. Watch and see what? Did it have something to do with the meeting that night? I asked Jesus about it several times, but all He'd say was, "Watch and see!" Then I remembered Genesis 18:17-18 "And the Lord said, 'Shall I hide from Abraham what I am doing, since Abraham shall surely become a great and mighty nation, and all the nations of the earth shall be blessed by him?'."

I pressed in and prayed, "Lord, don't hide from me," and then, a vision opened where I saw a woman at Patricia's meeting become healed of cancer. Then I received other healing words and saw the service as though I was already there. I saw myself pray for the sick and lay hands on hundreds of women who fell out under the power. Patricia was there and she called me out and then prophesied over my ministry and me. The Lord said that He would use that night's service to launch me into an international ministry, and that I wouldn't return to my secular job. I didn't understand what was happening, but I prayed, and the Lord reminded me of Acts 13:2, where the Holy Spirit said, "Separate to Me Barnabas and Saul for the work to which I have called them." Then He said, "I'll tell Patricia tonight at the service to take up an offering, to ordain you, and to call you into the ministry by a prophetic word. You will quit your job, and, as a sign to you, I'm going to heal a woman of cancer in that auditorium!"

Oh God, I thought, *how is it going to happen? I've never been to Bible school, I don't have any finances, and no one knows who I am. What am I going to tell my wife?*

God just said, "Watch, and see. My power is going to fill that auditorium."

Now friends, hear my heart. For the first time in my life, I actually had a great job working at the mill, and it was run by a Christian. I had medical and dental benefits, made great money, and was able to take care of my family. I was content to be faithful in the small things and worry about what God had for me later. I had been very zealous for ministry, but I laid that down three years previously. I had wanted things to happen quickly, but there was too much selfish ambition in me, so He had to kill it. Now that the full-time ministry desires had died, He said, "OK, I can give it to you now."

I'd never spoken in a meeting like Patricia's before, and arrived in my typical attire: ripped jeans, bandana, goatee, and earrings. Patricia emphasized the time restriction again. "Can you keep it ten minutes, Todd?"

I nodded but immediately went back to the Lord and asked Him how He was going to do what He had shown me. "I'm not even the main speaker. I don't want to look as though I'm trying to steal the show—there isn't even time for the words of knowledge!"

However, as I asked the Lord this question, I had a vision, and it gave me the "wisdom of the Lord." In it, I saw the stone roll away from Jesus' tomb—and out of the cave appeared a blast of light and glory! I knew it was The Resurrection. Then John 11:25 illuminated in my spirit, "Jesus said to her, 'I am the resurrection and the life'." Suddenly, I knew that there had been many suicides in that very city, and that they were dealing with a spirit of death. I saw that the Lord wanted to roll back the stone and release resurrection power. During the worship and praise time, I shared the vision with Patricia.

"You've got to share that," she said.

"After I share, can I pray for a release of that?"

"Yes! Break the spirit of death according to what you saw, and then share your testimony," she instructed.

I spoke out this word, and the Lord told me to call out the woman with cancer that I had seen in the vision that morning, and rebuke the spirit of death that was upon her. Then the wave of the Spirit moved into several other healings. Patricia recognized the move of God's power and ran to the microphone. "You need to hear his testimony, and then I'll have him pray for all wayward sons and daughters."

Everything unfolded like a television show. God did everything I'd seen in my vision. I gave the words of knowledge and the woman was healed of cancer. Hundreds of women were laid out under the power. Ten minutes turned into an hour and then Patricia rose to speak. The power of God hit me and I knew what was coming. She said, "The Lord just spoke to me. We're going to take an offering and lay hands on this young man. He's going to the nations. He'll never return to secular work."

God orchestrated everything! Not only did those people give a large offering—over fifty men and women committed to intercede for my marriage and ministry from that day forward. God supernaturally set it up and launched me in the ministry after my three months of preparation. I thank God that my wife and mother-in-law were in that service. If they weren't there and I had tried to tell them what happened, they might have said, "No way, maybe when you're thirty or thirty-five!" But they both witnessed how the Lord put together the events of that meeting piece-by-piece; they were convinced that it was really God's timing.

I thank God for my friendship with Patricia, and for how God used her as an instrument to ordain me into the ministry—but I always will know that the call came from God. I've since been ordained in Canada by my local church, and through the Christian Minister's Association. In the U.S., I'm recognized as a minister of the Gospel through World Ministry Fellowship in Texas.

THE POPCORN ANOINTING

It was weeks later before I understood that my launch into ministry was the fulfillment of the end-time army visitation, which I described in the beginning of this book.

Here's a quick bunny trail about what the Lord is going to do in the future. The way the Lord called me into the ministry is an example of what I call the "Popcorn Anointing." We see an example of this quick ministry launch in the book of Acts: "Now in the church…there were certain prophets and teachers…As they ministered to the Lord and fasted, the Holy Spirit said, 'Now separate to me Barnabas and Saul for the work to which I have called them.'" (Acts 13:1-2).

The time has come where those who have remained faithful are going to be thrust into the harvest. This is God's sending time. Just as Paul was snatched out of the Arabian Desert, many will be brought out of their desert season into their giftings and anointing. This is the "year" of the Lord's glory. The gold (finances) is going to be released for end-time apostolic ministries, which will bring in the harvest. Scripture links the release of God's power with financial blessings:

> *"And with great power the apostles gave witness to the resurrection of the Lord Jesus. and great grace was upon them all. Nor was there anyone among them who lacked; for all who were possessors of lands or houses sold them, and brought the proceeds of the things that were sold, and laid them at the apostles' feet; and they distributed to each as anyone had need." (Acts 4:33–35).*

In those days of the early church, not one of the believers was in need. Those who owned fields or houses sold them and brought the money to the apostles and the money was distributed to each one according to his need.

FIRST ROAD TRIP

After Patricia called me into the ministry, I said, "OK God, I'm going to quit my job." Even though everyone had tried so hard to see me employed and I didn't have one speaking engagement yet, as an act of faith, I left my job for traveling ministry. I'd been saved four years. Nobody knew Todd Bentley, and I was only twenty-two years old.

I remember my first road trip. Patricia invited me to William's Lake to be a part of her prophetic team. She said she couldn't pay me an honorarium and I'd have to pay my own way. She'd introduce me and let me prophesy and share my testimony.

In those first few weeks, I said to God, "My rent is due. I have no money coming in but I'm going to go on this trip with my wife." Shonnah and I drove to the interior of British Columbia in my lemon-of-a-MPV van. The road trip was a nightmare; the radiator wouldn't hold water, and we had to keep stopping. The five-hour drive took us seven or eight hours. I remember seeing Patricia and Ron's new red, air-conditioned van and asking, "God, am I ever going to be there?"

Each night I was able to minister at the altars. Patricia also gave me an opportunity to preach on prophetic evangelism. One morning she announced, "OK, this morning Todd is going to prophesy to everyone who has a last name that starts with A-D and he only has ten minutes to do it!"

That being my first traveling ministry opportunity, I purposed in my heart that I was going to live by faith, even though each day I wondered how God was going to provide. In one of the meetings, a woman had a vision and saw herself withdraw $500 from her ATM machine and then give it to me. The day before our rent was due, God gave it to me, down to the last exact penny. It so encouraged me!

The next month I asked, "God how are You going to get it done?" Again, just before rent day, Greg Dennison arrived at my house. He was one of the men in Pat's first meeting who had committed to pray for me. He said, "Todd I had a vision a month ago, and I saw myself writing out $500 post-dated checks. I want to be your first partner." He also became my first travel companion and disciple.

MORE THAN ENOUGH

Whenever I prayed that God would provide finances, something inside of me said that I should never believe for more than I needed at the time. The devil constantly reminded me of struggling ministries, and I thought, *Why should it be different for me? These were godly men who served the Lord, men who had character and passion. They had everything I wanted, but their churches didn't grow past sixty or seventy members.*

I felt guilty for wanting to have enough to help the poor, to hire staff, and to finance crusades and was constantly under guilt and condemnation for having dreams of a big international ministry. *What if the Lord called me only to reach one, I wondered. Who am I to think I can reach 10,000? I'm always thinking about more than enough but I should just be satisfied with enough.*

If anything happened that was good, I was afraid that it would slip away the next day. I felt unworthy of blessings—this mind-set stemmed from the great lack I had experienced from childhood. Even in my ministry vision I had to have that spirit of poverty broken. I'd think about Billy Graham and Benny Hinn and wonder why I couldn't do that too? Then I started reading: "If you abide in Me, and My words abide in you, you will ask what you desire, and it shall be done for you. By this My Father is glorified, that you bear much fruit..." (John 15:7-8). I then realized—God doesn't just want me to bear fruit; He wants me to bear *much* fruit.

The story of Jesus feeding the 5,000 (see John 6:1–14) also helped me. Think of it—that number just refers to men; it didn't include the many women and children who were also fed. And when everyone had eaten all they wanted, there were *12* full baskets *left over*. Hallelujah, there was more than enough! These Scriptures became a foundation for my life and ministry. At first I thought God would never provide financially. Then at each new level I had to believe for more finances and I had to work it through in my spirit. I had to increase my level of faith that He could do it again and that I could trust Him with my future.

HUNGRY FOR MIRACLES

My hunger for a more powerful ministry in the area of miracles continued to grow. I read the Gospels and the Book of Acts and said to myself, *This is what I want.* I became convinced that in Jesus' ministry and in the early church, the way they brought in the harvest was with signs and wonders. I remember, at times, coming home from meetings and wondering, "God why did You heal this one and not that one?" In this season of pressing in for healing, I became quite frustrated that one deaf person would hear and six others wouldn't. I wasn't always moving in super faith. There were times when I would lay hands on someone and wouldn't feel any anointing. In my mind I thought, *Are You even listening to my prayer God?* In my mind, I was repenting of unbelief while out of my mouth I prayed this great prayer of faith.

Often when it seemed like the meeting wasn't lining up with my preaching and with my idea of what a healing service should look like, I would wonder why it was so hard. Then I would release a healing wave and everyone would just stand there with their eyes open and look at me. I would pray a mass prayer rebuking devils and sickness and pray for the healing presence. Then I'd look at the crowd and they just stared back, so I'd say, "Do something you couldn't do before—quickly!" Still they just stood there, and I'd wonder if anyone would ever join their faith with mine. I've attended meetings where I wondered if there was anyone at all even remotely excited about the content of my message. If they were, I wondered why they weren't responding in faith. I'd return home thinking about how much work it was to get someone healed. "God, maybe we could just be a salvation ministry!" I'd say. But I couldn't ignore this compelling, burning hunger for more of the real Gospel—the full Gospel of power!

ABBOTSFORD CONFERENCE—AUGUST 1998

Even in those early days, I didn't want to wait for churches to call me. I was "gung ho" to host my own crusades. Today, our conferences attract sometimes as many as two to three thousand people from all over the world, quite a jump from my first meeting of 25 people, mostly women, in the Abbotsford Revival Center. I still hear the music we played in those early days—Clif Robertson singing, "Poppa, poppa, pour it out, pour it out, pour it out," or, "Lord of the dance, You're the dancing Lord!"

> Even in our earliest meetings, God gave us favor. A reporter from a local newspaper gave us a favorable review comparing our services as similar to those of the early days of the Toronto Blessing.

HEALING ANGELS, VISITATION, AND COMMISSION

As I've shared before, I studied T.L. Osborn's book, *Healing the Sick*, and also F.F. Bosworth's *Christ the Healer*. I preached the theology and principles of healing, I read the healing Scriptures, and I claimed them by faith. I confessed, "I am who God says I am and I can do what God says I can do. I believe God's word." I prayed for the sick wherever I met them. I really wanted to see people healed. I just laid hands on the sick based on the authority that I knew of in the Bible. I believed it, so I started doing it. I didn't have a special visitation, anointing, commission, or special words from the prophets about healing.

I started preaching on everything I saw in the Bible that had to do with healing—the principles of faith, theology of healing, hindrances to healing, and how to maintain your healing. I trusted that the Holy Sprit would confirm the word. I laid hands on and anointed the sick with oil. I believed God's promise in John 14:12 was for me: "Most assuredly, I say to you, he who believes in Me, the works that I do he will do also; and greater works than these he will do, because I go to My Father."

I copied the models of Oral Roberts, Benny Hinn, and T.L. Osborn. Healing is for every believer because Romans 8:11 says that the same Spirit that raised Jesus from the dead lives in me and He's going to quicken and bring life to my mortal body through that Spirit. It's for me and for you.

I purposed that if I prayed for a thousand and no one got healed that I would pray for another thousand. In those early days of warring and contending, it seemed as though I prayed for a thousand without anyone being healed, but I just kept praying until something happened. Each time a miracle happened there was something new that happened in my spirit in the area of authority and faith. The testimony of what I saw, gave me the confidence that I needed to believe God would do it again. Each healing breakthrough spurred me on to want to see more.

In the beginning, I had faith for backs, fibromyalgia, and crooked spines. "Anyone got any pain in their body? Arthritis? Come forward now!" At that time, my faith level wasn't where it needed to be for the blind, deaf, or crippled.

"GIVE ME THE DEAF"

Eventually I said, "God I'm not satisfied with my level of healing. I want the deaf to hear." Since my mother was deaf, I really wanted to damage the enemy's kingdom in this area. My area of crisis became my area of compassion. I went hard after that anointing.

Everywhere I went I'd call the deaf forward and pray for them. I prayed for the deaf and I prayed for the deaf, and I prayed for the deaf. For the longest time, when the deaf left my meetings they were still deaf. I prayed for hundreds of deaf people and occasionally the deaf heard—partially. I saw results maybe two percent of the time. I kept begging God, "Give me the deaf. Give me the deaf." Then, God gave me a key; He taught me about the deaf and dumb spirit. I saw it in Mark 9:25: "He rebuked the unclean spirit, saying to it, 'Deaf and dumb spirit, I command you, come out of him and enter him no more!'"

So, just as Jesus did, I began to command that spirit to "loose ears." The next time the deaf came, I had a little more confidence and expectation. When a few deaf heard, there was more confidence and expectation for next time. I learned that it was all about warring and contending, and I used this principle in every major area where I wasn't seeing results.

"OK God," I said one day, "I'm seeing breakthrough, but I'm not seeing breakthrough for tumors." In faith, I would sow into praying for tumors until people were healed. Then I would move on to another type of sickness.

I discovered that healing comes in levels and that, as believers, we need to contend and break through one level until we get authority. As we agree with God and see several deaf ears or tumors healed, then our faith-level for that infirmity grows. The more people I prayed for, the more were healed. I prayed in faith regarding a particular illness until I received a breakthrough—the deaf, the blind, and then those in wheelchairs. Now I'm contending for resurrections.

ON THE ROAD

Because of my first meeting with Patricia in William's Lake, I received my second invitation, to Prince George Family Worship Center in British Columbia. In the first eighteen months of ministry I visited there six times. At this time, I also ministered in Mission, B.C. and in the Yukon. These would be the first places where we saw demonstrations of God's healing anointing and glory move through our traveling ministry.

The following are a few reports of those early days.

WHITEHORSE, YUKON—JANUARY 1999

I'd already been in ministry six months when I went to minister in Whitehorse. Those were the early days when I would say, "God what am I doing here in minus 20 degree temperatures? I'm actually ice fishing with the pastors in my free time. No wonder all the Americans think it's only Eskimos and igloos here in Canada."

I remember when I stepped outside and my nose hair crystallized! I prayed, "God, please don't send me here a lot or, if You do, please let it be in summer."

But a small group of people there were hungry for revival. We held the first meeting in a Native Indian hall called the *Potlatch House*. People arrived in snow boots, some as far as Alaska. God gave us favor when a news reporter, Anne Pritchard from the Yukon News, attended the service…as a skeptic! Here is her article (with her summary of my testimony edited out for brevity).

Faith healer lays hands on Yukoners
by Anne Pritchard, news reporter

My hands ache. Constantly. It feels as if knives are being stabbed into my wrist. It's job-related, a result of banging out stories on a keyboard over the last 15 years. It's a four-Tylenol-a-day pain in the…well, wrist.

So when I read about evangelist and faith healer Todd Bentley's "miracle, healing, evangelism crusade," I thought I'd check it out. I was interested anyway. I wanted to see if the guy was a shyster, a snake oil salesman. You gotta wonder.

"Bring your lame, dumb and those with cancer and FAS-those with no hope of a medical cure," said Bentley's flyer, which was posted around Whitehorse.

In response, about 40 people—myself included—hit Mt. McIntyre's Potlatch House on Friday night to hear

Bentley preach—and maybe experience a miracle healing, or two. The mood is upbeat. The crowd warms up singing songs of Christian faith. Then Bentley gives his own testimony to the crowd. Finally the altar call! Most go up for healing. Are they healed?

Sometimes there are healings on site and, at other times, healing will happen later, he says.

Sometimes people heal only to revert back to their original ailment, he adds. "I will say that I have seen an incredible amount of people with bone injuries—a crooked spine straightened where God actually takes bones and realigns them." Bentley claims recent miracles have involved eyesight and cancer. He has prayed over folks at the Potlatch House, and laid hands on some. Tonight, he started out offering to heal folks with arthritic pain.

About 30 of the 40 people in the crowd went barreling up to the front of the hall. Bentley laughed, and called the rest up. The crowd lined up, and Bentley walked to each one. Sometimes he touched their heads, at other times he just held his arms over the person and uttered a prayer.

Sometimes he did it solo, other times he asked someone for help. And were they healed?

There's no way to tell, but everyone toppled to the floor and lay there in a seeming euphoric mood; they appeared to be drunk. Meanwhile, I'm hanging back watching the proceedings. I'm trying to keep an open mind, but this looks weird, people toppling over like tenpins at the hands of the young, stout earring-wearing preacher. He sees me, eyes my wrist supports and starts urging me to the front of the room. I think, 'What the hell,' and stride to the lineup. He anoints my head with a golden oil (it looked like olive oil) and lays his chubby fingers on the top of my head. I start to get dizzy, and am caught up in some sort of turbulent energy. It feels like the wind is blowing. Hard. I feel like I'm starting to fall over. I start resisting, pitching forward to avoid hitting the floor like the rest. Bentley starts to laugh, good naturedly—like he's seen it before. Then I give up, collapsing like the others. I feel woozy, like I've been drinking.

He leaves me there and then moves to the next person. I feel peace, and euphoria.

And, you know, my wrists feel OK. At least so far. Bentley's healing crusade goes on until Thursday night.

MISSION, B.C.—MARCH/APRIL 1999

My first experience with revival was within ten months of being in the ministry. Patricia asked me to come in as a guest minister for one night at Mission Foursquare Church. In the prayer service that evening the room smelled of refiner's fire and laundry soap. "But who can endure the day of His coming? And who can stand when He appears? For He is like a refiner's fire and like launderers' soap" (Mal. 3:2).

Patricia said, "Something's up." During worship the air became thick with the dew of the Lord and people were saying, "I feel sticky." It was as if dew had fallen from heaven.

The Holy Spirit said to me, "Todd you have not because you ask not. If I'm doing dental miracles in Toronto and Argentina I can give them here too."

Moving by faith only, I told some stories and asked for dental miracles of glory and gold. That first service seven people received them. Patricia said "There's an unusual presence of the Lord, let's continue the services."

These dental miracles went on for a year in our ministry—signs of God's glory. During the Mission meetings, we packed this church out to overflowing; visitors would come into the meeting and see people with flashlights looking in other people's mouths during worship. The unsaved youth started to come in; then some were saved. We grew out of that facility and had to move to a larger church. This was truly the beginning of what revival might taste like.

GREAT JOY IN THE CITY
MACKENZIE, B.C.—APRIL 1999
The following report is about this meeting (author unknown):

Mackenzie experienced the reality of the Scripture verse from Acts 8 as there was "Great Joy in the City." Evangelist Todd Bentley held meetings at Living Joy Christian Center, April 19-21. Unusual dental miracles took place, traces of "gold dust" could be seen on people's hands or face and people were healed of a variety of pain conditions and physical problems. The response was one of amazement and awe, and of course, joy. Fillings in people's teeth changed to silver or gold, and seemed to be highly polished—teeth even straightened. People with pain in their hips and pelvis received freedom from pain and could move in ways that were impossible before. Eyesight and hearing improved and people with asthma and respiratory problems reported great improvements. As a result of people experiencing the reality and power of God's love, many people acknowledged and accepted Jesus Christ as Savior and Lord. We continue to rejoice at God's goodness, His desire still is to heal the sick and the broken hearted, and to bring liberty to the oppressed. In a world that is experiencing such strife, tragedy, and senseless violence, hope can still be found in the reality of Jesus Christ.

GOLD TEETH HARD TO PROVE,
USEFUL FOR OUTREACH MAY 1999
Excerpts from an article by Peter T. Chattaway

The Great Physician may also be the Great Dentist. In the past two months, several dozen people have reported receiving gold fillings and similar miracles at churches and revival meetings throughout British Columbia.

They were having people come up to be prayed for, recalls Dorothy McKee, who says she received four gold teeth at the Mission Foursquare Church March 21. "My husband was checking people as they went up to the front, and he looked in my mouth, and voila, I already had them." Dental miracles have been reported around the world, most recently in Argentina, at various times over the years. The first instance of miraculous fillings in Canada took place March 3 at the Toronto Christian Fellowship. Within a week, over 300 people claimed to have received dental miracles there.

It took only a couple of weeks for churches in Langley and Mission to follow suit. Nine people reported receiving dental miracles at the Langley Vineyard's March 20 service; the next night, seven people reportedly received the same during Todd Bentley's revival service at the Mission Foursquare Church. And the reports keep coming in.

"We've had between 45 and 50 people who have reported some kind of dental miracles in their mouths," says Langley Vineyard pastor Jesse Padgett. Of those, he estimates about 15 to 20 have gone to the dentist for confirmation.

Bentley, an Abbotsford-based evangelist, says the Mission meeting marked the first time gold teeth have appeared at any of his meetings. "Since then they've appeared in almost every meeting that I've done," he says, citing his recent rips to Mackenzie, Prince George and Portland, Oregon.

In addition to gold teeth, churchgoers also report gold dust and oil appearing on their hands. Paula Spurr, a musician and former deejay, says her hands began to sparkle during a 'God Rock' service led by Todd Bentley at Burnaby Christian Fellowship March 16.

"It was like Tinkerbell visited. Everyone's hands were shimmering a little bit," she says. "It was funny, because that's not at all the kind of thing that I look for. I don't need bells or whistles to prove anything, but it happened anyway, so it was like a little present."

Phillip Wiebe, a philosophy professor at Trinity Western University, says the gold tooth phenomenon is not a new thing; he first heard stories of miraculous gold fillings coming out of California 35 years ago.

"And what meaning might such miracles have? For the person that would undergo this, it would be, I would think, wonderful and kind of reassuring, and it would make them think that 'God loves me, is thinking about me and cares about me,'" says Wiebe.

For everyone else, he suggests, signs such as these may be "teasers" pointing people back to God. "The Lord leaves these signs, here and there, that He's real, so that doubters like myself will have some obstacles and, maybe as a result of them, believe."

MACKENZIE, B.C.—OCTOBER 22–23, 1999
Pastor's Report, Andy Barnes, Living Joy Christian Center

Todd ministered this weekend to about 30 men. Almost every man was stretched out before the altar in a state of repentance. During ministry times, which usually happened before and after preaching, God displayed His love and power in a variety of ways. Some of the miracles that took place included a girl with a crooked spine becoming perfectly straight, shoulder problems instantly healed, people being freed of depression, fear, and anger.

In April a man got saved while Todd was here, his wife was already a Christian. They have been going to her church and he has remained free of any desire for alcohol and has been growing in his relationship with God. This time their three sons were saved and they rejoiced in tears over the fact that the entire family was now saved.

A lady came to Tuesday's meeting intending to have Todd pray for her mother. Her mother had an asthma attack, and while being rushed to the hospital, had a heart attack in the ambulance. At the hospital doctors discovered a hole in one of the heart valves, and also that she had diabetes. She remained in a coma for six days, during which time they gave her insulin and waited for her to recover enough to do heart surgery.

During worship and ministry time the daughter had oil on her hands and as Todd was praying for people, he gave several words of knowledge, one of which was for people with diabetes. She felt a real peace and did not feel she had to go for prayer. The next day she found out that her mother had been released from the hospital, and there was no longer any trace of diabetes. The heart problem had improved so dramatically that it would be more dangerous to operate than to let it remain. She was even strong enough to walk about four blocks. Praise God, both the mother and the daughter gave God glory for this miracle.

Monday night during ministry two of the people on the worship team heard wonderful high harmony joining with them in singing—it turned out that nobody else was there singing with them, it was angels joining in. Awesome!

Throughout the men's conference and the open meetings there were times when the joy of the Lord would break out all over, and the Holy Ghost would minister divinely to people in different ways.

A SUDDENLY OF GOD

Prince George, British Columbia—January 2000

On my sixth visit to Prince George, about eighteen months into my ministry, one of our weekend trips turned into eighteen nights of gold and glory. We called it a "suddenly" of God. We were expecting a good time in God's presence, and He came and gave us a taste of revival.

We were recording a live worship CD and at one point, the fragrance of the Lord filled the building. For about forty-five minutes people smelled vanilla, cinnamon, and roses. Psalm 45:8 refers to "the Lord's fragrant robes."

A deaf woman was healed. Diamond dust appeared on people's hands. The glory cloud came. The glory would still be in the church the next day. People fell out under the power in the parking lot or just on the walk into the building. The Evangelical Christian News reported on the meetings and people learned about it all over Canada.

Our worship leader, Clif Robertson, said that when people began to arrive at the building the presence of the Lord was already lingering there. People began to get "drunk" In the spirit. I had planned to preach on the glory of God, but I didn't. Why should I preach on it when it was already there? Yes, people are hungry for the demonstration of the Spirit of God in power. But the most important thing is the presence; even if He didn't come with the miracles, we would just love His presence.

Prince George & Mackenzie
A meeting report by Val Andres, (Todd's mother-in-law)

During those early Prince George meetings, Todd made several visits to the small northern community of Mackenzie. A native woman testified that she was healed of a back injury while standing by herself at the altar. The next day her daughter, who was sixty miles away, called to tell her mom that she was healed at work of her back injury. It turns out that both healings happened at the same time, 11:00 o'clock. God is not limited to a building. Many people are going to be healed miles away.

In Prince George Todd was able to minister to two sets of young people in youth prison. Todd received words of knowledge and prophecy to speak into their lives. He was excited about reaching out to those in a lifestyle that he once lived.

The healing miracles in the meetings were not just physical; many were healed emotionally and delivered from demonic strongholds. The Spirit of the Lord moved for over two hours in deliverance one night. He who the Son sets free is free indeed!

Todd believes that the healing anointing has come to another level. In the four weeks that he was on the road in October, the healing testimonies seemed to be greater than at any other time. A man came out of a wheelchair, a man had a growth come off his eye, and people reported hearing and seeing angels in services. October truly has been a month of harvest!

There were physical healings, spiritual conversions, and people intoxicated with the wine of God, falling over and shaking, gold dust and dental miracles. Several would testify to feeling the Lord's presence in the parking lot and many were hit with the presence of the Lord before they even got in the sanctuary to take their seats before the meetings began.

Following is a healing testimony from that time:

Cancer Testimony

My name is Maureen. The doctor had told me that there were spots on my liver and they were cancerous. Last night I went to the Turning Point to receive prayer and during the evening started to feel a burning feeling in my side, and a feeling like something was squeezing me. Today I went to an appointment that was scheduled two weeks ago with the doctor; the appointment was to decide about surgery to remove part of my liver. They did another ultrasound and could not find the spots on my liver, only what they described as some fatty tissue, which could be controlled with a better diet. The doctor admits he can't understand it because this is the second time in two months things have disappeared from x-rays and ultrasounds. I understand it; it is a miracle from God.

I NEED MORE!

Those meetings led to my first revival in British Columbia. Within nine months, God was visiting our meetings regularly with the glory and the gold. There were extended meetings that lasted several weeks. Each night people would receive gold crowns in their mouths and oil would manifest on people's hands as it happened in the healing revival of the 1950s. The presence of revival swept through our services—the fragrance of the Lord and the glory mist. It was in those early meetings that people began to see angels and receive healing in their body. Christian News Week reported this.

I distinctly remember one extraordinary and wonderful experience that happened in Fort St. John during that first year of ministry. After I prophesied over everyone in the service one night, at about one or two o'clock the morning, I returned to the place I was staying. I decided to worship the Lord for a while and give Him the glory for the meeting. I could sense His presence in the room. Then it was as if the door opened and someone walked into the room; I could suddenly smell the fragrances of the Lord. He fed me the fragrance from His hand. I remember the tears running down my cheeks as I smelled vanilla, cinnamon, roses, and many other heavenly aromas. I thought to myself, *I am so close to the Lord right now I can actually smell His fragrance.*

God caused tremendous growth in the ministry through these early meetings as well as fresh encounters with the Lord, especially on the trips I took to the Yukon. I was crying out to God during this time, "Holy Spirit I want to see more healing, like in the days of the "Voice of Healing Revival." This powerful revival in the '50s birthed hundreds of healing evangelists. The following article excerpt describes the beginnings of that revival:

> "There was a man by the name of Jack Moore in Shreveport, Louisiana in 1946. This angel spoke to him and told him to begin to bring people together and so he brought Gordon Lindsay, A. A. Allen, William Branham, Oral Roberts, and Jack Coe…all together and they started the 'Voice of Healing.' Five years later when the power hit (William Branham was commissioned in May 1946 but the corporate anointing began to take shape some years later), it hit the "Latter Rain" (movement) in '50 and '51…." [1]

Night after night in America tens of thousands would pack the tents of hundreds of evangelists, some well known and some not. The miracles in these meetings were as profound as miracles that some see today in Africa, India, and other third world nations. Thousands were being saved. Some reports spoke of up to a hundred people getting out of wheelchairs in one service. There were creative miracles; piles of discarded crutches lay at the altar, not just one or two here and there, but whole stacks.

WHAT'S A HEALING ANOINTING?

After reading stories about the Voice of Healing Revival and other healing revivalists like Smith Wigglesworth, Maria Woodworth-Etter, and Aimee Semple McPherson, I was hungry to see miracles like that. When the Holy Spirit first started using me in healing, I didn't know I had a healing mantle. I never heard God say I was a chosen vessel, that He wanted me to carry healing to the nations, or that I had a special gift. I just believed what the Bible said about preaching the Gospel, healing the sick, cleansing the lepers, and raising the dead. The Bible says these signs will follow those who believe. He is Jehovah Rapha, the God who heals. I also realized, from Scripture, that healing is part of the atonement.

I believed it was for me, and so, on the basis of faith in God's word, I just continued anointing people with oil and preaching God's truth about divine healing based on the principles of these six Scriptures:

- John 14:12: "He who believes Me will do the works that I do and even greater works than these."

- Isaiah 53:5b: "By his stripes we are healed."

- Psalm 103:3: "Who forgives all your sins and heals all your diseases."

- Mark 16:18b: "they will lay hands on the sick and they will recover."

- Romans 8:11: "The same spirit that raised Jesus from the dead lives in you."

- Hebrews 13:8: "Jesus Christ is the same yesterday, today, and forever."

It was clear to me that healing is in me and in every believer, but there's a difference between healing through faith in God's word and the gift of healing in First Corinthians 12:9 "To another gifts of healing by that one Spirit."

While I was ministering in the Yukon, Canada I had a Holy Spirit visitation. "Do you want the healing anointing?" God asked me. I had just finished doing a healing crusade.

I said, "God, what do You mean, do I want the healing anointing?" Then I remembered the story of Jack Coe, one of the most prominent healing ministers of the Voice of Healing Revival. He once said to the Lord, "I'm not satisfied with the level of healing. How can I get more?" God said, "You need a healing anointing." Jack asked, "What have I been doing all this time?" God said that Jack had been healing by his faith and the faith of the people, which is good, but that He had an anointing for him so that it wouldn't matter whether people believed, are saved, or have faith. God told him that there can be such an atmosphere and manifestation of His presence that whoever comes into His glory gets healed.

God was now asking me if I wanted that anointing so that it wouldn't be so much about whether people believe the principles of healing (although that's important). He was offering me an anointing, so that when I walked into a room people would be healed in an anointing that comes from His presence and the grace of the Holy Spirit. I said, "Oh, gosh, let me think about it." NOT! Of course I said, "Yes, God I want it now."

God continued, "The anointing is because of My presence; where My presence is, people are healed."

"God," I replied, "If I can get more of Your presence I know I can get more healings." Up until this time, my goal was more knowledge, formulas, teaching principles, and getting more faith.

I kept doing all the things that I did in the area of faith, healing lines, and so on but at the same time, I started operating in the dimension of gifting. It came into my life because I earnestly desired spiritual gifts. "Pursue love, and desire spiritual gifts," Scripture tells us in First Corinthians 14:1. God doesn't want you to desire something you can't have.

I continued to preach and teach the truth of divine healing. But when an anointing would come, people would get healed sitting in their seats. So that's how I began to understand the difference between the healing that comes by the faith principle and the healing that comes through sovereign atmosphere.

WHITEHORSE, YUKON—JANUARY, 2000

A great highlight of this trip was to see a lady I'd visited in the hospital the last time I was in Whitehorse. At that time, she was paralyzed from the waist down because of an incurable disease. Doctors, and her family, were waiting for her to die. After prayer, her legs received partial healing; she began to move them and regain some feeling. Now, she had her driver's license back and was even beginning to walk short distances with a cane.

Another highlight was my invitation into the Catholic School to share my testimony with the grade 11 religious studies class. God moved and eight people prayed to receive Christ. There was such favor that they invited me back the next day to preach to the tenth graders. This time 24 students gave their hearts to the Lord.

In the evening service, there was a new level of power. One man who was deaf had his hearing restored. Another man with a paralyzed leg, the result of a witchdoctor's curse in his home-land, was instantly healed. These meetings had such a level of God's presence that the demons would spontaneously cry out, throw some people on the floor, and cause them to flail and thrash about.

When I left the Yukon I had no idea that the Lord would move me into a new season of healing, send me to Africa to get John G. Lake's anointing, and show me a vision of the coming healing revival.

ENDNOTE

1. Bob Jones and Keith Davis, Eye of the Eagle II, 12/05/00.

CHAPTER 12

A PROPHETIC JOURNEY

I longed to see the apostolic power return to the Church, and I longed for an increase in my ministry. The Lord spoke to me about John G. Lake, so I studied his life and how God had used him. He had planted over 600 churches in South Africa.

He didn't just do miracles, signs, and wonders but *lived in union*, in oneness and intimacy with the Lord. Experiments were done where diseases and bacteria were placed on his hand and monitored under a microscope. They'd either dissolve or die. Lake carried an unusual anointing of the presence, the fire, and the holiness of God. The anointing on his ministry was transferable and tangible. People would often open his newsletter and begin to speak in tongues or get healed because the anointing would be released through the letters that went out. When I read this, I got hungrier. I said, "God I want to see whole cities overcome by Your power and presence. I want more in the area of healing."

The Lord gave me a new commission. "Go to South Africa on a prophetic journey," He said. "I want you to go and get the anointing of John G. Lake."

"God I don't know anyone in South Africa," I answered. But during our conversation, I had an open vision and I saw the dates when I would actually go—March 10-27, 2000.

When the invitation came from a local pastor, Keith Abrahams in Abbotsford, who was a prophet from South Africa, the dates matched exactly. Keith asked, "Todd do you want to go and minister in South Africa if I arrange some meetings for you?" I thought back to my first year of marriage—Shonnah and I were in a service with a guest from Ghana, Africa and we were overcome with weeping and intercession, and felt as though we would one day go to Africa.

THE GREAT CLOUD OF WITNESSES

Prior to our South Africa trip, the Holy Spirit gave me my first vision of the coming healing revival of signs and wonders. During worship in the local Abbotsford Revival Center, I felt the Lord's presence surround me. My ears were opened and I heard the tongues of a great crowd. I looked around the sanctuary; there were fewer than forty people and no one was speaking in tongues. I knew there was no way they could make this great noise. Then I knew it was the tongues of angels. I asked a woman beside me, "Jen, do you hear them? It sounds like angels." It was as though 70,000 people were praying in the spirit all at once. I felt waves of His glory and power come over me. I felt myself ascending, and I was lifted into the Spirit like the apostle John who was caught up in the Spirit on the Lord's Day (see Rev. 1:10).

Suddenly, I was standing on a football field in a stadium. I knew I was in a prophetic encounter. The stands were filled with angels, tens upon tens of thousands of angels. There was an immediate knowing that these angels were waiting to be released.

They were cheering on the advancement of the Kingdom in the modern-day Church. The Church was the team on the field and the angels were about to be released onto a last days' generation to bring about the purposes of God. "Bless the Lord, you His angels, who excel in strength, who do His word, heeding the voice of His word. Bless the Lord, all you His hosts, you ministers of His, who do His pleasure" (Psalm 103:20-21).

A VISION OF THE COMING HEALING REVIVAL

The Lord showed me that during this upcoming healing revival, an anointing would be released greater than that of the Voice of Healing revival years ago. God spoke to me about the coming healing revival in Canada and beyond. Next, I was caught up in the spirit over North America as if I was flying in an airplane. I saw many small rain clouds of healing and miracles. They were individually set up over many churches, cities, nations, and ministries, pouring down healing rain. The rain clouds looked like those in the cartoons where they pour down upon one person and follow him wherever he goes.

I saw many small pools of water and I asked, "What are these?" The Holy Spirit said, "I am releasing the pools of Bethesda. This is the release of John 5:1–4:

> *After this there was a feast of the Jews, and Jesus went up to Jerusalem. Now there is in Jerusalem by the Sheep Gate a pool, which is called in Hebrew, Bethesda, having five porches. In these lay a great multitude of sick people, blind, lame, paralyzed, waiting for the moving of the water. For an angel went down at a certain time into the pool and stirred up the water; then whoever stepped in first, after the stirring of the water, was made well of whatever disease he had.*

In the vision, I saw the coming healing revival. I saw angels like the angel in John 5 who would be released upon this last days' generation. I prayed it would be greater than the days of

Alexander Dowie and John G. Lake. "Let there be whole cities and geographic locations touched by Your healing power."

THE TRANSFERABLE TANGIBLE HEALING ANOINTING

Then I saw many ministers, ministries, and churches that are already flowing in this miracle, healing anointing, beginning to minister throughout North America. In my vision, as these ministers of healing finished ministering in one location and left, the healing miracle cloud remained upon that church or city, and continued to pour down healing rain.

It was a transferable, tangible anointing of healing being imparted to other ministries, churches, and even cities. It spread like fire. Everybody who encountered the healing wave started to minister the power of God.

As in my vision, I believe that many places are going to receive such an outpouring of healing rain that pools of water are going to form, like modern-day pools of Bethesda. This outpouring of miracles, signs, and wonders is a part of the apostolic move and will touch the four corners of the earth.

THE HEALING AND MIRACLE CENTERS

The literal meaning of *Bethesda* is "the house of outpouring and grace." The grace of God will give us an outpouring of the rains of healing and miracles, until the power of God increases and we have a flood of miracle rain and many pools of healing. The pool of Bethesda was in a geographical place called *Solomon's Porch*. The sick came from all over the nation. I believe the Pools of Bethesda the Lord showed me will be places of healing, miracles, and revival in many geographical locations.

Once again, great multitudes will come from all over the world to geographical healing centers, just as they came to Spokane in the early 1900s to receive from John Lake's ministry. In five short years of Lake's ministry, over 100,000 healings and miracles were documented. The mayor of Spokane called the city the healthiest in America.

WHO IS GOING TO RECEIVE IT?

There won't be just one pool of Bethesda or one Spokane, I believe, but over a hundred different cities that will be internationally known for the ministry of healing. The Holy Spirit spoke to me that these miracles and healings are for those churches and ministries that will fervently cry out for the rain, like Elijah on the mountain in First Kings 18:41–46:

> *Then Elijah said to Ahab, "go up, eat and drink; for there is the sound of abundance of rain." So Ahab went up to eat and drink. And Elijah went up to the top of Carmel; then he bowed down on the ground, and put his face between his knees, and said to his servant, "Go up now, look toward the sea." So he went up and looked, and said, "There is nothing." And seven times he said, "Go again." Then it came to pass the seventh time, that he said, "There is a cloud, as small as a man's hand, rising out of the sea!" So he said, "Go up, say to Ahab, 'Prepare your chariot, and go down before the rain stops you.'" Now it happened in the meantime that the sky became black with clouds and wind, and there was a heavy rain. So Ahab rode away and went to Jezreel. Then the hand of the Lord came upon Elijah; and he girded up his loins and ran ahead of Ahab to the entrance of Jezreel.*

Elijah heard the sound of the abundance of rain. He knew in his spirit that the famine for Israel was over, and it was time for the rain to fall. In the same way, we know today in Church that it's time for the power of God. In First Kings 17:1 Elijah prophesied, "As the Lord God of Israel lives, before whom I stand, there shall not be dew nor rain these years, except at my word."

This Scripture indicates that the rains would come according to Elijah's word. It's the same with the coming rains of healing. It will be at the word of God's people, hungry for healing revival, in intercession and prophetic proclamation that the rains of miracles will fall. Though Elijah knew it was time for the rain to fall, he still prayed fervently on the mountain—he had to birth and call the rain forth. Though he saw nothing, he persisted in fervent prayer until the rain came.

If you are to be in the rain of healing and miracles moving across North America, you need to preach healing. Though you see nothing, preach healing and preach healing again. When you pray for the sick and nobody is healed, pray again. Elijah persisted seven times and he saw nothing. When he finally saw the cloud, it was still only the size of a man's hand.

GOD'S PROMISE TO FILL HEALING ROOMS

In North America today, we have numerous healing room ministries—I know of over 60 of them. We are getting ready for the power of God just like in Second Kings 3:17–20:

> *Thus says the Lord: 'Make this valley full of ditches.' For thus says the Lord: 'You shall not see wind, nor shall you see rain; yet that valley shall be filled with water. And this is a simple matter in the sight of the Lord" Now it happened in the morning, when the grain offering was offered, that suddenly water came by way of Edom, and the land was filled with water.*

God told them to prepare during the drought for the water, by digging ditches (water canals). As we prepare the containers for healing revival, then one day—it could be today or tomorrow—with no sign of wind or rain, when it seems like we aren't getting the breakthrough we are looking for in healing, and we continue to persist in intercession, preaching, and prayers for the sick—boom!—the water canals will be full!

I hear the sound of the abundance of rain and I know in my spirit *IT IS TIME!* Climb up on the mountain, call for the rain and call for the storm. When the rains first began to come in First Kings, the cloud was only the size of a man's fist, but it grew to the place where Elijah told Ahab to get his chariot and get going before the rain stopped him.

God spoke to my heart that there would be healings at first. Then the rain would become torrential and we'd move into creative miracles. Will your church be a pool of Bethesda for the sick and the lame? Well then, let it pour, for the Lord says that truly the people will come from miles around. There will be many cities like Spokane—this time not just with a man or a ministry—but whole cities under the anointing. People will be saying, "If I can get to that city I know I'll be healed."

CHAPTER 13

THE HEALING ANOINTING

My first ministry opportunities were in British Columbia then in the Pacific Northwest. Shortly afterward, I received speaking invitations every day, and suddenly found myself booked six months in advance! I didn't have to say, "Who's got contacts?" It just happened.

Why? Because I beheld the face of God and the hand of God showed up! Intimacy, relationship, and the anointing resulted from spending time with God. The presence of God released the anointing.

After I received the vision of the coming healing revival, I knew that my trip to South Africa would ignite something in my heart for the healing revival. This would be my first international meeting.

The night before I left for Africa to get the John G. Lake anointing I was at the house of one of Patricia King's intercessors.

The phone rang and it was Patricia calling from England. When she found out I was there she said the Lord just gave her a word that I was going to South Africa to get the healing anointing of John Lake and that when I got it I was going to bring a healing revival to America. I hadn't shared any of that information with Patricia.

DURBAN, SOUTH AFRICA—MARCH 2000

I believed that I would see great things in Africa and receive this anointing from the Lord. I went to Durban, South Africa with my friends Giovanni and Clif Robertson. Clif led worship at our meetings. When we arrived, I told the pastor that I wanted to go to the inner city market place outside the church walls. I wanted to be in the ghetto with the drug addicts, gangs, the poor, and the prostitutes. All I needed was a sound system in the streets.

One of the highlights—the pastor took me to Hawthorne, where 20 years previously, there had been a revival, but now, it was the darkest part of the city. He set up the sound system and I started preaching right away:

"I came from Canada and have a testimony of the power of Jesus," I said. After preaching, I challenged the people to come down and see the power of Jesus so they would know that the things I'd said about healing and changed lives are true. I laid hands on, and prayed for, over 1,000 people. It took hours.

Here is my on-site, as-it-happened report of the day-to-day outpouring of God's power on that trip:

Over 800 Saved, Over 250 Recommitments
Durban Report

I'm going to concentrate this report on the open air preaching that I did. The other meetings were awesome too, but I love being out among the hurting people. We didn't advertise these meetings. We simply visited different locations (mainly lower income dwellings), set up the sound equipment, and played music. The flats (apartments) were arranged in such a way that, as the sound transmitted, it would resonate between the buildings. Each area contained hundreds of people.

Different people shared their testimony between songs, and then we'd give the message of salvation. At first there would be 50-100 people who'd come out to hear and see what was happening; but then as soon as people began to be touched by the Holy Spirit and be healed in their bodies, hundreds showed up! It didn't matter if it was sunny, cloudy, or raining; the people came and waited, sometimes hours to be prayed for. One lady was set free from alcohol addiction. She came to the meeting drunk and went away a free woman. She arrived at our other street meetings to give testimony of what God did for her.

Open Air at Hime Street (Wednesday)

We set up the equipment and began to worship God. We were in the midst of the projects known for the highest gang warfare and bloodshed. People were on the streets; some were hanging over their balconies listening to what was going on. Hundreds of people heard the message of salvation, healing, and deliverance. Once the miracles began, people came from all over.

The crowd grew. People were healed of all kinds of sicknesses and diseases, the blind, deaf, and crippled; devils were manifesting and being cast out—over a hundred people gave their hearts to the Lord. There was a man who had a stroke and could barely walk; he left that night carrying his cane! We ministered here in the street well into the evening.

Open Air at K1 Shopping Park (Thursday)

Today the people started coming when I began to preach. Some came right up to where we were, others stayed back; but when the miracles and healings began, they pressed in. Well over

fifty souls were saved, and many were healed by the power of
God while hundreds of others looked on. Here are some healings
that happened. A woman who was almost blind from cataracts,
also had an arm that was bent and frozen. She raised her arm
above her head, and she also began to see. Another had been involved in the occult and was set free. A woman who had painful
leg problems began to jump up and down. You could see the joy
on her face. A man whose facial skin was pulled toward the left
and had numbness and paralysis was healed. A woman who
could not see well enough to read began to read from the Bible.
Tears of joy filled her eyes as she thanked the Lord.

Open Air, Reger Road (Saturday)

It was raining, but we decided to go anyway. Hundreds
showed up as I preached. They stood in the rain waiting and listening as I ministered. Many were saved, healed, and delivered.
People fell under the power of the Holy Spirit and some landed
in puddles. The people here are so hungry for the Gospel that
some waited two hours to be prayed for. This day there were
forty-four saved. Those with impaired vision saw clearly again.
One man riddled with painful arthritis was healed. Many other
healings took place as the people came with an expectant heart.

Open Air, Hime Street (Monday)

The people of this place requested that we come back again
to minister. Many turned out again and were filled with the Holy
Spirit. We went after those that didn't come. We became, not
only fishers of men, but also hunters of men, going out and bid-
ding them to come. Some were saved or healed as we prayed in
their homes, while others were saved behind buildings. Those
that had been previously saved and set free were now also doing
the work of the evangelist. So much happened, so many healings, so many salvations. God was in this place.

Return Visit to Hime Street (Tuesday)

It just keeps getting better. Hundreds of people listened as different ones gave testimony of the power of God in their lives. They came to receive Jesus as Savior, they came to be healed, and they came to be delivered from the oppression of the devil. One after another they kept coming. Some of the believers began to go after those who were standing around. There were those who came to receive Jesus and before anyone laid hands on them they would fall under the power. It is revival. The church here is stirred, excited, and full of expectation of what the Lord is doing and what He is going to do.

The Barracks (Thursday)

This is old military housing that has been converted into homes. Hundreds came out to hear and see the Gospel of Christ in signs and wonders. After a deaf mute heard and spoke and a deaf lady received her hearing, the people crowded around and came for their own miracle. Eighty-three people gave their hearts to the Lord, and many others were set free from addictions and sickness.

Open Air at the Flats (Saturday)

During another outreach at an apartment complex, I noticed that all the windows had bars on them. The pastor said that was because husbands and wives sometimes threw each other out the windows so the city put up bars. A small crowd heard the music and gathered to hear me preach. We started praying for the sick and many were healed.

About twenty gang members on the other side of the street saw people shaking and falling out under the power of God and began to mock us. I challenged them to come and be touched by God's power. I said, "If you believe that this isn't real then prove it by letting me pray for you. But I'm so confident that this is real that if I pray for you, you will shake and fall under the power like these other people. If it happens to you, then you need to give your life to Jesus. Are you up to the challenge?" We prayed for them, they all fell under God's power and got saved. Many young people and gangster youth were on the ground crying—immediately after their salvation, they called for their buddies to be saved. Over forty souls were birthed into God's Kingdom.

South Africa—In Summary

God poured out the power of Sozo (Salvation, healing and deliverance) in mighty measure while we were in South Africa. By the end of our visit, we were receiving invitations to return to this sunny country. We also learned that the King of the Zulu people wants us to come and minister to him and the Royal Family.

While on this trip, I didn't do anything special to get the John G. Lake anointing; I was just obedient. I went to South Africa and did what the Lord wanted me to do. On returning to North America, I also went to some places where John Lake ministered in the United States. After visiting the healing rooms in Spokane, I prayed at Lake's grave, asking God to give me what he had during his powerful healing ministry. "Release it again Lord, that whole cities will be healed."

HEALING WELLS OPEN IN ALBANY, OREGON
JULY 17-19, 2000

When I arrived home from South Africa, the signs and wonders in my ministry began to increase. We had a growing sense of greater things yet to come. Within six months, our first visit to the Vineyard Christian Fellowship in Albany, Oregon would turn into a revival of healing that would attract international attention. Here's the pastor's report (Pastor Denny Cline) of our first week of meetings there:

As senior pastor of the Vineyard Christian Fellowship in Albany, Oregon, from the church's founding days in 1994, I and my congregation have been contending for the release of the miracle healing anointing. I believed in my spirit that asking evangelist Todd Bentley to come for a series of meetings would result in a significant breakthrough. Through my years of ministry I have seen many healings and miracles, but only sporadically. However, this week was filled with continual waves of healings and miracles. As the testimonies continue to come in, we expect to find that about 200 people were healed.

For example, in the first five nights, ten deaf ears were opened and many back conditions were healed including curvature of the spine, herniated discs, and whiplash. Four people testified that they have canceled surgeries. After visiting her doctor, one lady testified to being healed of Hepatitis C. There have also been many testimonies of the healing of fibromyalgia and arthritis. Another lady, after a word of knowledge, was healed of a brain injury and memory loss.

A lady from Sweden, walking outside of the church with her husband, stopped out of curiosity. When someone told Todd she was deaf he went outside, laid hands on her and she was healed. Another remarkable story of a young lady's hips and shoulder healed, as well as a ganglia cyst on her wrist healed. She reported being pain free for the first time in months. A teenage girl with shifted hips from birth reported heat as her hips adjusted. She said that the constant head and neck pain were gone.

Another notable aspect of the meetings was the presence of God. The meetings started with a Toronto-like outpouring of joy and manifest glory of the Lord. About Wednesday the meetings seemed to amp up in the anointing even though many healings had already occurred the first two nights. As the week progressed, the presence of God has increased and many are now being healed in their seats or at the front. Before hands are even laid on them, many are falling under the power of the Holy Spirit. The meetings are lasting until 11:30 PM or 12:00 AM and often people stumble out of the meetings still affected by the Holy Spirit.

We are planning to continue to have regular healing and renewal meetings and return visits from evangelist Todd Bentley.

Denny invited me to return as soon as possible, so I returned in August. I felt something was stirring. God ripped open the heavens; more Hepatitis C, food allergies, mental illness, and vision problems were healed. There was also deep emotional healing as God bound up the brokenhearted—people suffering from long-standing trauma, nightmares, depression, torment, and mental anguish. Some people were healed as they left, others didn't realize they were healed until they got a blood test back from the doctor a month later.

ALBANY OREGON—AUGUST 22-25, 2000

Here's another report by Pastor Denny Cline:

A young man, after responding to another word of knowledge on anxiety and panic attacks, was healed of a severe back and muscle condition that caused pain. He testified to feeling his back straighten out. Another lady reported that a serious car accident left her with a severe back condition that required her to make frequent visits to the chiropractor. She was healed in her seat. There were many other healings including a Baptist girl who was healed of a knee injury standing at the altar watching the power of God.

Not everything was that dramatic. However, there was great enthusiasm and the zeal for what God was about to do. Then came Alenna's miracle.

In one minute Alenna's eyesight was completely healed! At first, 68-year-old Alenna Nelson could see only 10-15 feet in front of her before everything went completely blurry. The next minute, Alenna, for the first time in years, could now see details on the leaves, painted on the wall, 60-70 feet away, in the very front of the church. Besides healing her eyes, God did so much more.

Yesterday afternoon, Alenna just wanted to go home. She was tired. Two doctor visits completely drained her and she couldn't face going to a long church meeting, even if it was for healing. But her daughter, who was unable to be there herself, had appealed to her to, "Please go to that meeting."

That day Alenna had actually been so tired that she had just wanted to go home early. Her daughter persuaded her to stay for prayer. She responded to two altar calls—one for blindness, another for anxiety. Not only was she dramatically healed of near-blindness, she was set free from a long-standing bondage.

These are her words: "I've suffered from anxiety for 20 years. My muscles are so tight they don't even relax when I sleep. But when I got up off the floor I felt the anxiety just disappear. It was gone." I just said, 'I'm going to do it by faith.' I just had the desire and so I went forward by faith. Now there's no anxiety and I can see all this detail."

And who was the channel for these miracles? It was 24-year-old Todd Bentley. Only saved six years, Todd brought no college education or great charisma, no backing from a huge denomination, or a life-long call—just a recent call to go pray for the sick to be healed. As he puts it, "Preach the Gospel, pray for the sick, cast out demons, raise the dead. I just went and did it," Todd explains. "One minute I was an employee and the next, I'm doing nightly healing meetings all

JOURNEY INTO THE MIRACULOUS

over the U.S. and booked for a year solid." Todd, who is now preaching all over the world, says that, "Healing must always accompany the Gospel when it's preached because healing is part of the Gospel!"

I remember when God began to move in the Vineyard church in Albany, Oregon and I sensed for the first time we should do extended meetings. I prayed, "God, the Vineyard should be the last church where You would touch down like this for me."

My style is not low key as you might find at most Vineyard churches. Although I do love the Vineyard beliefs and worship, my style isn't an exact fit—it's more loud, fiery, and Pentecostal. So, at first, when I felt the Lord challenging me to stay for those extended meetings in January and February (and eventually trips back each month until May 2001), I said, "God, are you sure?" Pastor Denny had felt that each time God moved the previous three visits (in July, August, and November 2000) that we should stay. Little did I know it would be these meetings and the publicity almost daily through the Elijah List, which would thrust our ministry to a new level. I remember asking, "God, if this keeps going, should I stay for revival?" It was difficult to think of staying on, especially with my passion for ministry and crusades in developing nations and considering all the other meetings already on our schedule. I had to be willing to say "yes" and God rewarded us for it.

Since those extended meetings, the ministry has now tripled in size and the healing power has increased in our meetings in America. These new blessings on our ministry, I believe, were largely because we broke through in those early weeks of the revival of healing in Albany.

CHAPTER 14

BACK TO AFRICA

I took my second international trip to Ghana and Nigeria, Africa in October of 2000. My team consisted of Shanee Clark, my disciple, and my friend Greg Dennison.

God opened up radio and TV for the preaching of the Gospel as we entered this new country. We started the harvest right away. Three people in the studio were saved—the head of production, the studio manager, and the Muslim DJ who interviewed me.

The radio station aired three separate radio programs throughout the central region of Ghana and within one day, we ran into people in restaurants, marketplaces, and even several workers in our hotel who heard the radio. Four to five million people in this region alone had heard the Gospel message I preached. It is impossible to document the thousands who have made a commitment to Christ through these broadcasts.

There has been a great outpouring of God's presence and power. Over 250 souls have been saved in the open-air services alone. We visited the local leper colony and 23 received Jesus; the remaining seven were already saved. As I prayed for them all I laid my hands right on the areas affected by their leprosy to show that they are accepted and loved.

In one open-air crusade well over a thousand heard the Gospel. It seemed as if every person being prayed for was healed. People were set free from demons, addictions, deafness, and vision impairments. As hundreds pressed in on us, healings happened so rapidly that it was difficult to keep track of them all.

The last evening of the crusade in Cape Coast, Ghana, I preached a new message God gave me called, "When the Holy Spirit Comes." There was a great manifestation of God's power at one point and I collapsed onto the stage. Many were healed and delivered. Another 37 souls came to Jesus bringing the total up to 287. During a second altar call for the baptism of the Holy Spirit, the people received the Spirit and spoke in tongues so easily.

Following is a report from Greg:

EL NIMA, GHANA—OCTOBER 25 TO 27, 2000
Report by Greg Dennison

This morning was the last of our crusades in this region. It was held in the old fishing village of El Nima. The supervisor of this area estimated the crowds at 5 to 10 thousand people. As Todd preached, over 350 additional souls responded to the call of the Gospel, bringing the total up to 637. Next, Todd led them in a prayer for mass healing and miracles. Many hands went up to testify of being healed and the people wanted to come forward to give public testimony of the healing power of Jesus. Hundreds of people pressed in when the miracles began to happen and it was difficult to move. Some of the healings included vision impairments, deafness (including a boy who felt a deaf spirit come out of his ear), arthritis, and various long lasting pains (one lady with an illness testified that she was healed as she felt the fire of the Holy Ghost go through her body, healing a sickness she'd had for over 11 years). Another man came with an illness in his chest so severe it left him coughing blood and his body so weak he could barely walk to the crusade. He reported that as he came to the crusade the power of God fell on him and he was healed.

KUMASI REGIONAL CRUSADE
GHANA, AFRICA—OCTOBER 29-31, 2000

We continued on to the city of Kumasi. God opened opportunities for me to preach at three different radio stations, which broadcast to five regions and millions of people. One of these stations broadcast two nights of the crusade live—the preaching, salvation calls, mass miracle prayer, and testimonies of people who were healed.

Once again God confirmed the preaching of the Gospel with salvation, healing, and deliverance—a boy who had been deaf and mute for over seventeen years started to hear and speak. A new convert was instantly set free from a continual shaking that had plagued him for over six years. The parents of a demon-possessed boy heard the radio broadcast and came from over thirty miles away. On the platform, the boy shook violently and shrieked loudly as the afflicting spirits came out. He was also healed of a speech impediment.

The last evening of the crusade ten people were healed of vision impairments and blindness. One of them was a man who had not been able to read the Bible for 12 years. He joyfully read from the Bible while on the platform.

One last great testimony of the manifestation of God's power came from a man who left his restaurant unattended to come to the crusade. He was the first to come forward for salvation. He told us that God had shown all three of us to him in a dream the day before we arrived. He saw Shanee holding a bag scattering seed. I placed a cross on his forehead and Greg hugged him and said, "Happy birthday." When we showed up the next day, it was indeed his spiritual birthday.

There were 387 recorded commitments to Christ over the three evenings in Kumasi bringing the total to 1,024 souls in six nights.

ACCRA CRUSADE
GHANA, WEST AFRICA—NOVEMBER 2-4, 2000

This was our last three-day crusade in Ghana. The first morning I appeared on "The Breakfast Show," the equivalent to the *Regis & Kathi Lee* morning show; it's about all there is to watch in the mornings. This was followed by radio programming on the local stations. During our two-week stay in Ghana there were 23 TV commercials drawing people to the Accra crusades. These 90-second commercials showed me giving a vigorous call to come to the crusade while the location was flashed across the bottom of the screen. At the end of the commercials there was an explosion of the words, FIRE—FIRE—FIRE!

As we went about the city of Accra, people continually recognized me because of the TV and radio commercials, and I constantly invited people to come to the crusades. There were 200 souls saved in the first two nights in Accra. Some of the instant miracles for these nights included a man healed of a blind eye, a girl healed of double vision, a man healed from a spine deformed for ten years, a man ten years blind in one eye healed, and a man who had pain throughout his whole body was healed.

It was difficult to keep track of the healings because the people crowded around us, and it seemed that about 18 out of every 20 people here were healed by God as we prayed.

TO THE MARKET WE GO

The next day I told the pastor, "The power of God isn't just in the crusades. Take me to the biggest market. I want to go to where the people live and work."

"How about the fish market? It has 10,000 people."

"Great, bring the sound system."

This meeting was unadvertised and spontaneous. We set up right by the seashore. I started sharing my testimony. People all around me were busy fishing and selling fish. When I said I would pray for the sick, hundreds pressed in. I gave an altar call and over 300 were saved. Then the miracles started happening— the blind, the deaf, and the crippled. People pressed in by the thousands, and they had to sneak me into a cab and drive me out of there as people followed me down the street. All together over 637 people were saved. It was these meetings in Ghana that would birth in me the passion to do mass evangelism and reach nations through TV and radio broadcasts of the crusades.

The third night of the crusade was spectacular—God began to move even before I preached. Over 80 souls came to Jesus this night. I have lost count, but I believe this brings the total souls in Ghana to just over 1300. This is not even including those who received Jesus through the radio and TV programs.

The miracles were amazing to see: A deaf and dumb boy heard and spoke; a thirty-year hip problem was healed; a deaf man was healed when a spirit came out; a growth on a woman's abdomen disappeared (she actually felt it go); a man, who normally used two walkers, was healed (he vowed to give both the walkers to the hospital), and a boy who was deaf and mute heard for the first time.

As often happens, God saved the best wine for last—people on this last night were healed and slain in the Spirit in greater numbers than any of the previous nights. Shanee and I then went on to Lagos, Nigeria, our first visit to this congested city of more than ten million.

LAGOS, NIGERIA—NOVEMBER 5-12, 2000

We were invited to The Redeemed Pentecostal Mission in Nigeria, Africa for a Signs and Wonders Crusade. I remember this event vividly because I found out that, at the same time, in this city, Reinhardt Bonnke was hosting his historic Great Millennium Crusade. Over one million people attended each of his services and over a million got saved.

I remember during the day the pastor saying, "We have to leave early to get back to your crusade, because they are going to shut down all the highways, and most of the city buses are going to the other meeting." Here I am in the early days of my African ministry crying out to God: "Will I ever reach 50,000, let alone a million?" However, God came down with His power and numerous people received their salvation, breakthrough, healing, and deliverance. I was pleased to know that God was with me as well as with Reinhardt that night!

Here is a letter that I received from the pastor in Nigeria:

Dear Rev. Todd Bentley,

Glory be to God for the crusade. Testimonies are all over the city of Lagos, Nigeria about what God did through Fresh Fire Ministries. Attached is the list of some of the miracles recorded during the November Crusade in two locations. We are pleased to give you this report of what happened during the your visit, Rev.

Todd Bentley, to The Redeemed Pentecostal Mission Inc, Nigeria, Africa that presented the Signs and Wonders Crusade November 5th-12th, 2000. Some of those that received their miracles are as follows:

Two hundred and forty people received their salvation and another 140 came to the Lord in Itire, part of Lagos!! A three-year-old deaf boy, healed. A woman with paralyzed legs, healed and ten people that are deaf and dumb, healed. Many people with Cataracts in the eyes, healed. Someone with Poliomyelitis and crippled legs for eight years started walking. An epileptic, delivered and healed. Twenty-five people with body pains, healed. A drug-addicted boy, delivered. Someone was delivered of demons and his swollen leg with water plus bacteria was released. A woman suffering from breast cancer—growths gone. Forty people that had waist pain, healed. Seven people with typhoid fever, healed. Fourteen people with intestinal disease, healed. Eight people that had fibroid tumors saw them dissolve and ten people were healed of malaria fever. A big lump in the breast was dissolved and healed, and another crippled boy was healed. Two people with body growths—gone; and eight people with eye problems, healed. A three-year-old boy, dumb, was healed, and someone healed, from unconsciousness. A serious hand injury was healed and a female lawyer who was bleeding for fourteen days—after prayers with Rev. Todd Bentley—the bleeding stopped instantly.

In another part of Lagos called Itire where you ministered for three days, Rev. Todd, this healing data was recorded: Six people that were deaf and dumb, healed; one person crippled healed; five people that had cancer, healed; four people that had fibroid, healed; 40 people with stomach pains, healed; a lunatic person, healed and 160 more people received salvation. The latest information from the ITIRE CHURCH LAGOS is that supernatural revival has broken out in that church and the whole area. Once again, we are so excited as God used you mightily for this Miracle, Signs and Wonders crusade with our church in Nigeria. We are looking forward to another bigger crusade which will be coming up March 2001 where you will draw a large crowd of 30,000- 40,000 with the power of the Holy Spirit.

Bishop John E. Amadi

UNBELIEF

I've got to admit that during those first few early African crusades I'd struggle with unbelief. I'd pray for someone and they would say they were healed and I wouldn't believe it. Often they wouldn't display huge emotion or shaking. Even though the miracles were before me I'd think, *It can't be that easy.* When they told me, "I used to be paralyzed," I really wondered if they were. I had to wrestle through this. I finally asked myself, *Why would they lie to me?* If they lie it's between them and God. My job is just to pray for the sick and God's job is to do the rest.

BACK TO ALBANY

Every time I returned from Africa our miracles seemed to increase, so I was excited to return to Albany for my third visit in November 2000. God did it again. One of the first healings in these meetings came by a word of knowledge. A woman who had no eardrum, who had been deaf in one ear for 50 years, was healed. Then a woman who had been deaf in one ear for 41 years, also with no eardrum, came forward—two creative miracles back-to-back. By the end of the November meetings, there were hundreds of healings again in Albany.

Here's an edited version of the healing report from Steve Shultz of the Elijah List:

NO EARDRUMS?

"What is it about older people that are getting God's *Healing* attention? I watched it again tonight. Oh, and teenagers too! It's as if God is making a point...as if He's saying, "I'm not done with the older generation—*Not even close*. At the same time, I'm just getting started with teens.

No ear drums and yet tonight, these ladies can hear! This is miraculous! I've never seen anything like it—at least not for a few months: Viola is 86 years old and she hasn't heard out of one ear for 50 years! The doctors, because of a problem, removed Viola's eardrum in 1950! That's it. No hearing ever since—until a few hours ago. I was there. I saw it with my own eyes! Todd Bentley prayed a few simple prayers, and yelled Jesus' name into Viola's ears. "Jesus!" Todd yelled. After a few attempts, suddenly Viola is hearing sounds. Pretty soon, completely covering her one ear, she is able to repeat the new sounds she is hearing in her "dead" ear. Sounds that Todd is now whispering, "Father," "Father," Viola repeats. "Holy Spirit," Todd whispers. "Holy Spirit," Viola repeats. The congregation is getting loud and excited. "Jesus," Todd whispers again. "Jesus," Viola says back. Now the Albany congregation has gone wild!

VERIFYING THE MIRACLE!

I go to Viola to talk to her because, if I'm going to write this to The Elijah List, I'd better verify it. That's when I learn about 1950, the "mastoid" something and the surgery. Her friends who brought her are beaming. She can hear out of her "dead" ear—which is no longer dead!

CHAPTER 15

Chapter 15

TOUCHED BY AN ANGEL

Years ago, Paul Cain and William Branham held powerful healing meetings in Grant's Pass, Oregon. A local businessman caught the healing vision and built a large, barn-like facility for these meetings. On December 5, 1950, William Branham dedicated this "tabernacle" to the Lord. At this time, (what is often referred to as The Voice of Healing Revival,) Grant's Pass was one of many places that held healing meetings however, they were held here quite frequently given the size of the location and the ability to host the great healing evangelists of the time. Thus, the Lord deposited a great well of healing there.

December 5, 2000 was the 50-year anniversary of this dedication, and several prophecies were given telling that it was time to re-open the ancient healing wells of those times. I recall so clearly ministering with Bob Jones, Paul Keith Davis, John Paul Jackson, and Bobby Connor at the Eye of the Eagle Prophetic

Conference there. We spiritually re-dug and tapped into those ancient wells of the 1950s.

A PROPHETIC SIGN

The pastor of the church in Grant's Pass, Oregon, Dale Howell, and a mutual friend, John Macgirvin, hiked two hours into the forest to fish in the Rogue River. John sat on a huge granite rock 15 feet above the river.

The Lord said, "Reach into the crack in the rock." John dug in the sand and pulled out a silver Roosevelt dime. He held it up for Dale to see. "The Lord just told me to reach in the crack of the rock. Silver represents jubilee, 50 years!"

Dale exclaimed, "I can tell you what the year is on that dime." He was correct—1950. That dime was minted the year God sent healing to the Northwest—half a century previously. The Lord told John that the dime was a sign that the healing revival was going to happen again and that the past revival was a tithe—a tenth of the healing power that He was going to pour out! The coin symbolized the Voice of Healing Revival, the first fruits of the coming healing revival. This sign confirmed the mandate of the conference and encouraged us to contend to open up the healing well.

BRINGING THE ANGEL

One day, a man who was a part of the Healing Rooms ministries in Portland attended the conference. Right in the middle of the service, he crouched alongside my chair and whispered, "I brought the healing angel from Portland—from John Lake's healing rooms. He's standing at the back of the tent."

To be honest, I thought the guy was nuts. But, I turned around and there was the angel. I ran to the back of the tent and fell out under the power. John Paul Jackson laid hands on me and then I had an encounter with the angel. The presence of the angel knocked me out of my body. Then it was as if my spirit left my body and I was watching my body on the floor.

I walked around the tent in the spirit, knowing what infirmities people had. Then I began to wonder, "How am I going to get back in my body?" Eventually, I decided I would just go and lay on myself. Prophetic experiences involve choices in the mind, so I had to purpose to enter in. I didn't know how to tell people what had happened—I thought they'd think I was nuts.

When I arose from the floor, I didn't realize that I was being taken up a notch in the spirit. I just thought, *Wow, what a great service tonight. I had an encounter with an angel!* I then received more accurate words of knowledge and discovered that I had received a gift of healing and of discernment. Today, there are times when I feel the angel's presence on my left side. When I touch someone with my left hand, I've been able to discern whether his or her sickness was a demon, disease, or a natural infirmity and what part of the body the sickness affected.

BOY COMES OUT OF A COMA

Right after that angelic visitation, I had an extraordinary experience that led to a powerful healing. The next night, while praying, I went into a trance and a woman visited me. She shook me violently and said three times, "The headlines report, 'BOY COMES OUT OF COMA.'" Then she ran from the room.

I asked the Lord, "What do you want me to do with this?" The Lord said, "There will be a man instructed to come tonight to take an anointing back to a boy who is in a coma in another city."

When I gave the word of knowledge I said, "There is a man here who was instructed to come tonight to take an anointing back to a boy who is in a coma?" Sure enough, a man ran down the aisle exclaiming, "You're not going to believe this, but I was just at the hospital with a woman whose son was in a coma, and she asked me to come tonight to stand in the gap—to receive an anointing for that boy's healing!'"

Later I heard the report that the boy was healed and rose from his hospital bed! The local newspaper even ran a headline, the same one I saw in my vision.

ALBANY, OREGON—JANUARY 2001

Three weeks after the Grant's Pass angelic visitation, I returned to the Vineyard Church in Albany, Oregon for the fourth time. This would be the beginning of an extended revival of healing there. For months, the church had been preparing for an open heaven through servant evangelism: giving out free gas vouchers and Colas, handing hot dogs to the skateboarders, and washing cars in the community. They did all of these things just to show the love of God to their community. I believe those acts really opened up the heavens because faith releases wonders and manifestations of God's power. Scripture tells us that faith works through love (Gal. 5:6). Blessing the city with loving acts, I believe, opened the heavens and invited God to give us an unprecedented miracle outpouring.

There was such a level of anointing for healing that we extended the meetings for weeks. People attended from Canada, Europe, Asia, and other countries, and representation from at least 25 states. Hundreds of pastors arrived, and night after night we packed out the church. In fact, some people lined up for hours before a meeting just to gain access to the sanctuary. A few people were healed in the parking lot!

There were profound demonstrations of miracles and healings each night—cancers, deafness, polio, various pains, and emotional maladies were healed. There were over 250 salvations, many rededications, and water baptisms. Here are some reports:

Report by Steve Shultz, Publisher, The Elijah List

Todd's back in Albany, Oregon and as usual you never quite know what will happen. The first of the series of 17 nightly meetings began at the Albany Vineyard, Wednesday 1st-3rd. As Todd began to preach he was so overcome by the Spirit he was unable to speak. The presence of the Lord came into the room powerfully; some began to laugh, while others reported, "I've never felt such a presence of the fear of God. I wanted to dive under my chair."

After about 15 minutes of trying to get it together enough to preach, Todd and the podium went to the floor together. While he lay there, an angel of the Lord appeared to him with a large bucket of oil and told him to lay hands on anyone who wanted it. Still unable to speak, Todd wrote Pastor Denny a message relaying what he'd seen. He wrote later, the muteness was a prophetic sign, like Zechariah who was unable to speak before the birth of John the Baptist. But the birthing at this time is a new level of the supernatural.

The level of hunger at these meetings is wonderful, and nearly all went forward that night to receive from the Lord. Here are a few highlights of the meetings to give you an idea of what God is up to.

Prayer Cloths, Miracles, and Other Testimonies...

Last August Todd anointed and prayed over prayer cloths for healing, and people sent them out all over the country.

Debbie sent one to her step-dad in California who had colon cancer. This week she received word there is no trace of cancer in his body. Her brother, who had cancer in his prostate and urinary tract as well as in his bones, also received a prayer cloth. He has been given a report from his doctor this week that he, too, is cancer-free.

Twenty-five-year-old Adrianne had been an addict for ten years. She testified Friday night: "There hasn't been a day where I haven't craved drugs. I've been in and out of jail and prison for seven years. Pastor Denny prayed for me on Wednesday night; I haven't had any craving since. I have been clean and with the Lord for 104 days, but I still had cravings everyday until this past Wednesday. Thank you Jesus!

Phil, a young man with an incurable condition (and an unpronounceable name), came for prayer. There was chronic pain in his knees for three years due to the disease. Todd laid hands on him and immediately the pain left, mobility returned, and he was able to run for the first time in two years.

Mary hit her nose in August resulting in continual headaches, and impaired sense of smell. Her neck, back, and shoulders hurt all of the time. When she received prayer, she felt her nose reposition, her sinuses drain, and her sense of smell return. Also, she felt her back and hips reposition and the headache leave.

Stephanie responded to an altar call for lung conditions. As Todd laid hands on her, God showed him she had asthma and a lung infection, confirming her doctor's diagnoses made just that morning. After prayer, her breathing was totally free. She also was suffering with chronic back pain from three previous surgeries. The Lord removed the pain. She is now able to touch her toes and bend from side to side.

Spontaneous Healings Occur Throughout the Congregation

Todd had a word of knowledge about stomach problems. Delores, had stomach problems, felt "activity" in her stomach and then the pain left. Two weeks earlier she had injured herself falling on a cement floor and had been using a walker. The Lord touched that too, and she now walks without assistance.

As the Lord has declared His intention to increase the level of the supernatural we look forward, with great eagerness, for what's to come over these next 14 nights. *WARNING! IF YOU SIMPLY WANT TO STAY SAFE AND COMFORTABLE KEEP AWAY FROM THESE MEETINGS!*

Todd has been sent here to stir up the church to do the work of the ministry. These meetings are not just for watching—they are for equipping and activating, as well as healing and restoring. With the release of the new level of the supernatural, great blessing is coming to the church. But God is also bringing a release to *go out*. Psalm 110:3 declares: "Your people shall be volunteers in the day of Your power."

Oregon Healing Meetings Become Healing Revival — Horse-Feeding Trough Turned Into a Baptismal

This Thursday thru Saturday, Jan. 25th-27th, 2001, healing meetings continue, led by the healing ministry of Bob Brasset from Victoria, B.C. Todd Bentley returns February 1 for more healing, signs, and wonders meetings.

How fitting that—just as the Savior of the world was laid at His birth in a cattle's feeding trough, a manger—the newest births into the Kingdom of God in Albany, Oregon are being laid in a horse feeding trough, dipped beneath the water in baptism and then raised to walk into their new *life*.

So many baptisms have begun happening at the Albany Healing Revival, *on the spur of the moment,* that a large horse watering trough has now been set up and remains in place, at the ready—as many are being healed, saved, and baptized—all in one night.

Is it a Salvation Revival—or is it a Healing Revival?

That answer to that question seems to be, "Yes, it is!" On Friday evening, a call was made for anyone who came prepared to be baptized. Only one came forward, but before he was baptized, more came forward and soon there were approximately 15 who came to be baptized, wearing only what they had on.

Later, while a group of teens (and there has been an amazing salvation move among the teens) was praying for a man in a wheelchair to be healed, suddenly a "SHRIEK!" came from the opposite side of the room. A young man had just gotten saved and the "crowd" attending to him shouted with delight as he was *immediately baptized in the trough*—still wearing his previously-dry set of clothes—as the work of salvation in his life was made public!

Transferable Anointing—of Both Healing and Salvations

Already, at least three or four groups are reporting revival and healing outbreaks in their own spheres immediately upon returning home from Albany. In the last 17 weeks, some 25 states have been represented, as those eager to receive a healing touch have traveled to this small, previously "unknown" town of Albany. Just as was hoped by those who prayed this anointing in, the anointing is transferable to other homes, churches, and home groups. One young man has taken to the streets and is seeing dramatic healing results in Gresham, Oregon.

Another group of teens have taken the anointing to their on-the-street ministry. But it's not just teens. One pastor is suddenly seeing revival break out in his church. He came for healing. He is now getting revival in his church.

The Origins of the Healing Revival

This healing movement—apparently launched when 25-year-old Todd Bentley came to Albany, Oregon from Canada (at the invitation of Pastor Denny Cline who was introduced to Todd by Patricia King, also from Canada)—now continues even when Todd is not present. There is what is being called a "corporate anointing," according to Pastor Denny Cline. The anointing remains and other healing ministries are preparing to come and impart even more healing. Randy Clark is slated to come in May and other ministries are being scheduled.

Prophecy by Bobby Conner

The attention now being given to Albany—was first prophesied when Bobby Conner visited Vineyard Christian Fellowship of Albany, Oregon back in late 2000. Bobby prophesied that the Lord was going to put Albany on the "M-A-P," Which Bobby said stood for, "The Master's Awesome Power."[1]

So many healings were breaking out that, at the end of December, Todd Bentley decided to clear his schedule in January and hold healing meetings for 17 days straight. As each night progressed, the anointing seemed to build on the nights before.

THE ALBANY HEALING REVIVAL CONTINUES
Report by Pastor Denny Cline

There have now been 91 first-time decisions to receive Christ as Lord and Savior, 50 recommitments with approximately 60 baptisms over the 18 nights including the last night after Todd left. We have already had people visit from over 25 states and six countries. Nearly a hundred pastors visited from all over the Northwest and around North America.

Every time we meet in consecutive meetings the power seems to increase as do the healings and miracles. These meetings are different than other renewal meetings. There is something fresh being imparted in healing, signs, and wonders—as well as a tremendous deposit of fresh revelation that is coming from Todd Bentley's ministry.

We have contended as a congregation for the ministry of Jesus for five and one-half years and have been on the brink of a revival-type outpouring at least four other times since our beginnings. But this is unique in the hunger that is being created in people as well as the fruit that is being produced. Not everyone is healed and not everyone is attracted to this type of atmosphere. There is a blend of the "fear of the Lord" mixed with the joy of the Lord and the meetings go very long, sometimes for five hours. But our fellowship is committed to loving and caring for all who come, as best we can, with our present facility and core group's involvement.

The worship leader brought different worship groups from around the city to make it a corporate thing. They enlisted intercessors from all over so it would be a Body of Christ move, not just a Vineyard move. We invited in other healing ministries so it was not a one-man show. It's more than a man having a gift. It's because of Jesus.

Let's believe that it can be transferable to a pastor or a prayer cloth. Pastors have hands laid on them and miracles break out when they go home. We mailed out over a thousand prayer cloths and three cases of terminal cancer were healed. The anointing is tangible and transferable. We want to see the demonstration of the Spirit of God in power.

Every night people bring the lost and some get saved. People were getting saved and then getting baptized immediately in their street clothes. We hit the street with prophetic evangelism and won backsliders to Christ. A 15-year-old prayed for someone whose back got healed. The Body of Christ got excited. Once you taste this you need more. The presence of God was thick throughout the whole building.

Salvation and repentance, renewal, signs and wonders, they're all an expression of God's "dunamis" power. The church will be at least what we saw in the book of Acts and even more. The glory of the latter house will be greater than the glory of the former house. (See Haggai 2:9).

This move is very much about teams, not superstars. It's about being in the presence of God, holiness, consecration, and then releasing it to the people. I call it a God-consciousness. We need the Gospel again with signs and wonders.

THE ANGEL IN ALBANY

In February, I saw an angel twenty feet tall. The angel stretched as high as the ceiling of the Albany auditorium. At the time, I didn't realize that the angel was the same one I'd seen in Grant's Pass. The Spirit gave me a sign that this angelic visitation was real. A woman in the audience, Muffy Jo Howell, (the daughter of Dale Howell, the pastor from Grant's Pass) also saw the angel. "Todd," she whispered, "There's a huge angel in the pulpit."

Muffy had been crippled with an infirmity in her hips from birth. However, suddenly she screamed out, "The angel just touched me," and she was healed. I really knew God was up to something.

The audible voice of the Holy Spirit, which accompanied the angelic encounter, instructed me not to speak to the angel. (In subsequent encounters, I also heard the audible inner voice of the Holy Spirit.) The angel had a key, just as a mayor holds the key to a city. The angel's commission was to turn this key over to pastors by imparting wisdom, authority, revelation, and anointing so that they could take healing back to their churches. The angel stayed in the pulpit and released a healing anointing while I prayed for thirty pastors that night.

HEALING REVIVAL

I knew by the Spirit that the angel's name was Healing Revival. He was like the angel in John 5 that stirred the pool of Bethesda. "For an angel went down at a certain time into the pool and stirred up the water; then whoever stepped in first, after the stirring of the water, was made well of whatever disease he had" (John 5:4).

This angel was a prophetic sign that God was going to fulfill the vision that I'd had the year before about the coming healing revival. I believe God sent the angel to Albany to establish healing revival and regional breakthrough. This angel is one of the many that I saw in the earlier vision of a stadium in heaven waiting to be released to fulfill end-time purposes. Albany is just one of many cities, and churches that will experience a great healing outpouring.

It was revealed to me that this angel is not an archangel, but ranks under them. He has authority to deal with powers but not principalities in the demonic realms. A power is a territorial spirit and it sets itself up over a city or region: "For we do not wrestle against flesh and blood, but against principalities, against powers" (Eph 6:12). A principality has a mandate over nations, just as the Prince of Persia written about in Daniel 10:13.

In Albany, I saw the angel open up a pool on the floor about 30 feet by 30 feet. A portal opened in the heavens and a shaft of light descended. I was under the power of the Spirit and too "inebriated" to minister, so I called Denny to take over. He gave an invitation for the sick to come. The Lord told me to call the people up to be healed because the heavens were open. So many people went forward to get in the pool and to get ministry, that the meeting went on for a few more hours as joy was poured out and people lay scattered under the power, all over the floor. As people drew near the pool, they fell down like dominoes—without a touch from a single soul!

One woman was healed from various injuries, including a fractured neck that caused other problems in her body. Another person reported that over twenty years of pain was healed, while a woman, whose breast cancer had spread to her ribs (it was so sensitive no one could touch her) was also healed. This was one of the most unusual and spiritually intense atmospheres that I'd ever seen! Here's more of Pastor Denny Cline's report about the meetings:

CONTINUATION OF ALBANY REPORT
by Pastor Denny Cline

I would not usually include a Sunday morning service in a report, but there was such a carry over from the night before that this day is noteworthy. At times, over the last few weeks the spiritual battle for carrying on these meetings has been intense. Many have been hit with minor sicknesses, even Todd's children and wife, and some who have been battling serious illness for years took a turn for the worse. But in the midst of it all, God seems to be increasing the intensity of His presence and routing out the enemy. This morning the worship leader called up the sick to receive healing during the worship time. I sensed that some were still in their seats and were feeling symptoms like nausea and breathing difficulty. This was, to me, an indication that the enemy was on the run and people were about to get delivered. That is exactly what happened. Over the next half hour, many were set free in their emotions and their physical bodies as they received prayer from the ministry team.

MY MOTHER PASSES AWAY

In the midst of this dramatic move of God's presence and healing, my mom contracted pneumonia and died in February 2001. This was the last night of the Albany healing revival, which had lasted almost two months.

This was a real test for me. Each day people were being healed of stroke. Why not her? She had experienced a massive stroke in November 1999. I prayed for her and within two months she was walking and talking again. But she lived in an apartment by herself, and she was depressed. She had a second stroke and came out of the coma to tell Shonnah that she didn't have the will to live. She was paralyzed on one side and had deteriorated to a place of complete incapacity. I had to decide whether to give in to confusion, discouragement, and anger. Her death challenged what I preached but finally I decided I was going to push through. At my next meeting I announced, "I'm going to go after this a whole lot more," and then I made a decision to press in and keep praying.

My mother's struggle with deafness was also like a signpost for me to diligently ask God for healing for the deaf. Consequently, one of the greatest anointings on our ministry today is for deaf ears. I've ministered in services where every deaf person begins to hear. In one crusade in India, we actually witnessed 139 deaf mutes receive their hearing during the six nights of meetings.

ENDNOTE

1. See http://www.elijahlist.com/words/display_word.html?
ID=55—released Sept 24, 2000.

CHAPTER 16

SCOTLAND HERE I COME

While I was still out on the floor in Albany, the Lord said, (as a confirmation to me that this was an angel of healing revival,) that He was going to give me the name of three revivals and the three revivalists that this angel had worked with. This word from the Lord would be a sign to ensure I would never doubt that He again is commissioning healing angels to stir up pools of healing revival in churches, cities, and regions.

The first revivalist that the angel worked with was John Knox in Scotland. I said, "I've never heard of John Knox. Was there even a guy named John Knox? Who is he?" I discovered that he was considered the "Martin Luther" of Scotland— a great Scottish Reformer and the founder of Presbyterianism there. He overcame the religious spirit in the 1500s and birthed protestant Christianity out of the Catholic Church.

The second revivalist the angel visited was William Branham. The angel, who helped release healing revival through Branham, visited him in 1946. Revival history records that Branham's international miracle ministry, and the great American Healing Revival of 1947–1955, began with an angelic visitation.

The angel told Branham: "If you will be sincere, and can get the people to believe you, nothing shall stand before your prayer, not even cancer." The angel also told Branham, an unknown preacher, that he would soon minister healing before crowded arenas of thousands. Branham received discernment of people's illnesses, thoughts, deeds, and specific sins requiring repentance.[1] Gordon Lindsay wrote in his 1952 biography of Rev. Branham's early life and ministry: "The story of the life of William Branham is so out of this world and beyond the ordinary that were there not available a host of infallible proofs which document and attest its authenticity, one might well be excused for considering it far-fetched and incredible."

The third person the angel worked with was John G. Lake who ministered in the Pacific Northwest of the United States. He started the healing rooms, which became wells of revival in Spokane and other parts of the northwest region of America.

VISION OF JOHN KNOX'S GRAVE

Although I'd been to the places where John Lake and William Branham's healing ministries in the U.S. started; before this word from the Lord, I had never heard of John Knox, had never been to Scotland, and had never particularly wanted to go. However, seven days later while in a church in Portland, Oregon and, during worship, I was taken into a prophetic vision to Edinburgh, Scotland. I saw a castle and a moat. The Lord met me and we walked two-hundred yards from the castle to the grave of John Knox. On the left hand side were three rocky outcroppings and beautiful rolling hills. I saw three specific sites: his grave and memorial, the castle, and the rolling hills of Edinburgh.

Two days later I received an email from a prophetess, Catherine Brown, who lived in Scotland. "Hey Todd," it said, "Are you coming to Scotland?"

I thought, *I guess I am now!* I replied, "How about April?"

Then the Lord said, "This is a sign to you that I am fulfilling the vision of the coming healing revival—about the 100 healing pools of Bethesda." He told me that the anointing would be transferable and tangible. "I want you to take it all over the world...every place you go, I'm going to open up and increase in miracles, signs, and wonders! It's not going to be just about what I do with you, it will be about transferring and releasing people into the ministry of healing."

That night in Albany, the Lord asked me where I'd seen the angel before. I replied, "God I've never seen him before."

"No, Todd, think about it."

"I don't remember the angel."

"In your apartment three-and-a-half years ago—remember that angelic visitation just a few weeks before I called you into the ministry? It was the same angel that you saw in Grant's Pass and Albany. That day in your apartment was when I commissioned you to take healing revival to the world. That's why I've done with you what I have so quickly; it's because of the angel that goes before you. This is your angel, the angel from John 5 (at the pool of Bethesda). Everywhere you go the angel goes. I want you to be a part of taking healing revival to the nations. I don't want you to have just a gift of healing. I want you to be a part of what has been prophesied, in breaking through and seeing the fulfillment of healing revival. I'm going to have over 100 healing centers. Albany is one of those pools. As a confirmation,

I took you to Scotland in a trance. Now I want you to get on an airplane and go find the grave of John Knox. Go to the sites that I showed you."

I toured five cities in Scotland and ended in Edinburgh the last night of my ministry trip. I told the pastor that I wanted to go to John Knox's grave and then recounted the story about the angel, describing the castle, moat, crag, the hills and the grave. When we arrived at the castle, it was exactly as portrayed in my vision! We walked into St. Giles church and I even led the pastor right to the location of the plaque and the memorial, without ever having been there in the natural before. Immediately, I had a strong visitation of the Lord and fell under the power of God for four hours. On a subsequent trip to Scotland, I saw a huge increase in signs and wonders!

CONFIRMING ANGEL SIGHTINGS

Ever since my angelic experience in Albany, people I don't know, including children, and even warlocks, approach me in different services and describe the angel. Countless times people tell me, "Todd there's an angel that follows you, and I believe it is the mantle and anointing that was with William Branham."

Sometimes the angel visits in strength and authority, pushing back the demonic realm. When his presence is manifest in meetings (it has manifested at least 25 times over two years), there's a definite increase in accuracy of the word of knowledge.

Before you get into unbelief about my angel and say, "There's too much emphasis on this angel stuff," you need to understand that the angels are the ones who do the work of the ministry. I want to emphasize that our meetings are all about Jesus and His ministry and love for people. However, angels are real and they are sent on behalf of the saints to minister to people.

For example, angels ministered to Jesus when He emerged from the wilderness, "Then the devil left Him, and behold, angels came and ministered to Him" (Matthew 4:11). And all believers, including you, have an angel. "For He shall give His angels charge over you, to keep you in all your ways. In their hands they shall bear you up, lest you dash your foot against a stone" (Psalm 91:11). In addition, Scripture tells us that the "angel of the Lord encamps all around those who fear Him..." (Psalm 34:7).

I believe in angelic ministry and angels who have different purposes and tasks. Angels are involved with so much of what goes on in the heavenly realm. I want to make it clear though, that Jesus is the one who does the healings, not the angel. The angels simply open up heaven and push back the warfare. They bind the devils of infirmity, they are aids of salvation, and messengers, but the source of the healing is the Lord.

THE RESURRECTION ANGELS

Some time after the Scotland trip, in January 2002, I was in Kelowna, British Columbia, at a conference. Bob Jones called me up to the platform. "Son, I have a word for you. In 1975 I had a life and death experience. I haemorrhaged and died and was taken to heaven but couldn't enter. The Lord said He was sending me back to prepare the church for a harvest of a billion souls. When I returned to my body there were two angels speaking to each other. These were the resurrection angels speaking about the harvest and about me. Ever since that time these two angels have accompanied me and I have been used to raise the (spiritually) dead. The Lord has commissioned me to release these angels to you."

When Bob took my hands I trembled, shook, and fell to the floor. I became light and weightless. The two angels lifted me toward heaven. I was not permitted to go in but suddenly, in this revelatory experience, I was on a brown horse in a harvest field of grain that went on farther than my eyes could see. Then I appeared before the stone that had been rolled away. I saw two angels sitting on the rock and they said to Mary, "The one you are seeking is not here." I felt the presence of Jesus who had risen from the dead. Then I knew I had received a true impartation of the Spirit that brings life from the dead, and these two angels were part of it. I also knew that God would release power to me to raise the dead, those dead in spirit, and even those dead in body. Bob said, "From this day forward, these angels will be a part of your ministry."

ENDNOTE

1. G. Lindsay, 'William Branham—A man sent from God', pg. 9

CHAPTER 17

HEALING REVIVAL IN THE NATIONS

As of 2003, I'd already traveled to 30 countries throughout the world, in Asia, Europe, Africa, North and South America. We've seen over 100,000 people saved over a span of five crusades. It's not unusual to preach to over 70,000 people in a single service in some countries, and as I've shared, even be favored with crusades that a radio broadcast.

The Lord has graciously brought me so far from those early days ministering to the youth in a church basement, or preaching to 50 or a hundred people. And I never did make it to that Bible school that my church had generously offered to send me to (ha-ha).

Our international headquarters are in Canada, and we have offices in the United States and Africa. God has continued to give us tremendous favor over the years. I've preached the Gospel with signs and wonders. The blind see, the deaf hear and the lame walk. Now our ministry emphasis has expanded to include humanitarian aid for the poor, mass feedings, building orphanages, and sending containers of food into war-torn areas.

We've journeyed into the miraculous globally and have seen the amazing faithfulness, power, and love of an awesome, supernatural God! As you read the following chapters, open your heart to the Holy Spirit and allow Him to impart to you faith and the tangible, transferable healing anointing!

MASAKA, UGANDA—APRIL 2001

Upon arrival in Entebbe, Uganda, we could feel the presence of the Lord. From the moment we touched down God poured out His anointing upon us. We were met on the tarmac by the pastors and then ushered into the VIP room where we cleared customs. Only the President and his cabinet members had ever used this room. The pastors had asked the government for special permission and received it. They had also asked for electricity at the crusade site for a good price and they were told we could have it for free. God is good!

Once we cleared customs we were taken into the restaurant where they had set up for a press conference. Various newspaper reporters and photographers waited for an interview. The pastors, 100 of them working in unity, had done the groundwork, placing thousands of posters throughout the city. I saw one large banner across the street, and I am sure there were more. Thousands of leaflets were passed out, and many press releases sent to newspapers and radio stations. They rented buses to bring in a thousand delegates from other cities, and also arranged meals and organized a Jesus march through the city of Masaka to announce the crusade. The crusade was to be held on the grounds of a golf course about seventy miles from Kampala. The pastors set up a large tent for leadership meetings during the day; and to house the extremely sick (and even the dead) in the evenings.

Shortly after our arrival, we noticed a newspaper headline that revealed the spiritual powers at work in the region. "LOCAL WITCHDOCTOR STONED TO DEATH," the headline announced. Apparently, the witchdoctor had run out of body parts for his traditional spells and had summoned the powers of darkness, placed a curse, and commanded a great accident on the highway. Fourteen people were killed when their van turned over, and then the witchdoctor gathered up the bodies. People were so enraged, that they stoned him to death, right on the street.

We realized that the enemy was at work but that the Lord was too. We were about to see great destruction to the works of the enemy in Uganda—Jesus style—through miracles, healings, and salvations!

First Evening Service

We had an initial crowd of 2,500, but it grew to almost 4,000. After I shared my testimony, we had an altar call and the hands shot up into the air. About 60 people gave their hearts to the Lord. Next, I loosed the anointing for corporate healing upon the crowd. The power of God fell and many were touched by the Holy Spirit. The miracles began. We do not have a total count on all who were healed but there were many.

People who were completely blind had their sight restored and many deaf began to hear. A woman who had broken legs was healed, and another woman's uterus was put back into place. One woman who had been in an accident suddenly could lift her arm, and another person's knee was restored! Many who had tumors watched them disappear, and cripples walked without the use of canes.

Many who were oppressed by the devil were also set free—those tormented in their minds, demoniacs, and others who thrashed wildly on the ground. One person was carried to the platform; her demons were speaking, threatening to kill her.

When she received prayer they screamed, *"We're leaving! We're leaving!"*

This was the first time that a crusade had ever been held in Masaka, and the first time for many of the pastors to witness the power and demonstration of the Spirit. So many healings and so many miracles! Afterward we stopped in at a local radio station and were interviewed in a live broadcast about the crusade and the wonderful works of God. This was only our first night, and we knew that greater things were ahead in the next few days.

The Following Morning

When we arrived at the crusade grounds on Thursday morning, April 5, a huge crowd of about a thousand people had already assembled and waited in the tent. Anticipation and excitement was high, as people arrived expecting to receive! The crowd called upon the Lord, their voices intense. They'd already been there for two hours, and the two national television stations were also present, waiting to report on the outcome.

Just before I rose to address the crowd, a man came forward, and it was obvious he was under some kind of demonic trance. Before he could do anything, the power of the Holy Spirit seized him, and his body went stiff and he fell to the ground. The enemy definitely was not happy or impressed by our meetings!

After praying for the worship team, I prayed for the crowd and to release miracles, rebuking spirits of pain, sickness, and disease. A man with a paralyzed arm was healed, another who a few moments previously could not bend his leg jumped up and down, and even did squats! A woman's vision was restored, and asthma and paralysis were healed along with many other diseases. Many people who manifested demons were delivered.

Nine people gave their hearts to the Lord and then I shared on the power of the Holy Spirit. I ended my message with a call for those who wanted to know Him more. Hands went up all over the tent. Everyone stood to their feet as I prayed for the crowd and called upon the Holy Spirit. Approximately 200 came forward and as they received prayer, they fell down under the anointing.

Thursday Evening—Outdoor Crusade

The crowd was larger with an estimated attendance of 5,000. After sharing my message, I gave an altar call for salvation. Many hands went up all over the crowd but only 45 came forward. The pastor later explained that the reason why many don't come forward and why the crowd continues to grow after it gets dark is because many are either Muslim or Catholic. They do not want to be seen by anyone.

There were many testimonies of healing that evening. We witnessed many cases of tumors disappearing, demonized people being set free, and the healing of blindness, deafness, as well as back, knee, arm, and leg conditions.

A man who received Jesus as his Savior and had been deaf for six months could hear. A little girl who was partially paralyzed walked. When a woman was hit with the power of God she vomited and was healed of a tumor that she had for over 15 years. A bedridden girl who had been brought from the hospital and carried to the crusade, who previously couldn't even stand, suddenly stood and walked off of the platform!

No wonder the Bible simply says, "He healed them all." Multitudes were healed at this crusade. We ministered to too many to keep count. Finally, we prayed for more sick, and another 13 people came forward and received Jesus as their Savior.

Ministry to Children

We had the opportunity to minister to about 600 children at Hope Nursery and Primary School the next morning, Friday. I shared what the Lord had shown me while in Moravian Falls

concerning children, and how HE was going to use them powerfully in revival and healing. A hundred and ten children received
the Lord that morning. I didn't want them to miss our crusades,
either, and rented buses to bring them in.

Later, we ministered at a secular secondary school for children ages eight to twenty. Over 800 students attended Stella
Marts School, and on the day we ministered hundreds more assembled outside the building. After I shared my testimony, 150
young people received Jesus.

Tent Meeting 11:30 A.M.

At 11:30 that morning, we headed back to the crusade grounds,
and the tent was already packed, the atmosphere electrified. At
least 1,500 people pressed together, and the presence of the Lord
was thick. I gave some words of knowledge, and the people eagerly
responded. The ushers brought many who were manifesting
demons to the front. We saw healings of many kinds, kidneys, stom-
achs, backs, and the lame. One lady who couldn't swallow attended
our crusade instead of going to the hospital and was healed! Tumors disappeared, asthma and arthritis were healed, a deaf and
mute girl was set free and could hear and speak, and seven more
gave their hearts to the Lord, although there were many more who
had raised their hands to receive Jesus.

Open-Air Crusade

On the third evening as my vehicle approached the platform,
I glimpsed a local witchdoctor in the audience. He was dressed
as a shaman, and had amulets and fetishes around his neck. His
hair was dirty and dreadlocked and his robes were torn and tat-
tered. He carried a large wooden staff with bones and other
paraphernalia on the end. As I neared, he challenged me, and
called on the power of darkness, then he shook his stick wildly in
the air, and cast spells and incantations.

Holy anger rose in my spirit as I ascended the platform, and I took authority over the power of witchcraft and commanded in Jesus' name, "You will not operate in witchcraft during this campaign." An angry cloud had already covered the grounds and it began to rain. Enraged, he shook his rod again, then he left. God had given us a tremendous breakthrough. The sun appeared again, and we rejoiced.

All total, almost 7,000 attended the night's crusade, and 90 gave their hearts and lives to God. After I shared a message on covenant relationships, I called for the sick to come, but many were being touched even as I spoke. Those who were healed made their way forward to share their testimony. Tumors disappeared—gone, dissolved! A doctor examined one woman and told her that the tumor in her spine was no more! A person who had lived with a swollen leg for four years was healed, and two women, completely deaf could hear! Many with heart conditions, pain, lung infections, and the demonized were set free. The meeting closed early, though, because the authorities were concerned for our safety and decided to take precautions after Muslim dissidents made threats

Saturday Morning

My team and I visited a public school where I shared my testimony with 250 young people; 48 souls came into the Kingdom. Later, we drove back to the crusade grounds and the tent, and people began to share their testimonies of the healings of the night before. Someone who had tuberculosis for six years shared his healing, and another shared about a withered hand restored.

I called out many words of knowledge, and also gave a salvation call and nine more went forward, including a woman who manifested demons. She went into a trance, and when the demon was cast out, she returned to her right mind. We saw tumors, goiters, and lumps disappear!

251

After I shared a message on the anointing, 2,000 or more people lined up to receive an impartation of the Holy Spirit! As the ministry team anointed them, the power fell and many collapsed, two, three, four at a time—there were "bodies" everywhere overcome by the power and presence of the Lord!

After the tent ministry, we traveled to Kako Public School, where over 800 students heard my testimony, with 42 giving their hearts to God.

Evening Crusade

For the evening crusade, 6,000 to 7,000 people had already gathered to listen to the worship team. I was surprised to see the witchdoctor on the platform with the pastors! I discovered later that while he was in the trance the previous night and communicating with his spirit demon guide, a "short, fat white guy, with a beard" broke into his trance and preached the Gospel to him! He gave his life to Jesus because he knew the power was real. The pastors had already prayed with him and he had laid down the power of witchcraft! Now he was saved, and in his right mind! I laid my hands on him, and he fell out under the power, trembling!

Then the heavens opened and it started to pour, in both the natural and the spiritual. Hundreds fled in the pouring rain while others stayed to receive their miracles from the Lord. A lady who was paralyzed in her right leg, which was swollen to twice its normal size, was healed and she walked. Two deaf mutes began to hear and speak and several who were possessed by demons were set free. Vision impairment, tumors, stomach problems, and more were healed. Our next stop after this crusade was Kampala, and Streams of Life Church.

Kampala

When we arrived in on Sunday evening, a large crowd had already gathered outside in the parking area. The sound system was set on high and the choir had commenced singing. Several blind had their vision restored and five deaf people began to hear. One woman, who was walking with crutches and wearing a cast, threw aside her crutches and took off the cast. Many breathing conditions, fevers and more were healed. There were so many healed, that it seemed as though everyone that we prayed for received their miracle from God. Another 60 surrendered their hearts to the Lord.

On Monday, we visited four schools, and had a great time; 830 accepted Jesus! At one school, the children pressed into the team asking for blessings! Their hunger for a touch from God overwhelmed us at times.

We returned to Streams of Life Church in the evening and yet another 80 were saved. Once again, miracles happened. A mute girl spoke for the first time, ever in her life. At first, her words weren't clear, but as she tried to speak and repeat words we gave her, they became clearer. Her mother jumped for joy!

Another girl had sickle cell anemia and could not close her hand. After prayer, she maneuvered her hand perfectly! A man born blind, and with a white filmy substance over his eye, experienced the joy of seeing as the white film dissolved! Many were set free of demons, as well.

It was our last night in Uganda, and we thanked God that we could be a part of what He was doing in the country and in the continent of Africa. It was only the beginning though, because later we visited South Africa, Nigeria, and Ghana—for we knew in our hearts that God definitely had a plan for our ministry there. We are forever thankful to the Lord for the faithfulness of our partners—those who have helped finance our Africa ministry.

KENYA MIRACLE CRUSADE—AUGUST 1-7, 2001

Before I even left for Kenya in August 2001, the Lord showed me someone I would pray for when I arrived. The vision came as I was ministering and speaking in Kelowna, B.C. The Lord took me to a Kenyan hospital where I prayed for a crippled man. Afterward, I yelled out to my friend Rob, "Hey, remind me that when we arrive in Kenya, we're supposed to go to the hospital to pray for a particular terminally ill guy to be healed."

Later, while in Kenya in August 2001, I visited that same hospital, where the doctors and nurses accompanied me from room to room as I prayed for the sick. I found the man the Lord had shown me, and learned that he'd been bedridden for six months, and was dying of AIDS. When I prayed, fire shot through him and he jumped out of bed, and ran down the hallway shouting, "I'm healed! I'm healed!" I turned to the doctor and asked, "What do you think of this?" and he just shrugged and said, "I guess we'll send him home."

Some people have a hard time believing how someone can be sovereignly moved by the Holy Spirit to "another place." It's biblical, though. The Lord can take a physical body to another place, and it's known as being "transported" This happened to Phillip when he finished ministering to the Ethiopian eunuch. "Now when they came up out of the water, the Spirit of the Lord caught Philip away, so that the eunuch saw him no more; and he went on his way rejoicing," (Acts 8:39).

This type of experience apparently happened a lot to Elijah because, in First Kings 18:11-12, Obadiah tells Elijah, "And now you say, 'Go, tell your master, "Elijah is here."' And it shall come to pass, as soon as I am gone from you that the Spirit of the Lord will carry you to a place I do not know; so when I go and tell Ahab, and he cannot find you, he will kill me."

The other way to travel is to be *translated*, that's where your spirit goes on a trip, but your body stays home. Paul refers to this in Second Corinthians 12:3-4, "And I know such a man—whether in the body or out of the body I do not know, God knows—how he was caught up into Paradise and heard inexpressible words, which it is not lawful for a man to utter."

Kenya was indeed a place of miracles and favor. When Rob Galbraith and I arrived, the nation embraced us warmly. National television commercials opened up the country for the preaching of the Gospel.

The first night of a four-night crusade in Eldorate, about four hours from Nairobi, was a huge success. Around 10,000 people gathered for an open-air crusade in the "64 Stadium." The city had never hosted an event on this level. Over 100 pastors worked together for the success of the crusade. After I gave my testimony and preached about the power of God to save, heal, and deliver, nearly 1,500 souls were saved. I prayed a mass prayer of healing and deliverance and many were delivered from demons.

One lady who was carried to the platform, demonized and mute, was delivered, within moments, of severe pains in her body as well as of several demons. After the service, she ran toward me, screaming with excitement, to tell me she'd been set free from years of torment and sickness! Many people were healed instantly by the power of God while standing in the field! A man who could barely stand or walk because of a dislocated knee for nearly a year and a half, felt the Lord heal his leg, and then he jumped up and down on the platform. A deaf girl, who couldn't hear in one ear, heard through it for the first time, and a man deaf for 11 years, could hear! Many were healed instantly of what we would consider "minor" illnesses, like ulcers, stomach conditions, migraines, and back problems, easily treatable in North America, but not so in the third world.

The next day, we visited a sad area of the city where drug addicts and alcoholics gather—young and old alike—a place so dreadful, that children sniffed gas there just to get high. A thousand souls gathered there for a time of spontaneous worship and preaching. Over 200 souls responded to the call of salvation. The power of God came upon us, and one young fellow fell prostrate. This was the beginning of miracles!

Rob and I conducted a healing line in the park, and deaf ears heard, a neck that could not move moved, a person who could not see at a very far distance regained eyesight, a paralyzed man could suddenly move the upper left side of his body and arm, joints and muscles were healed, and various other torments healed. Over 1700 souls were saved in those two open-air market meetings too. Glory, glory, glory!

Torrential Downpour Doesn't Phase the Lost

During the second evening crusade, an African storm rolled in bringing a torrential downpour. We believed the crusade would be cancelled, but when the pastor arrived that evening we were surprised to learn that nearly 11,000 people had assembled and although many had left, still thousands stood for hours in the rain to hear the Gospel. Another 200-250 souls responded to the altar call for salvation, bringing the total in two days to over 1,950 souls.

The miracles continued as before. Demonized people fell out under the power and manifested violently in the crowd. One young woman, so crippled with arthritis that she had to be carried to us, walked after the casting out of a demon. God healed a woman whose body was rotten with cancer. The fire of God touched her, the cancer left, and her arm was restored. We saw a dislocated hand come into alignment, and the fire of God touched another cancerous malignancy. God even healed a person instantly from the symptoms of typhoid fever!

After the crusade, we conducted a live national radio program to over eight million listeners! While being interviewed by two women, I laid hands on them, and they fell out under the power, live! Someone had to take over for them! After the broadcast, the station was inundated by callers sharing their

testimony of healing, and the next day, we heard countless reports of salvation. The station manager granted us a second live
broadcast the very next day, because of God's power.

The last two evenings the crowds swelled to almost 30,000,
and the crusade was broadcast live to over 8 million again. Many,
many shared their testimony of healing while listening to the
previous broadcast. A woman, Theresa, bedfast for three months
testified of the healing of her dislocated knee *and* deliverance
from drug addiction. The station's phone lines were plugged
with callers phoning in with healing and salvation testimonies.

The final night, 1,500 people committed themselves to Jesus,
and counselors worked for hours with new believers. In fact, the
pastor had to build more benches for the Sunday service to ac-
commodate all of the new believers. As I preached the evening's
message, before I even finished, people were being carried up to
the platform, having fallen under the power, and set free by the
message end. The miracles that night were amazing! An epileptic
since birth delivered, a deaf and mute man, after 28 years heard
and spoke, and a three-year-old baby boy born deaf and lame
could suddenly stand for the first time, as the Lord healed his
twisted, inward feet. It overwhelmed us to watch the little guy's
face as he heard for the first time. Even an infant, little Stephen,
born completely blind, received his sight. Many, many blind
were healed that night.

A woman reported that she was delivered from witchcraft,
and a demon-possessed woman shared that a flash of light filled
her soul as demons left her. I called four people to the stage
through a word of knowledge about their tumors, and they dissolved! A girl, Lydia, received instant healing for her broken arm.
Paralyzed limbs moved, and 20 years of ulcer pain, vanished.

In total during those final crusade evenings, 30,000 people
filled the stadium, and 2,000 souls saved. Reports were that

there had never before been a crusade of this magnitude in the city's history!

THE HEAVENLY VISION
ATLANTA, GEORGIA—2001

Still, our healing revivals continued. At a church meeting while in Atlanta, I heard the Lord say, "Lay down on the pew," and so I did. I felt myself ascend out of the building, and then propelled down a highway. I flew without a vehicle, passing over bridges, underpasses, and signs. Then I was propelled onto the North Chattanooga highway, and eventually alit outside of a large prison in Atlanta.

I entered the building, walked the corridors, and stopped at the cell of a 22-year-old man. I knew through a word of knowledge that he was in prison for crimes he committed before he was saved. It was a vivid experience, where I saw every detail of this young man's appearance, right down to his glasses. I prophesied to him about God's call on his life as an evangelist, and the revival that was about to come to the prison, and then, I was back in the church!

That evening as I ministered, I shared the experience and asked if it meant anything to anyone. One woman jumped up and said, "That's my friend's son. She rode with me to the meeting tonight and received a phone call that there was an emergency and she needed to return home."

"Call that woman right now," I instructed. She dialed the number and gave me the cell phone—a thousand people witnessed and overheard my conversation.

"Do you have a son in a prison in Atlanta?" I asked the woman, after she'd answered. I could have described him in more detail, but decided not to at that point.

"Yes," she replied.

I discerned witchcraft, rebuked the curse of death, and prayed. She cried out in praise to God for His loving attention to her son in prison, and for unveiling the darkness in her home. My call didn't only affect her son, but her home life, where that day, her 17-year-old son, a satanist, had attempted to kill his father. My phone call diffused the crisis. The woman drove right over to the meeting, to testify the word of knowledge was true.

THE MIRACULOUS
ECUADOR & PERU—OCTOBER 1–7, 2001

We arrived in Ecuador for a three-day crusade, before heading for Lima, Peru. We were to minister in a small sports stadium with a capacity of around 6,000 people. The Pepsi Cola Company wanted to sponsor the event, and asked me to visit their offices and pray for the company.

Favor and miracles continued to abound. Reporters clamored to interview me, since the city of Quevedo were hosting the crusade. A reporter asked me twice, "What is that energy I feel?" and I told him that it was the power of God, and prayed for him right there on television! Afterward, we were invited to do a radio program that would reach 60 percent of the country, and comprising millions of listeners. The interviewer received Christ when I prayed for the sick live. He said it was as though Jesus had walked into his body. He felt the fire of God! Then he testified to his listeners right there that prior to the interview, he had not known Christ, but that now he did! The station owners called in when they heard the broadcast, and although they shared how sceptical they were of God, they said that there definitely was a new, strong presence and fire that transmitted through the radio and that it greatly impacted them.

Within hours of being in the country and on the street having a coffee, the team and I were able to pray for three people to be healed and they were, and a man was saved. We called it the

"Sidewalk Cafe Healings." One man fell under the power on the street! We had plenty marketplace opportunities to evangelize outside of the evening crusades, and in one restaurant alone, eight employees were saved.

Some say Ecuador is the poorest country in South America. Many in South America cannot afford wheelchairs, and they don't go to doctors. Although we were warned that it was illegal to preach the Gospel and that we could be arrested, jailed, or fined, we preached anyhow. The crowd began small, but swelled to hundreds when miracles happened. One man totally blind received sight. The deaf heard, and 90 percent of the people we prayed for throughout were healed. Fifty more were saved right in the street!

One of the crusade time highlights was our invitation to a prison, where the worst criminals served their time. The moved us into the main courtyard, with the prisoners, and locked the door behind us! Armed guards with machine guns stood at the ready atop the wall as we preached the Gospel. That day, according to our count, 49 men gave their lives to the Lord and we prayed for at least a hundred healings.

The harvest continued wherever we went, in the streets, in hotel lobbies, in a taxi—wherever. We saw hundreds of souls saved and healings in our evening crusades, and of course, reached millions through the radio broadcast. The preaching of the Gospel was confirmed daily with signs and wonders. One little boy, mute his entire life, spoke for the first time. I had him repeat the English words I gave him, instead of Spanish, and my translator jokingly said that the reason the boy didn't speak all of those years, was because he wanted to learn English! God did a creative miracle in the bones of a cripple, seven deaf people heard in a single service, a woman blind for twenty years saw, and at least 1500 sick people were prayed for in one night. One of the most powerful testimonies was that of a taxi driver, who turned to the pastor after dropping myself and a team member off and said, "What is the energy coming off of those men? I feel something in the car!" This man, backslidden for years, returned to Jesus!

Lima, Peru

In Lima, Peru we hosted open-air meetings for up to 2,000 people. Some 150 people responded to receive Jesus at the very first meeting, and every evening we saw up to 200 souls saved. We also had a church meeting on Sunday, and another 80 raised their hands.

In these crusades, God came in unusual power. At the moment of salvation, many were instantly healed and filled with the Holy Ghost! Hundreds were filled with the Spirit without a hand laid on them. Fire fell on hundreds of people, causing them to weep, shake, cry, fall under the power, and speak in tongues.

Healing testimonies poured in every day. We verified one testimony of a woman, completely deaf and mute, hearing and speaking for the first time. So, we asked if anyone knew of the woman, and her neighbor came forward and reported that she'd always been deaf. This miracle and 75 percent of all miracles happened en masse: A seven-year old boy with a large hernia from birth, a woman who could hardly walk and with infection from two surgeries, more then eight tumors, including one on a woman's face that completely disappeared. In total, the Lord healed more than 50 deaf people and 40 tumors dissolved!

On the final day of meetings in Peru, we decided the ruling religious spirit and witchcraft needed to be broken, so we had a "no-holds-barred" service. After prayer, hundreds of youth were laid out under the power, including children weeping, shaking, and crying out to God. Almost 500 were baptized in the Holy Ghost at one time, breaking into tongues, with at least a thousand over the four days.

In much of Peru, and almost all of Ecuador, the people have no experience with the river of God, renewal, or revival. Most don't speak in tongues and have never seen manifestations of the Spirit.

On the final evening, my team and I got hammered in the Spirit, and staggered around "drunk" on the platform! The pastors, worship team, and hundreds of others in the crowd, who I taught to drink by faith, got "plastered" too. The crusade was so successful in these countries, that we were asked to return to Lima the following spring, to hold a large crusade in a stadium that holds up to 45,000 people!

BRANDON, MANITOBA—OCTOBER 10-14, 2001

After our return to North America, I traveled to Manitoba to minister. Here's a report by someone who attended our conference:

> It was such a joy to have you ministering at the International Healing Conference October 10th-14th. We certainly enjoyed having Ivan Roman with us too. It was an incredible time in the Presence of the Lord. When you spoke on the deaf and dumb spirit nearly 100 people stood to testify of restored hearing, including me (Ramona). I had 25 percent permanent hearing loss and God healed it! He also healed my directional dyslexia after 59 years!
>
> Andie Meyer, the young woman whose totally blind eye was healed, continues to astound her doctors. Her eye was shot out seven years ago and she underwent surgery, and was given a cadaver cornea to try to save the eye. The surgery failed and the sight in her eye was 20/400, totally blind. When she went through the 'tunnel of fire' on Friday night, her sight was restored! Her Jewish doctor examined her the next day and wrote a note to Andie's father letting

him know of the unexplained change. From 20/400 to 20/25! Not knowing what to do, he sent her to the University. Doctors there examined her thoroughly. It seems that she has a brand new eye, praise God! According to the doctor's report, they can find no sign of the injury or surgery!

Also, a woman at the healing Roundtable received a transfer of anointing (Yes, all saints can do this!) As a nurse, she was so concerned about all of the people she saw dying around her, she decided to do something about it. She went to work after the conference; when a baby was stillborn, and the doctors could not resuscitate the infant after about 45 minutes of trying everything from the paddles, to injections, and bagging, they handed it off to the nurse to prepare the baby for the morgue. She took the child aside and, as compassion welled up in her, laid hands on it and, in the name of Jesus Christ, commanded a spirit of life to come in. The child was raised to Life! God is so good!! This was not one of the traveling evangelists with a healing ministry, but a nurse who had faith imparted to her at the conference.[1]

TREMENDOUS MIRACLES AND HEALINGS ONTARIO, CANADA—NOVEMBER 14, 2001

I'd been praying for my father and his salvation for a long time, and even offered him a job in my ministry, editing tapes and videos, so that he would have to hear and watch the power of God at work. It would also expose him regularly to the anointing! I claimed the promise in Malachi 4:6, that God would turn the hearts of the fathers to the children. I kept asking the Holy Spirit, "How can I reach him," and I finally did.

I asked Dad to join me on the road, to a meeting in Ontario. He accepted, and looked forward to going back to his "home" province, to where he and my mom had first met.

For several nights, he heard testimonies of God's power, he heard and saw healings. I pulled him into the anointing, so to speak, and taught him how to "catch," people as they fell out under the power. There was a woman there who I laid hands on, who manifested a demon, and writhed on the floor like a snake. I'll never forget the look of horror on my dad's face, as though he were experiencing something right out of the *Exorcist* movie. Even though I had no doubt that this power encounter would be hard for my father to deny, I was still surprised when I gave the altar call, that my dad raised his hand and came forward for salvation.

I wept inside, and felt a little awkward. *Is this really happening*, I thought. *What's our relationship going to be like? What will happen tomorrow?*

I was afraid, and excited. To be honest, this was the first real emotional experience my father and I had ever shared. As we prayed the sinner's prayer, I wept, my lips quivered as I lay hands on him and he fell under the power. I knew in my heart that this was the beginning of a powerful work of healing.

MEETINGS IN ST. CATHARINES, ONTARIO

Ray Young, pastor of *The Father's House*, in St. Catharines, Ontario, said that our days there were best described as miracle days. People with every kind of sickness and infirmities were healed every night. A man with a severely damaged heart (it operated only one-third of its capacity), was healed, and a girl born completely blind in her right eye, could see through it after prayer. Many people were healed of ear conditions and degrees of deafness, and a young woman received a tremendous deliverance after years of struggling—the transformation was immediate.

A pastor from Quebec reported excitedly to Pastor Ray that after the meetings, God moved powerfully in healing and outpouring in his own church. Ray, too, reported that he saw an increased outpouring in his own church, and that a mother and daughter with stomach afflictions were set free—able to eat anything without ill effect. Words of knowledge and healing flowed, people healed in their arms, legs, backs, knees, bladders, and in all manner of illness.

"We witnessed major emotional healings of people who suffered trauma and abuse," said Ray. I had preached on the different levels of anointing, faith, and the sovereignty of God.

TRAVELING CANADA

Toward the last part of 2001, we traveled to Alberta, Manitoba, Ontario, and clear across the rest of the nation to Newfoundland. At a healing conference at the Toronto Airport Christian Fellowship (TACF), there were at least 300 and as many as 500 healings. In one day alone, 70 people shared healing testimony, most of them creative healings: a severed retina reattached and vision restored, partial paralysis to full mobility, a woman with Bell's palsy healed as the Holy Spirit created new nerves. God also healed some 12 cases of severed or detached nerves. There were also many vision impairment healings; cataracts healed, and people putting away their prescription glasses. One man, deaf for five years, received healing in his right ear as he drove home from one of our meetings in New Market. We saw many more healings in Ontario, from multiple sclerosis to ear tumors. God did a creative miracle in a man from Manitoba with internal injuries that had damaged his stomach and digestive system. He responded to a word of knowledge, and for the first time in 14 years, ate a piece of his wife's apple pie, yummy!

ENDNOTE

1. *Ramona—Brandon, Manitoba.*

CHAPTER 18

HEALING AND MIRACLE HARVESTS

BATTLING FOR MIRACLES
NEWFOUNDLAND, CANADA—JANUARY 2002

Our Newfoundland meetings got off to a slow start. It was my first meeting ever in that part of eastern Canada, and the words I preached simply seemed to bounce off the walls. I didn't sense a strong anointing for healing, let alone faith that something would happen. The meetings were a lot smaller than I anticipated, too.

My mother's family is from Newfoundland, and several of my uncles and other extended family members attended. Since they were from a Salvation Army background, I was concerned that if any manifestations happened, they'd be scared off. But God showed Himself strong, and as difficult as it was to minister, we saw several breakthroughs.

Every evening, we pressed in for detailed words of knowledge. (I believe that the prophetic ministry and revelation are important to break religious strongholds.). In Springdale, a community of only 3,500, the church exploded on the Sunday morning after I received an angelic visitation in the pastor's office, from the "Harvest" angel. I released a prophetic word for the church and prophesied most of the morning to the rest of the congregation.

Then it happened—one young man was taken into a vision of Jesus and people ran around the sanctuary as though they were in a marathon! Some prophesied, others experienced drunkenness in the Holy Spirit, and one elder, who was pinned to the floor for over two hours, received a creative miracle. The doctors had planned to surgically repair the crushed bone and cartilage that completely blocked his nostrils. He felt an intense burning sensation through his sinus cavity, and he was healed. A man who used pain medication every day for two years testified that his hips and sciatic condition were healed.

That Sunday evening, right in the pulpit, I was overcome with the drunkenness of the Spirit and laughter. So, it was right to start and lead a fire tunnel that laid out 90 percent of the people in attendance—yes, Lord!

We also ministered in neighboring towns and saw the power of God at work. A woman responded to a word concerning damage to the rotator cuff in her right shoulder. God not only healed her so that she could use her arm, and move as she use to, but He also exposed the injury and the hurts associated with it.

An elder's wife received a word of knowledge and prayer for back and neck pain, and for days afterward felt a "heat glow" around her head, and is now pain and pain medication free. At one location, miracles happened even between meetings! While four friends were having tea, the Spirit manifested, and an egg-sized lump disappeared from one woman's calf muscle, as well as a small lump from her thigh. Another there had her shoulder and arm muscles healed, and they witnessed gold dust!

FIGHTING DARK POWERS
REINOSA, MEXICO—FEBRUARY 2002

The first of two nights in Reinosa, Mexico were difficult, however, God gave us several key miracles and over 100 salvations. That evening in my hotel, I felt spiritual backlash. We discovered that the local witchdoctors covenanted together to release the power of witchcraft against the meetings.

At 2:30 A.M. I saw the form of a woman and I felt her presence at the foot of my bed. She had "astral projected" to my room. I knew the power of witchcraft was being released against us, and I took authority in the Spirit over its power. "Every curse, spell, and sorcery: you will not prevail against me and this campaign. Greater is He that is in me than he that is in the world. I will go forth in His power and prevail."

Breaking the Power of Witchcraft

The Holy Spirit spoke to me and told me about these witches who had gathered. The next evening at the crusade I said, "A witch came to my hotel room last night to challenge the power of God. I know there are many witches and warlocks in this meeting. I'm going to confront you and the power of witchcraft now."

I took authority over the atmosphere and climate of the room in Jesus' name. I broke and rebuked its power and commanded every devil associated with witchcraft to let go.

Individuals were thrown two rows back. Twenty-eight people writhed like snakes on the floor. The team carried these manifesting people to the altar. One woman, with blood in her mouth, screamed and shrieked! Another young woman, now set free, looked to her left and saw a grotesque demon step out of a local witch. She fainted. When she regained consciousness, she said she wanted to know Jesus.

God gave us an open heaven and miracles happened. The local town cripple, paralyzed from the waist down for 11 years, and bedridden for two, arrived in her wheelchair. Such was the intensity of her chronic pain, that she couldn't even hug her children. The Lord healed her and she pushed her wheelchair herself, out of the meeting! That day, we indeed experienced an open heaven of miracles—over 200 were saved!

THE MIRACULOUS IN
CALCUTTA, INDIA—MARCH, 2002

I traveled to Calcutta with our team member Ivan, my father Dave, and our associate Jeff Vosgien. We didn't take a full team this time because of the danger. India is unlike any place I had preached the Gospel. We ministered in a village just outside of the main city of over 15 million people. The Indian government opposes Christianity, so we had to come into the country for the purpose of visiting our friend Dr. "X." We could not, therefore, hold public meetings, large or small, as we could do elsewhere. The Hindus actually held a festival to oppose our coming.

We heard Hindu chants and prayers play day and night over the loudspeakers throughout the village. Idols were everywhere, especially along the roadsides; spiritual oppression was great. But we held on to God's word in Isaiah 60:2 which says that when "darkness shall cover the earth, and deep darkness the people...the Lord will arise over you, and His glory will be seen upon you."

The Christians and missionaries who were there for the healing impartation faced beatings and sometimes even daily threats on their lives. Only a few years ago, foreign missionaries were burned. Many new converts are chased down and threatened, made to deny Christ, or are persecuted in other ways. In addition, the common deception that Jesus is just one of many gods, makes it difficult to have large meetings and harvest here. However, we will have victory.

We stayed on a large compound patrolled by armed security. People were hungry for the power of God. Some of the pastors and evangelists attending the conference traveled five days from Nepal and the Himalayan mountains; some even walked three days to catch a bus for a two-day ride just to be there. In the first morning session, 145-150 responded to the altar call after I made it clear that they would need to forsake all other gods, religions, and idols. Most of the converts were children (aged 5-15), school teachers, and a few villagers.

The Miracles Begin

One pastor's wife was healed of a tumor on her left side when a word of knowledge was given. A man and a woman, who were new converts, were both healed of deafness. This man's wife, who wore a brace around her back and hips and could barely stand from the constant pain, was healed as well. One man with tuberculosis was blind in his right eye. He gave his life to Christ and God opened his vision more. There were many other healings as well.

Harvest

After three days in India, we began to overcome the resistance to the meetings, and the number of salvations reached 706. The new converts were followed up on and discipled by the team in India and Bibles were distributed. Most of the converts were Hindu and Muslim, and daily faced intense persecution for their newfound commitment to Christ. As I preached the Gospel nightly, we told them that a commitment to Christ meant the forsaking of all other gods and idols. Many began removing idols and making steps to be delivered. One young woman, after receiving her eyesight, ripped off the bandage on her wrists—a fetish that carried a curse, even though it was supposed to protect her husband.

More Miracles—Deaf and Mute

Hundreds pressed in nightly to be healed and many fell under the power, including hundreds of young children; it was precious to see them receive. The miracles were straight out of the Bible and created a stir throughout the village. The first miracle happened to a local man, widely known in his village as a deaf-mute—he heard and spoke. The second healing was a Muslim woman, also deaf and mute. She was only 16 years old and already married. God healed her and she wept with tears of joy on the platform. Then three deaf mutes, all siblings, began to receive their healing and speak. A woman paralyzed on one leg for over eight years, testified of her healing and the healing of another sickness. An evangelist's wife from Nepal gave a testimony of a tumor of four years dissolved at the very moment I spoke the word of knowledge. Then she had a visitation from the Lord in which He told her she was also being healed of other infirmities.

Miracles abounded and after the third service, at least 400 entered into the Kingdom—a total of 700 in three days. Thank You Jesus!

The Team

God used my team members Jeff, Ivan, and Dave mightily. He also used my dad to open deaf ears, even though and ironically so, he had trained in sign language several years previously. When a demon growled at him, my dad roared back, "Every devil GO!" and the man was set free! Ivan prayed for a young woman who was in constant pain, and she received a partial healing. The Lord instructed Ivan to ask her what it would take for her to follow Jesus, and she said, "I want to be healed, and

Healing and Miracle Harvests

then I serve Jesus!" Right then, right there—BAM—under the power; up, and healed!

Jeff prayed for an elderly lady who could not bend her left knee for twenty years. After prayer—BAM—healed, kicking and running across the altar.

Miracles happen nightly here in India! In a few nights, we witnessed 19 deaf mutes hear and speak. Over nine completely blind people were healed, and more received healing of their partial blindness. Cripples began to walk and many healings of various sicknesses occurred. We prayed for hundreds nightly, one by one.

More Souls

In five days, over 900 people prayed to receive Jesus. The resistance to the Gospel was strong in India. The Muslim and Hindu faiths are predominating—many come just to receive healing and believe they can have Jesus and their gods too. Every night we made it clear in the altar call that turning to Christ involves forsaking all. We also explained what it would cost to be a Christian because many face persecution for deciding to follow Christ. Many people who wanted to be saved were afraid of the radical Hindus and Muslims.

The first breakthrough came Saturday morning when I was led by the Spirit to preach on the subject of demons. In the service, Ivan had a vision of one of the Hindu gods; Jeff and Dave saw a large demon. That night, a woman violently manifested a demon that we discovered was the most powerful spirit in the Hindu culture. She was married to a Christian, and with the help of two of her brothers, had her husband beaten because of his faith. However, two hours later she was set free, and she and her daughter accepted Jesus.

275

Incredible Baptism of the Holy Ghost Service!

Saturday afternoon, at a meeting attended by over a hundred leaders, pastors, and evangelists, I preached on the Holy Ghost and power. The power of God fell, and the pastor and I shook and jumped up and down under God's fire like pogo sticks.

The Holy Spirit seemed to be rushing or, as someone said, "Swirling in from the roof like a small tornado." At the beginning of the service we heard a sound like a generator—then it hit. People fell out of their chairs and literally rolled across the floor for several minutes. One wave of the Spirit after another rolled in—leaders became drunk in the spirit and many started to laugh. I could not preach on the baptism because it was already happening! Fifty to sixty individuals responded to a call for the infilling of the Holy Spirit. As God's Spirit rolled in, a roar-like sound ascended to Heaven and row upon row of people were whacked onto the floor.

People assembled on the side of the road outside; I imagine it was like the day of Pentecost. Some Indian leaders who received the baptism of the Holy Spirit and the gift of tongues were even heard speaking in English...and we understood it!

Others were taken into visions. One woman ran to the altar, "I see the fire of God!" she exclaimed. An hour and a half later, the visitation lifted, and several received deliverance from devils. One woman hissed like a snake; even her tongue made a snake-like manifestation, until she was set free!

The Lord performed outstanding miracles during our time here. A five-year-old child, crippled in the left arm from birth, healed. A nineteen-year-old deaf-mute girl received her hearing and spoke. She was so excited, she wouldn't stop shouting as she spoke out all of the new sounds she heard. A little girl blind from birth and a man as well, both began to see. The man was very excited to see the flash of a camera, praise the Lord!

EASTER RESURRECTION CELEBRATION
SAN JOSE CALIFORNIA—APRIL 1, 2002
Summary of meeting, by Senior Pastor Greg Babish
Celebration Community Church

Glorious Resurrection celebration weekend, beloved Revivalists! As the Jewish community sings the Passover song, "*Dayenu* (It Would Have Been Enough)," we acknowledge that our gracious Lord of Glory keeps on sending us His best...keeps on pouring out His River...keeps on revealing triumphant, conquering, victorious Christ in us...and keeps on releasing grace for grace!

And now God has sent beloved, prophetic, healing evangelist Todd Bentley back to the San Francisco Bay Area. Last night, Thursday, March 28th, he began an Easter weekend of POWER-filled meetings. Discerning regional spiritual warfare, 26-year-old Todd Bentley identified the constricting, choking, suffocating python spirit (of cursing/witchcraft/divination) over our entire area—and went right after it, breaking the assignment of death and rebuking the python spirit and all its effects.

He absolutely nailed it for so many of us who had been wondering *what* was wrong with us! That spirit that had been trying to slowly squeeze the life of the Spirit out of us was broken; we were given a supernatural, divine strength to overcome. Todd called for the angels to minister to us as angels strengthened our Lord Jesus on earth.

Todd obviously really loves releasing the anointing that heals and teaching the revelation of our Kingdom authority...biblically-sound, experiential Christianity in the fullness of the manifestation of God's presence.

As he said, "Do you know who you are? Do you know what you have? Do you know how to give it away? God wants to move us into the authority of the rule and reign of JESUS! Don't be a victim of circumstances, your feelings, or what anybody else says! Most of us are satisfied, apathetic, or afraid to press in: "For as he thinks in his heart, so is he, 'Eat and drink' he says to you, but his heart is not with you" (Prov. 23:7). This hinders the manifestation of the life of God. Occupy, seize by force, and militantly *POSSESS THE LAND!* Make it happen! As Caleb says in Numbers 13, we are *'well able'* to overcome; we're not grasshoppers (vv. 13, 33)!

"Well able" means in the Hebrew *to have power, have the capacity to have success; could and can.* This Scripture emphasizes that we can have as much of God as we want now instead of waiting for Heaven. Todd made the important point that Christianity is not centered on the past or the future. God is here and now. We won't need healing in Heaven. Healing is for *now*!

Todd Bentley inspired us with his flamboyant fun, his wild testimony, and his attitude: "I'm gonna have the fullness of what You say I can have, Lord!" This lines up with the apostle John's prayer: "Beloved, I pray that you may prosper in all things and be in health, just as your soul prospers" (3 John 2).

GOD'S POWER TOUCHES MWANZA, TANZANIA
Summary and Report by Brian Hill

Welcome to Mwanza

Our 39-member Fresh Fire team arrived in Mwanza to a spectacular welcome. A huge gathering of over 200 pastors, church officials, along with others greeted Todd and the team warmly. Todd was given an ambassador's welcome with a garland of flowers placed around his neck. Later, we were told that no other "westerner" had ever received such a tremendous greeting. After a short press conference, the team was loaded up into passenger vans and Land Rovers. The crusade was now officially "in country."

Severe Poverty, Great Unity

The infrastructure of Mwanza is in shambles. Poverty and squalor reign supreme over these beautiful people. Many of our team members were heartbroken at the living conditions (or lack of) that prevailed. After an arduous trek over terribly rutted dirt roads, dodging other cars, carts, people on heavily laden bicycles and countless pedestrians, our team arrived at the Hotel Tilapia; a veritable palace compared to what we had just witnessed. Humbled by the experience, our hearts were being prepared for our commission.

The following day, Todd met with the council of church leaders. They informed him that an incredible 80 percent of the churches in Mwanza had gathered to support Fresh Fire's crusade! One idea that gained great momentum was to rent large trucks or buses to pick up as many crippled and sick people as possible and bring them to the Crusade. As the crusade budget had already been taxed heavily by ongoing expenses, many of the leaders and, later, team members, donated their own money to rent over three large buses for the entire time of the crusade! The local church contingent gave us more incredible news. They had canvassed the area with posters, calendars, radio announcements, etc. In some of the radio spots, it was being announced that although AIDS does not have a cure, Jesus could cure anything!

As a 'grand finale,' they informed us that the High Commissioner of Tanzania was coming to personally open the Crusade with a speech. With his arrival, representatives of all the media, including national television, would be attending. This would, in fact, give national attention to the event!

Child Crippled from Birth WALKS!

During Todd's leaders meeting, a small group of Fresh Fire Ministry team members visited a local orphanage. Numerous children gave their hearts to Jesus and several received healing in their body. After prayer, one child, crippled from birth, rose from his chair and began to walk shakily on his own! Other children—blind, deaf, and dumb—began to see, hear, and speak!

Gift Shop Deliverance

While they were in the hotel gift shop, team members prayed with a Muslim man who wanted to give his heart to Jesus. As they did so, he began to writhe around and hiss, like a snake. They commanded the demon to leave, and the man was delivered and saved! During the days before the crusades started, the team went into the market to do the works of Jesus. People were saved and healed everywhere we went. In one home for street kids, over 30 children and two staff members prayed to receive Jesus into their hearts!

Prison Warden Set Free

We also visited the largest prison (2,200 inmates) in Mwanza. The top officials of the prison, including the Chief Warden who was also in charge of six other prisons in the region, greeted us. We were given the opportunity to offer prayer to the staff members. Before she even left the states, a member of the team, Pastor BB Rail had a word of knowledge regarding someone in the government that had a disabled child. At first no one responded, but then the Director called up one of the women guards into the room. The team member prayed for the woman, who received it well. Then BB asked if any one wanted to receive the gift of Salvation. Again, no one moved. Then, unexpectedly, the Chief Warden stood up from his desk and announced that he would accept this gift. One of the officials standing behind the Director looked shocked as his superior prayed the prayer of faith! Upon receiving his salvation, the Director said, "I feel happy." He grinned widely as he shook the hands of numerous team members.

Healing and Salvations in the Hospital

Other Fresh Fire Ministry teams went out to the AIC Health Center and to the open markets on the street. At the AIC, the team reported three salvations and ten healings. Of the saved, the first woman was delivered from hearing voices and being tormented with continual nightmares. With the aid and confirmation from a local pastor and the interpreter, the woman said she felt something leave her body and now felt happy and peaceful! A man with an IV in his arm was healed of malaria then asked for salvation. The man was visibly strengthened and was beaming with joy as the team left his bedside. A Muslim man gave his heart to Jesus and then was healed of chronic stomach pains. A child of about four or five years old, had malaria and over 80 different parasites in her body. When the team arrived, she was unresponsive, almost catatonic. After receiving prayer, she was smiling and happy. Flora, another patient, received salvation and was healed of malaria and migraines. Several of the women on the team were in tears of joy, reporting that her face was actually glowing when they left.

Street Ministry Miracles

Next, we took God's power to the street, where we saw many miracles and salvations. Here's one notable story: A Muslim man had injured his leg in an auto accident and the other leg was crippled from polio. He received prayer and the injured leg regained its strength. As a result of his healing, he gave his life to Christ! The team discovered that the area that they had chosen to minister in was about 85 percent Muslim.

THE CRUSADE BEGINS
First Night: 25,000 Estimated Attendance—Over 500 Saved!

I have never experienced such a joyful time in worship as I did this evening (and I'm on a worship team!). Though a video camera and all the gear that goes with it encumbered me, I couldn't stand still. The choirs from Uganda and Tanzania were awesome. The crowd danced and sang with all their heart.

The High Commissioner of the Tanzanian government arrived shortly before the last choir was up on stage. He joined in the praise heartily. Afterward he addressed the crowd, giving his endorsement to Fresh Fire Ministries and encouraged the people to heed the evangelist's words. He then proceeded to give a Gospel message of his own, and challenging people to repent for their lack of commitment to following God.

Salvations and Healings

Rather than going into preaching, Todd launched straight into releasing a wave of healing over the crowd. He also gave an altar call in quick succession. About 270 people surged forward to receive salvation. Hundreds more were waving their hands to signify that they had also received healing or salvation but the crowd up front was so tight that they were unable to press forward. A few people, healed in the crowd, were able to come to the stage and testify.

Eight or nine deaf people received either partial or full restoration of their hearing. A young crippled girl pressed toward the stage, waving her crutches over her head in victory. She had been in the middle of the crowd and was healed in the first wave of healing. The crowd went wild! Another woman began to receive her sight. A man with a skin disease that inhibited his movement was able to bend and jump easily. Several demons manifested in people, and the team joined in to cast them out and deliver their hosts. One woman was very violent as she spat and raged, writhing like a snake on the stage. She was set free and began to rejoice and praise God.

The Fresh Fire Ministry teams continued after the power was shut off around 7:00 P.M. Many more testimonies will be forthcoming in the days to come as the leaders gather information from their respective teams. This has been a fantastic day!

Fishing for Souls at the Docks

The next day got off to a great start as teams gathered for intercessory prayer and worship. We have been meeting in a small open-air restaurant in the hotel complex that is right on Lake Victoria. It is also a favorite place for local fishermen who paddle their small boats into the cove to drop lines for Tilapia, a local fish. This setting seems prophetically appropriate for our work here.

After prayer, we loaded into our sturdy vans and bounced and careened our way to one of the open markets of Mwanza. This one is on the lake where local fishermen and cargo boats full of grain and other produce come to sell their goods. Mid-morning is a busy time for the market, and people filled the streets.

Today, Todd conducted the open-air meeting in a highly concentrated Muslim fishing village. Local pastors and Christians from Uganda came along as interpreters and musicians. As they began to play lively Swahili music, a crowd of about 500 or so gathered. Todd was introduced and he began to preach. The atmosphere was heavy with unbelief or fear, so Todd continued encouraging the crowd to give their hearts to Jesus and to also meet the challenge to come up for God's healing. By the time the meeting was over, we had around 150 saved souls and several healings of damaged bodies and many opened ears!

NIGHT 2 OF THE CRUSADE
50,000 Attendance/700-800 Saved/Numerous Healings

The word had obviously been spreading throughout this city of over 1 million that something very unusual was happening. This night, the crowd swelled to approximately 50,000 people. An air of anticipation grew as the worship teams danced and sang jubilantly.

Confronting the Powers of Witchcraft

When Todd came up, he immediately attacked the powers of witchcraft and sorcery. The previous night, we found out that curses had been placed against us. Blood and animal parts were found on the stage that morning, which is evidence of the evil that oppresses this area. Todd, through a word of knowledge, began to fast and pray, starting the previous night, to get a breakthrough against the local powers.

Todd gave an altar call for those who wanted deliverance from witchcraft, including witchdoctors who desired to give up their occult practices. The front area, roped off for ministry, was soon filled to overflowing. In that altar call alone, around 400 people got saved! When Todd led them through a salvation prayer, many people began to manifest violent demonic activity. Prayer teams to help deliver them from their torment immediately encircled these people. Approximately 40 demonized people were delivered.

One woman was extremely violent and thrashed about for about 45 minutes while the team prayed over her. When she was brought to the stage, she tried to attack Todd! After more lengthy deliverance, she was restored to her right mind and gave the following testimony: A witchdoctor had blown powder in her face and up her nose, which caused her to lose her sense of smell and hearing. Also, she said it felt like a knife was constantly being driven into her back. When she was delivered, her hearing and sense of smell returned. The back pain was gone as well.

Miracles Increase

That night hundreds of people were healed in a mass wave of healing. Here are a few of the testimonies:

A three-year-old boy, called up by a word of knowledge, had never walked in his life and also had malaria. He received dramatic healing and ran back and forth across the stage several times!

A man with a paralyzed right leg was healed after I grabbed his leg, and cast out the demon oppressing him. A woman, with a tumor protruding from her stomach, received healing. The tumor shrivelled up and disappeared! Several crippled people were able to walk on their own. A woman with polio was able to stand straight for the first time in years! Several deaf/mutes were healed. This brings that count up to well over 12 so far! A woman with a stunted leg gave her life to Jesus as she watched her leg grow!

Hundreds of others were healed of various pains and sickness but were unable to get to the altar and testify because of the crowds pressing in for healing! An estimated 700-800 souls were brought into the Kingdom by the end of the night!

Fresh Fire Ministry Team—Street Reports

Reports from the Fresh Fire Ministry teams are now flowing in fast. In addition to what has already been reported, there have been at least 300 more salvations through street ministry, visits to hospitals, orphanages and schools, ministry in the crusade crowds and one-on-one encounters throughout the day! The reports of healings are incredible: two people with AIDS freed from chronic pain; 28 deaf ears opened; 21 blind eyes healed; 15-20 cripples healed; 15 tumors either shrunk or disappeared; 12 demonized people set free; 8-15 people with various lung diseases healed; 12 wombs restored and too many general healings to mention!

CRUSADE NIGHT 3
At Least 700 Saved—Healings Abound

We are now at the halfway mark of the crusade, with only two more nights to go. The crowd has consistently been around 30,000-50,000 people. It is hard to get a solid count, as there is a constant ebb and flow of people coming and going.

Todd shared his testimony with the people. It was much like what many in the crowd were dealing with in their own lives. When Todd gave the altar call, hundreds of hands went up all over the field. They began streaming down towards the altar until there was no more room. Still hundreds in the crowd waved their hands as they gave their lives to Jesus.

As has happened in all the previous nights, when the prayer of salvation is shared, dozens of people begin manifesting demons fighting to keep their hosts in bondage. A special tent was dedicated to delivering these people, but the numbers were so many that some were dealt with right in front of the stage.

Spontaneous healings also took place all over the field. Here are a few: a woman, crippled for over a year received healing and walked on her own; dozens of deaf ears were opened; numerous blind eyes were restored and a woman was healed of a tumor on her stomach, the size of a baby's head!

Here are some more notable healings:

- People witnessed their tumors disappear during the mass healing wave.
- A thyroid goiter shrank to half its size.
- A woman's stunted leg grew two inches.
- A baby, paralyzed in her legs and blind from birth, received both her sight and strength to her limbs!
- Another girl of about 4 years of age was deaf from birth. When she got healed, she began to cry and tug at her ears.
- Many people, crippled from disease or injury received healing and regained use of their body.
- An eight-year-old boy was demonized so badly that six grown men couldn't hold him. Though he didn't speak English, a voice erupted from the boy, growling, "Who are you!" at one of the Fresh Fire Ministry

team members. Eventually he was delivered and later testified on stage that something was strangling him.

The current tally of salvations exceeds 2600. The healings are innumerable!

Intercessors and Pastors

We drove up into the hilltops where a small group of local Christians had been fasting and praying for over ten days, interceding for the Crusade and the people of Mwanza. These dedicated souls were gathered in a tiny room at the back of an orphanage for children whose parents had died of the AIDS virus. We blessed and prayed for the intercessors as well as the children gathered in the front yard.

For three days, Todd met with about 500 Pastors and Church leaders from all over the region. He taught and exhorting them about the Elijah Anointing: the transferable gift of healings, signs, and wonders. On the last day, he preached out of Matthew chapter 10: Preach the Gospel, Heal the Sick, Cleanse the Leper, Raise the Dead, Cast out Devils. He ended the conference by laying hands on each and every person, transferring the Healing anointing to them all.

CRUSADE NIGHT 4
Still 30,000-50,000 Attending / Over 1,000 Saved This Night!

As with the previous nights, the crowd surged like the ocean tide. At all times there were at least 30,000 people in the field' but when word spread about a particularly spectacular healing or deliverance, the people would come running off the streets to see what was happening, driving up the attendance to around 50,000!

Salvation = Healing

Todd opened the evening by teaching the people how to receive God's miracles and healings. He explained how, in Scripture, the word for salvation speaks of healing of the spirit, soul, and body. "If you can ask Jesus for a healing, why can't you receive everything else that He has?" During the call for salvation, demons began manifesting and the ushers started carrying people out of the crowd and into the deliverance tent as the demons caused their hosts to thrash about violently. At least 1,000 people prayed "the sinner's prayer" in that moment.

The Miracles Come Forth!

Soon, people began coming forward with testimonies of healing. In just a few moments, there were the testimonies of a blind eye, a deaf ear, and a tumor all being healed! Other miracles that were testified to on stage were:

- A man with a tumor for 15 years—the tumor disappeared!
- A young man, deaf in his left ear for three years, received his hearing.
- A woman with a tumor for 28 years—healed!
- A man with chronic back pain, unable to work for five years—healed and jumping around!
- A man, deaf in his right ear for 25 years, was healed instantly!
- A woman who went blind in one eye a month ago received her sight!
- A woman deaf for 30 years instantly healed!
- Another woman with two tumors in her abdomen for two years; again, they had disappeared after prayer!

- Twin boys mute and deaf from birth speak and hear for the first time in their lives!

- A young boy, afflicted with AIDS, showing classic symptoms (nausea, lack of appetite, weakness) prayed for at the crusade two days earlier. He was brought forward by a relative (both his parents had already died of AIDS) and testified that the boy was now eating and regaining his strength! After more prayer, Todd instructed the woman, who brought the boy, to take him to a doctor for testing.

Tonight the count is approximately: 8 tumors, 2 blind eyes, 7 deaf ears, 3 mutes, 1 AIDS victim, 1000+ salvations, and many, many more that went undocumented...*all in one night!*

5 DAYS TOTAL ATTENDANCE
OVER 210,000/ OVER 5,000 SALVATIONS
Countless Healings, Miracles, and Deliverances

Sunday Morning Services

On Sunday morning, the Fresh Fire Ministry teams ministered in approximately 20 churches throughout Mwanza. In those services more salvations and healings continued. In one service, Todd and Dave prayed for Mary, a paralyzed woman. Todd prayed over her, cast out some demons, and Mary was set free. She was able to get up and walk on her own!

FINAL NIGHT OF CRUSADE
50,000 ATTENDANCE/ 1500 SALVATIONS/ PENTE-COSTAL FIRE/ INCREDIBLE MIRACLES

The Best Wine of the Party

God always seems to leave the best for last. The final night of the Crusade was no exception. The attendance was high, approximating 50,000 people. Todd preached on salvation and being filled with the Holy Spirit. At the altar call, over a thousand people surged forward and half that many waved their hands from the crowd behind the roped partition. The estimated number of salvations for Night 5 was approximately 1500!

When Todd prayed with the crowd for the Holy Ghost Baptism, thousands more were filled and speaking in tongues! As with all the previous nights, when people began to press in to God, the demons came out of the woodwork! At least 16 people were rushed to the special deliverance tent for intense prayer and another 10 demoniacs were set free right in front of the platform.

Miracles Upon Miracles

When the Holy Spirit fell on the ripened field of souls, the manifested power of God blazed forth! There were so many healings and other miracles that it became difficult to keep track of them all. The following is a partial list:

- 32 tumors healed and disappeared!
- 18 cases of deafness healed and hearing!
- Several mutes healed and speaking!
- Several cases of partial blindness healed and seeing!
- One man was paralyzed for two years, unable to walk. After receiving prayer, he stood on his own and jumped around on the platform!
- A woman, near the front of the crowd, was suffering horribly from AIDS. She couldn't move and could barely breathe. Some of the Fresh Fire Ministry Team members prayed for her, and she was able to stand up and climb the stairs to the platform. She testified

that her breathing was easy and she felt strength coming back into her body!

- Another man had been insane, not knowing right from wrong. He said he would eat garbage from the street, not realizing what he was doing. In the past, he had spent some time in American hospitals but was not cured of his condition. After receiving the Holy Spirit, this man came into his right mind! He stated that he was going to start living a normal life and was hoping to find a job soon.

Summary of Miracles during the five-day Crusade (approximations only):

- Salvations: 5000
- Deliverance: 100
- Tumors: 60
- Deaf and/or Mute: 80
- Blind Eyes: 25
- Paralytics & Cripples: 25
- AIDS (obvious symptoms reduced or eliminated): 4
- Various other healings: Too many to count!

Tanzania Highlight: Invading the Fish Market

My fondest memory in Mwanza was a day I said, "Let's go to the marketplace," even though the police said that the Muslims were enraged and had killed Christians in the past. The police recommended against it. The local pastors said it would be better if we just stuck with the campaign in the evening and not go to the markets.

I asked, "What would Jesus do?" I decided to take our team to the heart of the Muslim district to present the Gospel with signs and wonders. I knew that this would shock these precious Muslim people.

We set up at the local fish market; hundreds were there and the local leaders gathered. Wearing their white robes and religious head covers, they crossed their arms, as if to say, "Who do you think you are coming into this area proclaiming Jesus?" There was an angry stir in the air.

We preached the Gospel with boldness. There was urgency— we had to snatch a few from the fire. I shared my testimony, and 157 Muslims pressed in to know Jesus. But there was a confrontation in the spirit, a wall of resistance, the greater core of the audience continued to mock and scoff. I knew we needed a power encounter. The Lord gave me a download of faith so I issued a challenge, "The first person who steps onto this platform will be healed right now, whether blind, deaf, crippled, whatever the infirmity. If not, we will discontinue our campaign. We will turn our backs on God, say the Bible isn't true, and my team and I will go home. If the first person isn't healed then everything I've preached in this city is a lie."

The Muslims were confused; they murmured angrily. They were caught off guard over my boldness. No one moved. I issued the same challenge a second and third time. "Bring me a sick person. Why am I so bold? I challenge you today. If my God doesn't heal the first one here, everything I have preached is not true."

Finally, three people came forward. One blind, one crippled, and one deaf. As the Lord sovereignly performed these miracles, my team all breathed a big sigh of relief. (Oh ye of little faith!) The heavens opened; there was a shift in the Spirit. We were shaken to the core and spoke the word of God with boldness. Our team prayed for over an hour for many others to be saved and healed. In this city we preached to over 210,000 in five days.

A NEW KIND OF POWER EVANGELISM
SOUTH KOREA—AUGUST 8-30, 2002

After training, equipping, and teaching on the prophetic, how to hear God's voice, and prophecy we released over 1,000 Koreans to prophesy over one another for over thirty minutes. I said, "If it can work in the church, why not in the market?" "For you can all prophesy one by one, that all may learn and all may be encouraged" (1 Cor. 14:30-31).

Hundreds converged on the food courts at the mall. We hung up a sign that advertised "Free Spiritual Readings" and set up six tables, with two people and a translator at each. We gave prophetic words over the lost for two hours, while hundreds of others went throughout the mall praying and gathering more unbelievers. There were 174 souls saved in two hours. Several of them were Buddhists.

The prophetic anointing carries in it the power to convict, convince, and reveal. Even if the word is "Jesus loves you!" delivered under the Spirit of prophecy, it reveals God. Hearing God is as easy as Psalm 139:17-18: "How precious also are Your thoughts to me, O God! How great is the sum of them! If I should count them, they would be more in number than the sand."

All you have to do is ask God for one of His thoughts for a person. You may just have a mental picture. Sometimes you may not understand what God is showing you, but the person will.

Most times, we cannot operate in the gifts of the Spirit in the marketplace because we turn it off outside the four walls of the church. We need an increased prophetic awareness. Let's start asking God for words in unusual places, especially restaurants.

God wants us to make ourselves available to Him. It's time for the Samaritan Well anointing. In John 4:5-42 Jesus shared a word of knowledge with a Gentile woman about her many husbands and her response was, "Come, see a Man who told me all things that I ever did. Could this be the Christ? Then they went out of the city and came to Him." The whole city came because one woman received a word from God.

POWER EVANGELISM STRATEGIES

Christians need to invade the world with God's power. We need to try prophetic, dream interpretation, or "free prayer" booths in flea markets, malls, coffee shops, or juice bars. God is going to anoint street preaching again, like in the old-time revivals. Servant evangelism is powerful too—acts of love carry power!

God can use anybody. I was teaching on prophetic evangelism once and a business man and his wife decided to make themselves available, gather some prophetic people, and go to the market for ten days. They set up a booth offering "Free Spiritual Readings." After each prophetic word they offered salvation and 650 souls came to Jesus. Its time to take it to the markets— that's where Jesus had some of his greatest miracles and healings.

OVER 5,575 PEOPLE COME TO JESUS
PERU AND ECUADOR—OCTOBER 2-11, 2002

Most of the 24 team members who accompanied us on this trip had never been overseas or seen the type of miracles that they witnessed. One pastor from the Midwest said, "I saw more genuine miracles than expected; when one says the word 'miracle' it can be used pretty loosely."

There were over 80 deaf mutes healed and some 20 cases of blindness, over 40 lame and crippled healed, tumors and more. There was deliverance from demons, and the sick on beds and mats were carried into the stadium. There were sick people everywhere carried in from hospitals with the nursing staff, and the IV still in their arms. Hundreds of crippled bodies, sick children with deformed heads, exposed sores, growths, and wheelchairs covered the crusade grounds each night in both Ecuador and Peru.

The crusades, held in two sports stadiums, were put together over a six-month period by hundreds of volunteers, more than 600 pastors, over 500 counselors, and several full-time coordinators. As always, our partners and intercessors made this crusade a success— their prayers and financial support helped us reach over 45,000 people in the crusades alone.

Headline news footage of the event was on the number one rated TV show, "Video Control" in Ecuador. During the interview on the show, the host returned to God after being backslidden for two years. He even added to the interview, preached, and gave a prayer for salvation. This TV show is like "Much Music" in Canada and "MTV" in the U.S.A. that reaches mostly teens and people in their early twenties.

Crusade and Team Highlights

The first day in Lima, Peru the FFM team went into the local prison. Most of the prisoners had committed rapes and murder and were young men in their early twenties. Over 20 souls were saved. One couple on our team, unknown to us at the time, was told by a guard they'd not get out alive unless they paid about $50. Of course, when we found out the ministry reimbursed them!

The first night at the crusade grounds was a little overwhelming for some on the team. The platform was set up in the middle of a housing neighborhood and there was traffic all around, a few thousand gathered on the grounds and the sick were everywhere. The team didn't know they would step nightly into the masses to pray for thousands. Demons threw people on the ground. One woman wailed, kicked, and screamed through her deliverance and another, after two days of manifestations, coughed hers out. A teenage boy paralyzed from the waist down from a car accident was healed on the spot as I called out a word of knowledge.

What really undid the FFM team was the outreach to the hospitals. When they prayed for one, hundreds of others would crowd around for prayer. There were nights they pushed and pulled at our clothes by the hundreds and it was necessary to push our way out of the service or back to the platform.

The people were so hungry and desperate each night. Some live on only a hundred dollars a month and are sick and crippled with no means of medical assistance. Relatives were weeping as their loved one on a stretcher was prayed for or cried tears of joy when cancer was healed.

One night a dying woman was carried into a crusade service on her hospital bed. She received prayer, sat up, and said, "The pain is leaving my body and the fluid in my lungs just emptied." Her breathing was restored and strength began to return to her body. The daughter pressed through the crowd with tears in her eyes and helped her mom try to stand up out of the hospital bed.

I remember the first night of the crusade in Chicayo, Peru, I saw Jesus in a vision step into the cripple section. When I prayed for mass healing, instantly six or seven, who could not walk, walked for the first time in years. Jesus did it! We took crutches, walkers, and canes up on the platform when we could each night and waved them in the air in the devil's face. "Jesus is the same today, yesterday, and forever." God used the team and they saw blind eyes and deaf ears open almost every night. We encouraged them to keep a nightly journal and e-mail what they could of how God used them. My heart is to impart, train, and see others do the ministry of Jesus.

One other favorite miracle was of a mother and her seven or eight-year-old daughter—both had tumors in their bodies. During the mass prayer from the platform, where hundreds of healings happened, with no hands laid on them, she and her daughter were both healed when they felt fire go through their bodies.

Some nights there would be twenty deaf mutes healed in a service. Sometimes Jesus touched them in the crowd, other times we would pray for them on the platform. I can still remember the precious children saying "hello" or "mama" for the first time. I'm just about to weep writing about it now.

In the final service after I preached, "What kind of Jesus do you have?" over 1,400 responded to the altar call. The last night together the team shared how excited they were to bring this fire back to their churches and that their faith level was increased to believe all things are possible. Others are already praying about how they can come to India or one of our upcoming missions trips.

Hundreds were saved each night. On one other occasion over 1,300 responded to the Gospel call. We saw over 5,575 souls saved and many more than this healed. The Holy Spirit still confirms the Gospel with signs and wonders!

JINGA, UGANDA—NOVEMBER 2002

Even though it had been sunny all day, the first evening of the crusade, at 3:45 a dark black cloud poured rain. We'd been expecting 50,000 people that evening. Only 8,000 showed up and when I gave an altar call, only 76 got saved. I was discouraged, and I was feeling discouraged for the team we'd brought.

Early the next morning the team prayed and the skies were blue. That afternoon when we got to the crusade at 3:45 the clouds rolled in and it rained. The attendance was about the same as the night before. Usually we can expect growth of 10,000 each night. That evening during the altar call 100 got saved, and the Lord did bless us with some creative miracles.

I don't remember doing a mass crusade with only 176 people saved in two nights. I was used to seeing that many saved in the open-air markets. I wondered if this was the kind of witchcraft

I'd faced in Uganda two years before, when a witch doctor chanted on the other side of the river. Those practicing witchcraft have power over the weather and accidents.

That night at the crusade we had several amazing miracles. During the mass prayer I said, "If you're being healed come to the altar." The first miracle testimony was a man who had had a massive growth over his male extremities. This affected his relationship with his wife, and she was getting ready to leave him. During the prayer his tumor shrank. He was ecstatic. The next miracle was a woman who had visible breast cancer—skin and tissue had eaten away the breast. She was totally healed; a new layer of skin appeared. The third miracle was a woman who had breast cancer for three years and had tried all avenues to get healed—multiple trips to witch doctors and soothsayers. Many people in Africa go to witch doctors like we go to doctors. Finally, after trying everything, they surgically removed her breast. She was known as "the woman with one breast." This woman had a new breast grow out during the mass prayer!

"Holy Spirit, why are you healing all these reproductive organs?" I asked. "I want to open the womb of the church," responded the Spirit, "and begin healing its reproductive function and the breasts that nurture. It was a sign of the birth of the coming harvest."

The next day the skies were blue. The Holy Spirit told me, "Fast today for the Spirit of Elijah so you can overcome the spirit of witchcraft working against the crusade." I fasted all day and at 3:45 P.M. the sky was still clear. At the crusade, the crowds swelled to 20,000 or 25,000. When I arrived at the crusade grounds at 5:15, I thought I'd gotten the breakthrough: "Praise God, we've made it."

All the talk of the town during the day had been, "Let's go see the power the white man possesses that even breasts grow in the meetings." Soothsayers and witch doctors were there because of the creative miracles. The Holy Spirit had told me to give an altar call for witch doctors, anyone who had practiced it or come under the power of its curse.

When I got on the stage at 5:30 P.M., I grabbed the microphone and it started raining on me. Thousands of people ran for the exits. It was pandemonium. I said, "Today in prayer the Holy Spirit told me He wants to break the power of witchcraft. If you're a witch doctor, a soothsayer or practice witchcraft or come under the power of witchcraft come to the altars now." Eighteen hundred people responded.

I prayed for the Holy Spirit to come and rebuked the power of witchcraft, "Devil let go of the people now in Jesus' name." Nothing happened. I just went after it again. I said, "In the name of Jesus, power of witchcraft let the people go." Nothing happened. I prayed the third time. "I command every devil of witchcraft and sorcery to let go of the people now in Jesus' name. In that moment it was like something snapped in the Spirit. Hundreds were thrown to the ground in one swoop. There were violent demonic manifestations—foaming at the mouth, vomiting, writhing, contorting, rolling and slithering in the mud—but simultaneously, in the heavens above, the rain cloud split in two and rolled away.

The sky became blue and there was a double rainbow. Hundreds were being delivered. The ministry teams were throwing people up on the muddy platform. I could barely move. Team members were running everywhere; three hundred were carried into the deliverance tent, and our Ugandan team ministered to them. The rest lay on the grass down front where they experienced sovereign deliverance.

Then the testimonies came. A woman paralyzed in the neck and one paralyzed from the waist down were healed; several people also testified of being healed of insanity and madness. We went on to great victory. For the next few days the skies were clear and the crowds swelled to 60,000. About 34,000 people made life commitments to Christ during our ministry in Uganda. Truly, the Lord had revealed Himself to us as healer, deliverer, and mighty warrior.

BOMBAY, INDIA—DECEMBER 2002
Report by Pastor BB Rail, Fairfield, Iowa

Millions of gods occupy the hearts of the people of India; hence India itself has many faces. Multitudes of people, pressed together, overcrowd the streets and marketplaces. Hoards of vehicles dart unpredictably from the left to the right side of the road. Small black and yellow taxis aggressively swarm like bumblebees through bumper-to-bumper traffic. Everyone honks in agreement with the sign on all the trucks: "Horn OK Please." Pedestrians appear to be fair game.

The local authorities did not allow the word "miracles" to be used in advertising the services. Instead, colorful flyers invited people to come to a "Jesus Festival," and experience the peace and love of the Christmas Season. Christmas trees, tinsel, ornaments, even frosty the snowman, did not distract us from focusing on the harvest!

God immediately revealed His nature as "the Lord who heals you" in the very first service by causing tumors, growths and cysts to instantly dissolve. The conservative crowd, predominantly Roman Catholic and Hindu, stood in amazement and grew each night as God faithfully confirmed His healing Word with accompanying signs and wonders. Armed guards became so overwhelmed seeing the miracles, many requested prayer and some were born again! Faith among the people rose to such a high level that on the last night a young girl, paralyzed from polio, spontaneously began walking. Everyone cheered as we all watched her "staggering run" through the crowd!

The people are unbelievably kind, grateful, and humble. Many of the ladies who had been healed were so thankful they began bowing down and wanted to kiss my feet. We made sure they understood Jesus alone was their Healer and to worship only Him!

A final highlight before leaving Bombay was a visit to St. Lawrence's private school. They gave us VIP hospitality. The students were captivated by Todd's personal testimony and allowed us to pray for each one of them. Approximately 1000 were born again that morning, bringing our harvest total to 4,525 as we departed for Goa.

GOA, INDIA—DECEMBER 2002

Our arrival in Goa, India was like stepping into another world. We were met at the airport with flower leis, fresh coconut milk, and a group of students playing Christmas songs. Were we really still in India? Clear air, white beaches, and tropical landscapes dotted with plantation type homes.

Expectations were high as we headed off to the "festival" grounds. God did not disappoint us. Once again, as He demonstrated His power over sin and sickness, the crowds doubled each night! The Lord had put in my heart that the Church was like the lame man outside the gate named Beautiful. Just as that man received a miracle, the Church would be filled with the power of God and rise up. Many cripples received healing that night; it was as though Goa would be the Gateway for God's healing revival!

As in Bombay, many blind, deaf and dumb were healed. There was such an explosion of joy the musicians could not hold back from playing. With each healing report, the music would explode and everyone would begin shouting and dancing before the Lord. Fortunately, the platform was of solid construction. The hunger of the crowd for salvation and prayer was of such a magnitude, the people all but trampled on another to come towards the front. Desperate for Jesus, unlike anything we see in North America. Meetings for pastors and leaders were held during the day. Todd gave me one of the morning sessions in which I shared my healing testimony, and the Lord healed many backs. It is quite difficult to adequately report all the wondrous events that we witnessed.

We left India with a conservative count of ministering to a total of 16,450 persons, of which 10, 825 were born again and placed in Churches. One hundred and 39 deaf and dumb were healed, 11 blind eyes opened and 8 cripples began to walk. A medical doctor on the platform verified all healing.

After ministering in Goa, India, I awoke at 2 A.M.—a demon, fourteen feet tall, manifesting as a menacing black shadow stood at the end of my bed. Chills went through my body. The whole hotel room was dark, but the demon was even darker than the night. The room had turned chilly. I yelled, "In the name of Jesus, devil, go." After I blurted out this command, the spirit left my room.

I found out later that the spirit went to the room of three other staff members and tried to take their lives. My dad was struck blind: "I was bumping into dressers. I couldn't find the phone; I panicked, my heart started fluttering. I'd only been saved about 14 months. I really thought I was going to die, but after several minutes it left."

It went to the room of my mission director, John Macgirvin. The shadow passed his door three times and then came in. "I felt like I was drowning in fluid in my lungs. I tried to pound on the wall to get Dave's attention, but I couldn't. I couldn't even breathe. I finally staggered to the bathroom and expelled some clear liquid. I couldn't speak; I could only rebuke it in my mind."

Jim Drown, my South American coordinator also felt the dark presence enter his room.

Here's another India report from a former doubting Thomas:

OVER 10,825 SOULS SAVED/ 139 DEAF HEALED—DECEMBER 8-19, 2002
Pastor Ken Greter, Abbotsford City Fellowship, BC, Canada

A team of seven from the USA and Canada embarked on a trip of a lifetime to Southern India December 8-19, 2002. This was undoubtedly the most profound evangelistic crusade I ever had the privilege of being part of. Quite frankly, my heart was somewhat skeptical regarding the testimonies I had heard from Fresh Fire team members involving miracles that were just like in Bible days. Well I am here to testify that with my very own eyes I saw the most amazing miracles, signs, and wonders in India. I turned from a "doubting Thomas" to an "authentic, Holy Ghost, Bible-believing believer!"

In all of my 22 plus years in pastoring, my Christian walk has never been so shaken to the core like it has been as a result of this crusade. I believe that every pastor needs to experience for himself the same miracles Jesus performed while on the earth. Jesus truly is the same yesterday, today, and forever! I can hardly wait to go on the next overseas crusade, where souls will be saved, pastors and leaders will be encouraged during the teaching sessions, and numerous signs and wonders will take place!

CHAPTER 19

JESUS—THE SAME YESTERDAY, TODAY, AND FOREVER

GOMA, DEMOCRATIC REPUBLIC OF CONGO
CONGO REPORT 1—MARCH 1-10, 2003

I had never been so overwhelmed. We had just arrived in the city of Goma, Democratic Republic of Congo, a border town of about 500,000 on the Rwanda border. In 2001, a volcanic disaster destroyed or damaged more than 50 percent of the entire city. Volcanic rock and ash some ten feet high buried and crushed churches, schools, homes, and businesses. The twisted metal wreckage of half-buried vehicles sticks out from the hardened lava. Hundreds died and tens of thousands are still homeless.

One young woman shared her story of how her father, who is a pastor, cannot enter Congo to be home with his family. The rebel government calls him an exile. Her home was half destroyed in the volcano and she had taken fifty other people into her home because their homes were completely destroyed. They had nowhere to live and nothing to eat.

Another story I will never forget is, how 75-100 Christians gathered into a Catholic church when the volcano first erupted, to pray for God to have mercy. They were all buried alive in the church.

People there were totally desperate. After years of civil war, the country split into three pieces. A natural disaster destroyed what was already desperate lives coping with hunger and third world conditions. Thousands of children were without education. They could not even afford the five dollars a month for school, and thousands more were without the basic school supplies for an education.

As we crossed the Rwanda/Congo border we were welcomed with a band and Jesus parade. As we traveled through the ruined city, in the midst of volcanic boulders, ash, and destruction, the city came to an abrupt halt with traffic jams and shouting and dancing in the streets. Jesus had arrived! I knew in my heart that God would give Goma beauty for ashes and the oil of joy for mourning. Isaiah 61:4 says, "and they shall rebuild the old ruins, they shall rise up the former desolations, and they shall repair the ruined cities, the desolations of many generations."

Since the devastation in 2001, promise after promise of humanitarian aid and relief efforts have been pledged. However, the people have seen very little relief. I was asked to meet with the president of this region of Congo and pray. There were three governments and they tried to sign a peace process and build one unified government. Fresh Fire Ministries said, "We will help." Even today we will take food to 2,500 families in a refugee camp for those left homeless after the volcanic eruption.

There were more than 12,000 people hungry and living in conditions so inhumane that our animals live better. I saw homes that were nothing more than plastic tarps, sticks, and mud. We told the president that Fresh Fire desired to build an orphanage, put roofs on churches, feed the poor, and send a 40-foot container of cranberries and school supplies for the children.

Shonnah, the FFM team of 16, and I were broken, so overwhelmed with the needs that we were speechless. I was so impacted that for a week after I would break down and cry. I have never wept so much. I am weeping even now.

As our team and seven truck loads of food made our way toward the refugee camp, the children ran to the roads with their buckets in their hands or whatever they could find to hold food. It was heard among the hungry crowd, "We aren't going to get the food and eat tonight even though we see the trucks of food!" Corrupt pastors and thieves have taken the food from the people so many times before, that these people wept saying, "Will we really eat?" We distributed the food to all the families. James 1:27, "Pure and undefiled religion before God and the Father is this: to visit orphans and widows in their trouble, and to keep oneself unspotted from the world."

Years of civil war and the Rwanda genocide of the '90s has left thousands of children without families. Many lost their homes and families in the volcanic disaster of 2001; thousands more are without education, and even in some desperate cases, food.

Jane's Orphanage

Shonnah, the team, and I were taken to an orphanage. A woman, Jane, and her husband, have such a heart for theses children to feed them, clothe them, and house them. She had opened up her home to receive the children even though she received no assistance from the government. They house about 125 children and 325 children are expected to eat there. The facilities are terrible; the boys sleep in no more than what I would call a rented old barn, without windows or insulation. The beds are so full; they sleep sometimes eight to a bed. I saw faces of these children broken and many maimed from the civil war. I saw children with scars across their foreheads hacked open by machetes and children without hands, arms, or fingers.

I said, "How do we feed these people?" And the woman replied, "There are times when we can't even get food from the city to this rural area. One, the roads are buried in molten rock, and two, we have no truck to transport food."

The kitchen was nothing more than a 6' x 6' shed with a huge cooking cauldron and the firewood stacked in the corner. As I walked through the orphanage, I saw no toys, and when we brought out biscuits, the children were so desperate; they stepped on, pushed, and screamed at each other.

That day, Fresh Fire bought one truckload of corn, rice, beans; a three-week supply. There is no government aid, no ministry support, nothing. We need to do more. Fresh Fire Ministries has committed to building new orphanage facilities and to provide food for the orphans.

God has given us tremendous opportunity in Congo. We were asked to meet and pray with the general of the entire rebel army. There are more than 80,000 soldiers. They asked us to train evangelists in the military so they could better evangelize the army. They also asked us to build a church on the military base.

FFM opened a pilot office in Goma and took staff from the Ugandan office to work with the government in Congo. The advisor to the president, a born again spirit-filled Colonel, aids and administrates leadership of each project.

CONGO REPORT 2

The First Miracle Crusade Night

A small Fresh Fire team of 17 drove four hours through Rwanda over the border to Congo. This would be another life-changing experience for both the staff, and those who had never been a part of a mission's team in Africa.

It was hot; the air in the city was still filled with volcanic poison and pollution. The poverty and desperation here was the worst that I have seen yet in any country in Africa. Over 200 churches worked together with our Fresh Fire Ministries crusade team based in Uganda to host this five-night miracle campaign. The first evening, a small group of 20-25 thousand people gathered, Baptists, Anglicans, Pentecostals, revival churches, Protestants, and unbelievers came to hear the word and to be healed.

The Crowd Grows, Miracles and Healings Begin

Over the next five days the crowd swelled to over 60,000. Each night thousands were saved, each day people would testify to being healed the evening before while listening on radio.

Each night the crusade was broadcast live to those living in Congo, and parts of Rwanda. One night I asked how many people here tonight got saved via the radio message at home the previous night, and a hundred plus hands went up. Each night, there were healings, miracles, and even signs and wonders in the heavens above. The first evening a deaf school of thirty-two students lined up on the platform, each was prayed for and 26 deaf and mute heard and spoke in that one wave.

Disrupted by Witch Doctors

After two days of breakthrough, the third evening I noticed the crowd had dropped by several thousand. There was a report in the city that day that during the third evening of the crusade local witch doctors had planned a violent confrontation.

Then the rains came and during that meeting once again we offered fervent intercession and petitions up before God. "God break the power of witchcraft, we rebuke the rains, and pray for heaven to open." In that instant not only did the rain cease, but the temperature of the wind changed.

Six or seven people were cast to the ground simultaneously under demonic influence, each one was carried onto the platform, devils were cast out in Jesus' name, some screamed, shook, and even spewed spit from the mouth, we believe that these ones were sent by the witch doctor to disrupt the meetings.

The Crowd Grows Again

The next day the crowd swelled and the report of the local Congolese was "we saw with our own eyes, they broke the power of the witch doctor."

Each night the Fresh Fire Ministries team would wade their way out into thousands who had made their way forward for prayer. When the miracles broke loose, a press of people ran up to the front. People were grabbing, pushing, and shouting. A Fresh Fire security detail, a gift of troops from the president himself, had to break up several fights.

Each night the Fresh Fire Ministries team, even ones that have never prayed for the sick, shared testimonies of the deaf that heard, and the blind that saw. When the team would return to the hotel, they would share testimony of what took place that evening. Two nights the team agreed that it was as if every single person they prayed for was healed. Each night there were testimonies of tumors healed, various pain, sickness, TB, and paralysis healed.

Cripples Are Healed

One night two cripples were placed on the platform, one boy whose legs were twisted from birth, received prayer. My wife heard the Lord whisper to her, "Pick him up." His legs straightened and he began to walk! Within moments the crowd screamed and cheered again as the second cripple stood and walked twice across the platform.

Sunday morning each team member was given an opportunity to preach in their own church service. Each team member shared testimonies of healings in their service and testimonies of salvation. One pastor, during the Sunday evening crusade service, testified, "I now know this anointing is not just upon Todd Bentley, it is a transferable, tangible healing anointing."

When my dad and John Macgirvin, the Mission's Coordinator, preached at a church on Sunday, they prayed for one cripple, his legs straightened out, and he danced around the church. Dave gave several words of knowledge, even calling out first and last African names! Whew!

The Pastors' Conference

The pastors' conference, consisting of 1,500 to 2,000 pastors, leaders, evangelists, and ministry workers, gathered each day. Each service built until the anointing service took place, teaching on soaking, the healing anointing, spirit of revival, holiness, and repentance. In one service Pastor Ken, Mission's Director, gave an altar call to repent of sexual sin, and more than half of the people came forward to get their life right with God. In the final service, 1,800 leaders stood shoulder to shoulder in the hot sun in a line one mile long winding down the streets of the city to receive a fresh touch from God.

REVIVAL IN THE LAND
CONGO REPORT 3
by Pastor Ken Greter, Abbotsford City Fellowship

"The Spirit of the Sovereign Lord is on us, because the Lord has anointed us to...bestow on [Goma] a crown of beauty instead of ashes" (see Isaiah 61:1,3b, emphasis added).

As I sit here, I wonder if it's really possible to give an accurate description of the devastation that we saw while in Goma, a city of about 450,000 situated near the Rwanda border. This city was once a tourist hot spot for people from all over the world, but due to a massive volcanic explosion that occurred over a year ago, Goma now lies in ashes.

For approximately three days during the eruption of Mount Nyirracongo, tons and tons of volcanic lava spread like a black blanket covering a huge section of the city and brought it to an absolute stand still. Gerald Mwebe, our African coordinator, wept when he first came into the city to prepare for the Fresh Fire crusade. I now have a bit of an understanding how Nehemiah felt when he was told the wall of Jerusalem was broken down and that the gates were burned.

The evidence of destruction brought about by this volcanic eruption could still be seen everywhere. Entire downtown sections were completely wiped out; twenty-foot steel telephone poles were partially immersed in six feet of hardened lava rock; churches, homes and schools were completely demolished. Understandably, because of the magnitude of this catastrophic event, thousands and thousands of people were left homeless, and many, even to this day, are living in some of the most deplorable conditions imaginable.

Todd and Shonnah knew that the Holy Spirit had brought them to Goma for such a time as this and the entire Fresh Fire Ministry's team, consisting of 17 from US and Canada, were ready to roll up their sleeves and begin the long process of restoring beauty from the ashes of total devastation.

Due to the physical, economical, and psychological impact of the recent civil war and continuing tensions, Congolese pastors and Christian leaders were in desperate need for encouragement.

We arrived in Goma, Congo on March 3rd. Multitudes of people greeted our arrival with cheering, whistling, and singing. We were escorted through the downtown with a first-class parade and then rushed into a building where the media was waiting to interview Todd.

Right from the start, Todd and Shonnah wanted to visit some of the most devastated areas and help out in humanitarian efforts. Contacts were made immediately and in short order truckloads of food items were purchased, filled, and ready for distribution. The Congolese pastors took us to a camp of 12,000 displaced individuals living in conditions that the average American would consider inadequate even for animals.

We formed a convoy consisting of pastors, military personnel, and the media, with seven trucks loaded with beans, corn, soap, and other necessary staples. Upon arrival, children everywhere were shouting and raising their hands, ecstatic that the trucks had finally arrived to fill their empty tummies. The interpreters were telling us that the kids were screaming, "Now we don't have to go hungry anymore."

Enough food was given to this camp to feed them all for approximately two months. If there was ever a time that I've seen the fulfillment of James 1:27—"Pure and undefiled religion (is) to visit orphans and widows in their trouble..." this was the day.

During the week Todd and Shonnah were inundated with interviews with governors, colonels, presidents, and pastors. Talk about favor! In most places we went, there was total security protection guaranteed; what a relief this was as tensions between governments and the different military factions were still at an all time high.

The morning meetings were scheduled for pastors and Christian leaders, with over 2,000 registered for the sessions. After some initial resistance, one morning Todd delivered a message with great fervor entitled, "The Fear of God, The Ministry to the Poor, and God's Mercy." The pastors were riveted to their seats, their hearts were deeply touched, and the place was blown wide open. We concluded the final morning by lining up all of the registrants outside the church building to receive Holy Ghost impartation from Todd and the Fresh Fire Ministry staff.

On the first evening of the crusade we saw crowds of up to 25,000 eager to hear "the man of God from Canada" share about his past background. A bizarre and humorous rumor that circulated for a short time was that Todd was a professional wrestler. Many of the team got a kick out of this and for a while Todd was subjected to some good-natured ribbing.

As is common in many cities in Africa, the people are steeped in magic and witchcraft is widely practiced. The city of Goma was no exception. Word reached us through the interpreters that the "man of God from Canada" was a challenge to the witch doctors and that a war was brewing.

Apparently, the witch doctors were trying to shut down the meetings by sending out curses and by subtly planting some of their cohorts in the crowds. For a brief time it appeared that they were succeeding as rains fell on two different nights, causing somewhat of a damper on the attendance. But glory to God, during the Saturday evening crusade, Todd began to operate under what

I call a "breaker anointing" and after the altar call was given, hundreds responded. It was then that Todd went after the spirits of witchcraft and oppression.

We were now in the pouring rain, which had held off until after the altar call. Next, five women, tormented by demons, were carried onto the platform where their bodies twisted and contorted in a manner not possible for a normal person. Oh thank God for the Blood of Jesus! One by one their bodies and minds were set free from the demonic strongholds, and they were gloriously filled with the Holy Spirit. We found out that these witches had hid in the crowd every night. However, the Holy Spirit exposed and set them free. Truly this was like an "Elijah and the prophets of Baal" confrontation.

The final evening of the crusade was a surprise to everyone. The pastors estimated that between 60,000 and 70,000 people crammed into the soccer stadium ready to hear the Word of God. As a result of these five nights of crusades, over 15,000 souls came to Jesus. This figure did not include those making decisions for Christ as a result of radio broadcasts. An awesome harvest! Also, hundreds received the baptism of the Holy Spirit, the lame began to walk and the blind received their sight.

On Sunday morning many of the team members preached in the churches, and reports came back to us once again of numerous salvations and healings. One Fresh Fire team that preached in a Methodist church was able to pray for the pastor and his wife; this couple was gloriously baptized in the Holy Spirit!

Revival Among the Pygmies

One highlight of these meetings was when a group of tribal Pygmies walked 60 kilometers from the jungle to attend the crusade, dance for the team, and bring gifts. These four feet tall, full-grown adults are considered to be the lowest of the low in their society and, in fact, there is even a common belief among some Africans that the Pygmies don't even have souls. We've heard reports of recent inhumane acts against these people including murder and even cannibalism.

One African woman has been so touched by God's love for these people that she provides them with food and disciples them. She is called 'Mother Mary' by the Pygmy tribes she has adopted. Mother Mary has been spreading the Gospel for several years to this people group, traveling as many as 50 kilometers one way to reach their villages with the Gospel of Jesus Christ.

The Pygmies live in the jungle and by faith, they sometimes survive days at times without food. Their testimonies of God's miraculous power of provision are right out of the Bible. Here's one example: once they were out of food for eight days and the Lord instructed them to eat dirt. As they did, it had the taste of corn and beans in their mouths.

When they arrived at our hotel, they sang a special song to us called "Jesus is My Winner-Man." These people had more heart, soul, and fire as they danced and praised the Lord, than just about everyone else. At the conclusion of their song, Jim Drown invited them to pray for the Fresh Fire team. There was not a dry eye among us as these precious Pygmies laid hands on each Fresh Fire participant blessing us with the power of the Holy Spirit. The other Africans at the hotel were shocked that we would even allow the Pygmies to touch us.

Up to this point, Mother Mary has led more than 900 of these Pygmies to Jesus, and she believes that this is just the beginning of what God wants to do among the Pygmy people. Hallelujah! People from every tribe, tongue, and nation will be found in the Kingdom of Jesus Christ.

Miracles in the Open-Air Market in Rwanda

We were all deeply impacted during the last leg of the journey as we left Goma and came into Kigali, Rwanda. Todd spontaneously decided to have an open-air crusade in a busy section of the city. We connected with one of the local churches in Kigali, and after a sound system and speakers were set up, Todd blasted away with his testimony. In no time at all, hundreds began to crowd in to hear Todd's story about how Jesus set him free from drugs and a wild lifestyle, and when the altar call was given, dozens came forward to receive Jesus. Miracles began to take place all around us as the Fresh Fire team prayed for people in the crowd.

The harvest was so ripe; it was like the fish were literally flying into the boat. Altogether, between the cities of Goma and Kigali, we recorded 15,277 souls coming into the Kingdom of God. What we experienced in this open-air market was just the first fruits of a much bigger harvest that Fresh Fire believes to reap as we go back in September 2003 to hold a crusade in Kigali, Rwanda and Kisingani, Congo.

Remembering the Poor

Last but not least, Todd and Shonnah along with the Fresh Fire team were taken to a very special place that brought tears to everyone's eyes. An African lady by the name of Jane, along with her husband, both ex-government employees, have answered an amazing call to feed and disciple 125 orphans, permanently residing in some makeshift shelters (how's that for a contradiction in terms?). As many as 200 more orphans are fed daily by their ministry, with no government aid. As many as six to eight children sleep in one bed.

I had never seen so many children with hands and fingers chopped off by machetes. Huge scars could be seen on dozens of children criss-crossing their faces and bodies. These children are the victims of a brutal civil war in which over a million people were killed. Shonnah was overwhelmed and in tears—totally speechless. She absolutely fell in love with this couple and with the orphans.

We thank God that we were able to quickly gather together a small truckload of food and goods for this precious orphanage. Todd pledged in his heart to go back to the Fresh Fire partners in US and Canada, and to share the vision of providing another building for this orphanage and to assist in the establishment of a regular feeding program. Todd also felt impressed by the Holy Spirit to raise funds in order to put some roofs on some of the churches in Goma, and to build a school in order to facilitate the education of underprivileged children. Plans have already begun in conjunction with other ministries to send a 40-foot container loaded with cranberry sauce, and school supplies to help with the children's education and physical well-being. What a massive project! We serve a mighty big God!

Many of the Fresh Fire team members shared with us that they had never experienced miracles of this caliber in their entire Christian life. It was almost as if we were living 'smack-dab' in the middle of the Book of Acts. Who says God doesn't perform miracles today? Jesus is the same yesterday, today, and forever. If you need convincing, plan to come on a trip with Todd and Shonnah for a future crusade and watch and see with your very own eyes. To God be the glory!

GREATER BATTLES, GREATER VICTORIES
LILONGWE, MALAWI, JUNE 4-7, 2003

"For dominion belongs to the Lord and he rules over the nations" (Psalm 22:28 NIV).

This was one of the most amazing mission trips I have ever experienced, as over 90 people from Canada, USA, South Africa, Austria, and Australia joined with Shonnah and me to feed the poor and to live out Matthew 10:8, "Heal the sick, raise the dead, cleanse the lepers, drive out demons."

I knew that this long awaited Malawi crusade was going to "go over the top," because of the constant opposition before we arrived. Just days before the crusade was to begin, Gerald Mwebe, our African Coordinator, sent an urgent request telling us that the Malawian health department would deny Canadian entry into their country because of the fear of SARS (Severe Acute Respiratory Syndrome). However, we praise God because Gerald was able to convince them that if we would get a medical check-up indicating negativity to SARS, we could come. All 24 Canadians scrambled and were able to get these reports just in time. Other complications among team members included stolen laptops, accidents, stolen vehicles, and delayed flights.

It was only later on in the crusade that we learned from a local pastor that this region is a paradise for witchcraft and that most North American evangelists go to Blantyre, a neighboring large city where the churches are much bigger and the crusades larger. Having 2,500 in our evening crusade would be considered a great success.

The opening night about 2,500 attended. The local pastors were very encouraged by the turnout as they repeatedly told us that Lilongwe was a preacher's graveyard. Approximately

500 responded to the altar call. I knew in my spirit we needed a breakthrough, so I invited all team members to fast over the next few days.

The second night of the crusade the attendance was higher. Before preaching, the Holy Spirit told me to call forward those who had made blood covenants to witch doctors. Over 400 responded to the call. In addition, hundreds of children received the baptism in the Holy Spirit, with the evidence of speaking in tongues. Children could literally be seen all over the crusade grounds, totally intoxicated with the wine of the Spirit. That night there were over 1,000 salvations recorded.

These Signs Shall Follow Them That Believe

It was an honor for Fresh Fire Ministries to partner with Rolland and Heidi Baker of Iris Ministries on this trip. We engaged in the largest feeding program either ministry has ever attempted. The Holy Spirit has given Iris Ministries tremendous favor in the nation of Mozambique and the surrounding countries in Africa. Through the generous contributions from those who have given toward the Malawi Outreach and Humanitarian program, FFM was able to donate a 2003 flatbed large truck to Rolland and Heidi's ministry. This truck was put to constant use while we were in Malawi, including hauling generators and sound systems for the open-air market meetings, carrying local worship teams around, and as a pulpit for preaching.

The Lord promised a great harvest if we would preach the Gospel and feed the poor in Malawi. This nation was just coming out of a severe famine due to drought during the last couple of years. The 90 members of our group were divided into eight teams. Every day they fed the poor and preached the Gospel. Even after the first day of the outreaches, team captains came back ecstatic with reports of the blind seeing, the crippled walking, the deaf hearing, and the sick recovering.

Every day, teams were sent out to local villages, hospitals, and other remote areas, where miracles and healings took place, and where thousands upon thousands of bags of maize and beans were distributed to the poor. At the hospitals we distributed the maize and beans to everyone, including the patients, who are required to provide their own food during their stays. The main building at one hospital had four floors, and of course no elevator. Thanks to our huge team of ninety, we were able to form a line winding all the way up the staircase and pass bags to the top floors.

In many cases, food was given to the local leaders of the camps or village in order to ensure everyone received their fair portions. In fact, in a number of situations, potential riots began to brew during the feeding process, forcing us to solicit the efforts of the local Malawian police authorities for assistance.

There are few things in the world that are more satisfying than having the privilege of providing precious souls with both the natural and the spiritual Bread of Life. We were excited to be able to feed hundreds of Muslims as well and were able to plant the seed of the Gospel into their hearts.

On one of the morning outreaches, as the Gospel message was preached and the salvation invitation was given, thirty village chiefs came forward to accept Jesus. Another 500 from the crowd responded. Revival had come to the land.

At every crusade that I host, I encourage the locals to bring the dead, so we can pray for a resurrection. During one hospital outreach, a handful of team members sneaked into the holding room of the morgue. Although there was no resurrection, I know many more opportunities will be waiting in the future, and yes, the dead will be raised in Jesus' name.

A Young Girl Healed of Polio

A young girl stricken with polio received Jesus into her heart, and immediately burst into a big smile. When a team member prayed for her, she felt the power of God hit her body and experienced circulation for the first time in two years. What an awesome sight as she left the hospital totally healed, carrying bagged food on top of her head that had been donated by FFM partners.

Refugee Camp Hears the Gospel

Dzaleka, is a refuge camp of 20,000 people who have fled civil wars and other catastrophes in their homelands—Somalia, Burundi, Congo, Rwanda and Malawi. After preaching, hundreds of children were born again. However, many adults in the crowd were very skeptical. By the unction of the Holy Spirit, I invited those who needed a miracle to come forward and assured the crowd they would witness the power of God. A number of deaf and mutes came forward, and when the first miracle happened, the crowd surged forward, almost suffocating some of the team members.

Immediately after we prayed for the sick, we distributed bags of beans and rice. What a blessing it is to fulfill the Matthew 25 mandate of Jesus, to "feed the poor, clothe the naked, visit the sick and imprisoned."

The Orphanage

Several team members visited an orphanage and prayed for Tullie, a 14-year-old boy with a blind left eye. They witnessed a progressive healing—he could see "men like trees walking." After continuing in prayer, Tullie was able to identify a small piece of candy, and said, "I see a sweet." He immediately began to cry, which caused all of the team members to break out in tears of joy as well. The supervisor of the orphanage said Tullie had been thrown into the city dump at six months old and his eye was pierced. Imagine not having sight in one eye for over thirteen years. What an amazing miracle!

Confronting the Powers of Darkness

Though we were met with much resistance at the evening crusade, (some of the stage and platform collapsed, injuring people) Friday night was truly the breakthrough we were looking for. Over 3,700 came forward for salvation and the baptism of the Holy Spirit. Lilongwe had never experienced anything like this before.

Before I could direct the new converts to a special area for further prayer and follow up, a backlash of demonic power erupted. Those who were demonized began manifesting and creating commotion in the crowd. Over one dozen demonized people, mostly women, were hurled onto the stage where they writhed around like snakes, screaming and flailing in every direction. I prayed for a woman, commanding the evil spirit to loose its hold on her body and mind. The evil spirit defied me, spit, and cursed me. I actually felt an evil substance, like poison, shooting up my arm. Thank God for the Blood of Jesus and His resurrection authority. By the end of the evening, all of the demonized were no longer victims but victors, all because of Jesus.

One of the more outstanding miracles was a local witch doctor who heard the radio broadcast of the crusade, and responded to the altar call. He also received a physical miracle in his body—oh yes, truly, greater is He that is in us, than he who is in the world.

Jesus Appears In the Crowd

Saturday was the final night of the crusade, and again, approximately 2,200 received Jesus in their hearts. I will never forget what happened. I saw an open vision of Jesus, clothed in a scarlet robe, walking among the new believers. Wherever Jesus was standing, dozens of people in that area fell under the power of the Holy

Spirit. The presence of God came as a glory cloud and hovered over the crusade grounds. Truly Malawi will never be the same.

Creative Miracles

Every evening the team prayed for the sick and cast out devils. During one of the evening crusades, a number of team members witnessed a creative miracle as an 18-year-old team member laid hands on a little baby's head, commanding the healing virtue of Jesus to flow into the body. The baby had what is called "water on the brain." His head was noticeably enlarged. Instantly, the head began to shrink back to normal size, to the amazement of the parents. To God be the glory! He does all things well.

Malawi, as well as many other African countries, is plagued with AIDS. At the crusades, I invited those afflicted with AIDS to come unashamedly and receive forgiveness and cleansing. Three different individuals (one who was listening at home on the radio) were tested by their doctors who pronounced them totally healed of this dreaded virus. AIDS can be beaten!

Hotel Supervisor Healed

At the hotel where we were staying, the grounds supervisor desperately wanted to attend the crusade meetings, but was unable to because of his conflicting work schedule. He was experiencing excruciating back pains, and during one of the evenings, was taken to the hospital hoping that some medication would alleviate the pain. However, nothing seemed to help.

He was taken back to the hotel lobby and heard the crusade over the radio. At the exact time he entered the lobby, I asked for those who needed healing to put their hand on the radio as a point of contact. He immediately felt the power of God surge through his back. There was no small stir among the staff in the lobby that evening as he shared his testimony again and again.

Is it true? Is Jesus the same yesterday, today, and forever? A little child, paralyzed from birth received a miracle and began to walk for the first time. As in Scripture, we were starting to see the sick "walking and leaping and praising God" (Acts 3:8).

I know that reading a big list of statistics can be boring, but remember that every number represents a person loved and touched by Jesus, a person whose life will never be the same! Here are the final totals from Malawi:

- Over 10,000 responded to the call of salvation
- Thousands received baptism in the Holy Spirit
- 124 Blind received sight
- 18 Healed of HIV (AIDS)
- 61 Healed from dreaded Malaria
- Over 120 deaf and/or mute heard
- 11 People healed from tumors
- 52 Healed of the "killer" Tuberculosis
- And many more miracles and healings

A TEAM MEMBER SHARES
Report by Shara Pradhan, Kansas City, MO

Perhaps these numbers seem distant or unfathomable. I hope that in the following accounts you can hear the heartbeat behind the multitudes, and see how God touched thousands, one precious life at a time. Here are a few accounts from my trip to Malawi.

God's Love for Muslims

One afternoon, we were at a school preaching and praying for the sick. The Lord whispered to me, "A 14-year-old girl is here who is Muslim and afraid of receiving Jesus because her family will persecute her."

Looking around at the beaming smiles and hungry hearts, I was a bit alarmed at how I would find this girl in the circle of faces. Holy Spirit highlighted one bright shining girl named Roshan. I asked her if she was Muslim. She said yes and told me that she was orphaned years ago and had to stay in the care of her very harsh, very Muslim (Sikh) grandma. Holy Spirit warned me, that Roshan was afraid to talk to me in the crowds for fear that her peers would squeal to her Grandma, and she would face painful repercussions. So I smuggled her on the ministry bus!

She was desperate for Jesus but petrified at the costly persecution facing her if she chose Jesus. Suddenly my leaders announced that we were leaving. A decision had to be made. Roshan decided that she wanted to accept Jesus. So we prayed together and then she had to leave. Holding her hand through the window, I pleaded with her to come to the crusade that night. We drove off, tears streaming down my checks. I was devastated at the thought of what awaited her at home.

Hours later, we arrived at the crusade; at least 50,000 people blanketed the fields. Roshan was waiting for me as I stepped off our bus! She brought her aunt and two little cousins (all Sikh Muslims!) who wanted to be healed from their full-blown AIDS. Her aunt's right eye was blind because of the HIV virus. We preached the Gospel to them and they accepted Jesus. Then we asked the Lord to heal her AIDS and fully restore her sight as an indication that the virus had left her body! We prayed fervently and nothing happened. My heart sank, and the crusade started so we were whisked to the stage.

On my knees, crying out to God for wisdom of what to do, I just worshiped Him. Then the Lord dropped one word into my spirit, "Prostitute!" This aunt definitely did not appear to be a prostitute; she was conservatively dressed in nice clothes. "Uh oh! Help God." I wavered, trying to decide whether or not to risk losing the relationship by offending her. Finally I asked her the question and learned her story.

Her husband had sold her into prostitution before he died! This trade was the only way she could support her family. Now both of her daughters had AIDS! After wrestling through worries about how she could ever take care of her family financially, she finally repented of prostitution and decided not to go back to this life of sin. We prayed and her sight was fully restored! Can you believe the kindness of God? Here was a partially blind, Muslim prostitute with AIDS and her two sick children not even looking for Jesus when He looked at the devastation the enemy wreaked in their lives and healed her!

Three Blind Women

One afternoon in a village, I was praying for a 90-year-old lady whose skin was weathered and cracked, and who was about 90 percent blind in both eyes. She loved Jesus desperately.

With fiery faith, I prayed for her for awhile and nothing happened. Distraught and desperate, I started crying. Immediately, the Lord reminded me of the account in the Gospels when He spit in the dirt, made mud, and used it as salve to heal a blind man.

"If you want to see healing, this is what you do. Why not today? Why not now?" So, I took some dirt, spit in it, made some mud and gently put it on her eyes. Seconds later, she started jumping up and down screaming, "Hallelujah! Hallelujah!" She could see!

Immediately, another lady with one blind eye approached us. In order to prove to the village that this was about Jehovah Rapha—not our American team—I had the 90-year old lady pray for the next blind lady and she received her sight!

Then another woman with only partial sight in both eyes approached the three of us. I wanted the saints to be encouraged to pray for each other after we left, so we all prayed, and she too was healed!

Johannesburg, South Africa—June 8-10, 2003

Johannesburg is a big modern city, a total change from Malawi, which was years behind. At night we ministered in church in a rough part of the city and during the day we did outreaches.

After a meeting one night I told the pastors to take us to the street children. Unemployment is so high (over 50 percent) that many children and adults live on the streets. It was about midnight when some team members bought food at a local grocery store, started making sandwiches and passing out food. The rest of the team just loved on the children and prayed for them. It was early morning before we returned exhausted to our hotel room.

There is continuing white/black tension in South Africa. We went to minister in a park where whites would never go. Even the pastors had never done anything like this before. The park was a high crime place—stabbings, shootings, carjackings, and drug dealing. Apparently, no insurance company would cover vehicles in that area.

While we were evangelizing there a crippled woman was miraculously healed. This woman was carted by her husband on something like a skateboard—a piece of wood on four lopsided wheels with a rope handle. She was completely healed and walked two blocks with the team. Many were saved and healed in that street outreach.

Open Market Ministry

Another day, during an open market ministry, 150 people were saved. These outreaches are my favorite. We chose a desperate, dark area of the city and set up a small sound system in the busiest area. Music always draws a crowd of people. So one of the worship leaders from church started off by singing and dancing to some upbeat worship songs. I preached, gave an altar call, and we all prayed for the sick. During two of these open-airs, the blind saw, the deaf heard, and the lame were healed!

Several weeks after returning from Malawi and Johannesburg, I was ministering in Kansas City when I asked several team members in the audience to share about the trip. I jumped for joy on the platform when I heard the following report which had just come in by e-mail:

TUBERCULOSIS WARD EMPTIED IN MALAWI!
JUNE 22, 2003
Report by Linda Pallone, Iris Ministries

Oh hallelujah!!! I just got word from Malawi of an incredible report and had to tell you right away!

Two weeks ago while in Malawi, Iris Ministries partnered with Fresh Fire Ministries to hold open-air meetings in the city of Lilongwe, Malawi for four evenings. I was in charge of organizing outreaches to take place during the day in which the Gospel was preached and food was distributed in each of seven locations. One of these locations was a "hospital" with very poor humanitarian and sanitary conditions. Many of the patients in this particular hospital had to sleep on the floor, and we found many desperate people there. We distributed food to every patient and every member of the hospital staff. This brought much joy and word of what we were doing spread throughout the city.

We also went through the entire hospital and prayed for every patient to be healed. Well, I've just received word that within 24 hours all the patients in the tuberculosis ward were healed and discharged from the TB ward!! All of them! There were over 65 patients in this ward, many of them on oxygen and in advanced stages of tuberculosis! Not one patient remained in the hospital!

More and more reports are coming in from people in Lilongwe, Malawi about how they were healed. God is so amazing! God is so good! There are many other testimonies...the next one I will send is regarding the salvation of 30 village chiefs!

I know that after reading these tremendous reports of revival, healing, and harvest, that you are no longer satisfied with the normal Christian life; there is a hunger in your heart to say, "God I want this anointing to come upon my life."

My purpose for sharing so many healing testimonies isn't just so you hear my story, but so you understand that Jesus is the same yesterday, today, and forever. I am just one of many first fruits of the promised healing revival the Holy Spirit has spoken about through many prophetic voices. A revival generation is still rising up as a healing army to the nations. My life is just one of many divine signposts pointing to the greatest times in church history yet to come.

CHAPTER 20

HOUND OF HEAVEN
ON DAD'S TRAIL

This is my dad's chance to tell his story. If you remember, our relationship wasn't very strong as I was growing up. Well, God is very gracious and this story has a very happy ending. If you've been to any of my meetings since September 2001, you've seen my dad ministering right along side me.

Sitting on the stairs in the church, I had no idea what to do. Everyone was worshiping and praying. This was totally foreign to me. I was at my first conference with Todd and I wondered, "Why am I here? What are all these people doing?" They were singing and dancing and praising the Lord. This was not something I was used to seeing. This was not like anywhere I had ever been before. The hairs on my arms were standing up; a cold chill entered my body. "What was this?" I had no explanation. "Was this my first experience of Jesus?" It was September 19, 2001 and from that day on my life would never be the same again. But I didn't know that yet. My name is David Paul Bentley and this is my testimony:

I was born in Toronto, Ontario, Canada in 1956. I had a 13-year-old brother and a 6-year-old sister. Both my parents worked but they still struggled financially. Even though it was hard they tried to keep us all fed and clothed.

In Toronto there was an outbreak of Tuberculosis. At this time a lot of people were isolated for signs of TB. My parents were both hospitalized for about two years. When I was about five-years-old my father passed away with tuberculosis. My mother couldn't care for us all. Much to her dismay she sent my sister and me to live with her sister on a farm outside of Toronto that was called Lang Staff.

As a five-year-old who had just lost his father, to now be taken from his mother was excruciating. This was something I will never forget. I ended up living with my aunt and uncle for about four years. My uncle was an alcoholic. He had his own family, two boys and one girl to take care of. There was not a lot of food there and they lived off of the land. He was not a nice man and treated me like an outsider. I was the youngest one living on the farm. It was too far to go to school so I never attended.

When I was about nine years old my mother remarried a man in Nappanee, Ontario. He already had children. They sent for my sister and me. There were two girls and one boy and the youngest was 14-years-old. His name was Jimmy and he was deaf and dumb. This was going to be even harder than normal. How do we communicate? We didn't get along at first but a while later I started to learn sign language to communicate with my stepbrother. (I didn't know that this would come in handy years later when I pray for the deaf.)

Summer was over and it was time to start school. I was nine and going to school for the first time. They decided to start me in grade one. I was in class with five, six, and seven year olds. Because of my size and age I became a bully, showing off, fighting, and getting into trouble. That was my way of getting attention. This only lasted for a year then they transferred me.

They decided to put me into classes with kids my own age and size. But I continued to fight. Learning was not a priority for me. I had to show these kids that I was tough. I would find the biggest kids and start a fight. I was transferred from one grade to the next even though I was failing classes. I was getting too old for primary or middle school, so they put me into high school. It was going to be tough now there were so many kids there. How was I going to be the bully? I tried to get into fights on a daily basis. One day I broke a student's leg. We were fighting in the hall, and I threw him down a flight of stairs.

I'd had a couple of warnings about fighting so I was suspended for two weeks. I didn't bother telling my parents. I had a friend living on a reserve and he didn't go to school so we started hanging out. We got a hold of a bootlegger and started drinking wine every day. Then we started smoking, so each day I took a few of my parent's cigarettes. It didn't take long until I got caught. My stepfather thought he would fix me and make me smoke a cigar. He didn't know that I had smoked them before. My friend and I would steal them from the drug store a couple times a week.

We started hanging out back of the bars and watched for people to put beer or anything of value in their cars.

Then we'd take it. Drinking, drugs, and stealing had become our daily activities. Being drunk and stoned made that two weeks go by fast. I went back to school and within two days I got a broken arm in a fight. Even with a broken arm I was still fighting. In gym class one day the teacher grabbed me from behind. I reflexively turned around and hit him in the nose with my cast. His nose broke.

I was blacklisted from all schools in Ontario. My life as a 15-year-old changed fast. Now I had all day every day to do what I wanted. My friend and I started drinking more and smoking more just to stay high. It was taking more and more just to get where we were the day before. Soon we were trying other ways to get high, we started inhaling everything we could find, it didn't matter what it was—glues, stolen gas from cars or lawn mowers, Cutex, etc. This was a new high.

One day three of us were in my stepfather's shed. We were all sniffing and drinking wine. One of my friends, Gary, said he had enough, that he was going to go home and commit suicide. We thought he was joking. About ten minutes later we heard a big bang. We ran to his house, but it was too late. He was lying on his back porch where he had shot himself in the head with his dad's shotgun.

This incident didn't have an effect on my behavior. By this time I was willing to try anything and everything. I was sent to a physiologist, but he just said I was an angry young man. At 16 I was well known by all the police. I was always in trouble. They decided to take me for a day stay at the Kingston Prison, as they did with a lot of kids who were in trouble. This is one of the most dangerous prisons in Canada.

That was a day that I would not soon forget. Now this tough kid didn't look so tough. Unfortunately, my behavior didn't truly change. I didn't want to go back to that place so I got a job in a bowling alley to get money so I wouldn't have to steal my cigarettes, liquor, and drugs. This lasted for a while, but I decided it was time to leave this small town where everyone knew what everyone else was doing. My brother was trying to be helpful and said I could move in with him. He tried to get me in school in Toronto but couldn't. I ended up getting a couple of different jobs. One was stocking shelves in a gas station. I was able to do this and still do drugs and booze daily. In Toronto there were even more kinds to try.

I started hanging out with my cousin. He was the leader of the Toronto Hell's Angels. There I tried marijuana and acid. I would get it from my cousin and even sell it to the people I worked with. Now my newest thing was pot and acid and alcohol. At nights I baby-sat my niece and drank vodka from the cupboard. Then I'd fill the bottle with water. I thought I was being very sneaky, but my sister-in-law figured it out.

At 17 I wanted away from my brother so a friend and I rented a place together. Now no one could tell me what to do. I went to the bars with my cousin and that started a new downward spiral. I got myself some false ID and started hanging out at the bars all the time. This would be where you could find me every day after work. On the weekends I would be there all day until I was so drunk they would kick me out. I started drinking beer for breakfast.

I met a girl who worked next to where I worked so we met daily at the bar. We stayed there until closing time every night. We started hanging out together all day and night. About a year later she became pregnant.

What to do? We took a holiday together to British Columbia to visit my brother. I fell in love with B.C. so we decided we would stay. We never went back to Ontario, not even to get our belongings. We married and settled in. This was hard for me as I liked being a single man, but I knew I had to take care of her and the baby that was soon to come.

I got a job in the mill. She thought this would give me a break from drinking for at least eight hours a day. I just had to learn how to hide my addictions. I hid my beer and pot in the garage where no one went but me. On my way home from work I couldn't pass the bar without stopping. Most of my drinking was hidden.

On January 10, 1976, Todd David Bentley was born. Now my life had changed, married and a new son—I was just 19. Now it was time to grow up fast. My job at a mill enabled me to take care of the family financially.

My wife was slowly losing her hearing. We couldn't communicate. Things went from bad to worse and we fought constantly. This gave me an excuse to even drink more. I stopped coming home and started hanging out in bars more and more. Soon we were separated.

Todd was now about five years old. We only got together on weekends but not for long periods of time. Todd and his mother moved to Newfoundland where he began school. When he and his mother moved back to B.C. I had already moved to Alberta with Darcia (who has been my wife for the last 20 years). During these years of living apart, Todd and I would not see each other for long periods at a time. This was not what I had wanted but divorce bring a lot of painful baggage. Through these years I still drank and did drugs daily. Todd and I were not as close as I had hoped and he had been told things about me that weren't true. This talk kept us apart even more.

As a rebellious young man he started getting in to trouble—stealing, setting fires, etc. until he was sent to jail. I thought that would straighten him out. But little did I know he was a lot like me! He was doing drugs and drinking, all the things I hoped he never would.

When he got out of jail we tried to get him back into school but that didn't work. I would see him just hanging uptown doing his thing. I told him if he was going to do drugs he should do them with me. At this time it seemed like a good idea. This would keep him from getting in to bad drugs on the street. We did drugs and drank together. This seemed to be an every day event. I now became my own son's drug dealer and bootlegger.

He was getting so carried away with drugs, he had lost all the jobs I got him. Now he was stealing my drugs and he had overdosed several times. He progressed to street drugs. We talked about it but that did no good. After his third or fourth drug overdose he just disappeared, all his belongings, everything we had given him in his apartment was gone. Even the furniture that was not his was gone.

I'd pretty much given up hope for him. Darcia and I figured the next time we heard anything about him it would be from the morgue or a prison. A year passed and he phoned me to say that he was reborn. Well I thought he was high, plus I didn't know what it meant to be reborn. He tried to explain it to me but I didn't believe.

The next time he phoned he told us he was getting married. This was not what I expected to hear. I still didn't believe he had turned his life around. I told him we couldn't make the wedding, but we would set up a honeymoon for them. I really didn't think he would get married, but he did. When Todd came to the island he had the most beautiful wife, Shonnah. We all spent a week together, the first time in years.

Todd started telling us about God. This was not the Todd I knew! At this time I told him I was not at all interested in, "his new God thing." Well Todd soon started a Ministry called Fresh Fire and he kept telling me about it. He sent me some tapes of his meetings. I watched with disbelief—people screaming, falling (pushed?) over and supposedly being healed. "What kind of scam is this?" I wondered. I thought he was in some kind of a cult. But, I had to admit he was doing great. This God thing had made him a happier person. I still didn't believe it, but if it made him happy that was great. Todd went on to have three children, which made me a proud grandpa. For many years Todd tried to teach me more about God, but I didn't think that was me.

At age 45 it had been almost 30 years that I had been drinking, doing drugs, and smoking cigarettes. I hadn't cut back over the years; in fact I did more than ever. I would still have my beer for breakfast, pot and beer at lunch; I was drinking about a dozen beers a day, and smoking more than a pack of cigarettes. For many years I thought I was getting away with all this. I was fooling my self thinking that Darcia didn't know what was going on. She knew, but she also knew that the more she tried to stop me the worse I would get. She stood by me for all these years, and I do thank God for her.

In December 2000, on Christmas Eve, we got a call from our son in-law. They had just taken my step-daughter, Barbie, to the hospital. A few days earlier at a doctor's exam they had sent her back home, thinking she just had a bad back. Two days later they rushed her

to the hospital and found that her appendix had ruptured days before. Darcia and I drove two hours. I
stayed with the two grandkids, Matt and Taylor. Darcia
went to the hospital.

At the hospital where they sent Barbie there was no
doctor who could help with her condition. She had so
much poison in her they told Darcia that there was
nothing they could do. They rushed her to the next
hospital where there was a surgeon. He said there was
nothing he could do for her, either. She told me to call
the family and let them all know. I phoned Todd and he
said he would pray, and told me I should do the same.
"Todd I don't know how to pray." He said to just start,
so I began to pray saying: "God, I ask you to save Barbie
from death. If you do this I will seek and search for
you." I prayed this over and over thinking, "Why am I
wasting my time doing this?"

The doctors told us that her chances of living were 30
percent at best. "Don't keep your hopes up." Barbie
went into a coma for two weeks. During that time I did
as Todd asked, and kept praying the same prayer every
day. On January 17, 2001 Barbie came home! That is a
day I will always remember. Thank you, Lord, what a
great birthday present!

A month later Todd's mother passed away. Todd asked
me to help him with the arrangements because he was
out of the country. This would be the first time Todd
and I would be together in a long time. A month after
her death my own mother passed away. This was a hec-
tic six months that I wouldn't want to re-live.

A month later driving home one day I had the strangest
thing happen. A voice out of nowhere spoke to me in
the car. This was not at all what I was used to. "DO

NOT FORGET YOUR PROMISES." I went home, lit a joint, and opened a beer. When Darcia got home I told her what happened. She said I should follow what I felt. She was hoping that she would see the same change come over me that came over Todd and she was afraid, but also excited because she knew I really needed a touch from God.

Todd called me and said he was coming to town for a couple days and wanted to get together. It turned out he had a position open in his ministry and wanted to know if I would work for him. I had been out of work since Barbie was in a coma. I had worked for this company 12 years and they let me go. After thinking about it for a while I said yes.

Driving to the airport the voice came to me, "DO NOT FORGET YOUR PROMISES." I called Darcia. "It happened again." (Later I realized that God was reminding me about my promise to seek Him out if Barbie lived.)

It was a new experience walking onto a job that I knew nothing about. Todd had me listening to all his teachings to find bad tapes and to fix them. I didn't realize I was being set up! I learned more about God everyday. But this was Todd's plan from the beginning!

On September 28, 2001 Todd prayed for me to quit smoking, drinking, and doing drugs. The next day God delivered me. No cravings; no withdrawals; all gone; thank you, Jesus.

I traveled with Todd to a couple of conferences. I'll never forget my first experience, which was with a demon-possessed woman. She was screaming, rolling, and biting at Todd. He asked me to help him with her. I was new at this and wondered, "Why not just knock her out and stop all this?" I held her down. Todd prayed and she calmed down some. But that wasn't the end of it—night after night the same thing would happen. The fourth night she came in and I thought she looked different. She was calm and happy. Then I knew what a difference God's power could make in the life of a person with a demon. She had been set free.

One night at a meeting in Ontario, Todd gave an altar call. Everything seemed normal when all of a sudden I was standing in the front of the church with a few other people. This was November 14, 2001. I gave my heart to the Lord that night. Still, I do not remember walking to the front. But I was there and have not regretted it since. The Lord has shown great mercy in my life and I am thankful for that day.

This was the beginning of a whole new life. The Lord was about to show me all I had been seeing in Todd's videos was true. I used to ask Todd, "How much do you pay those people to fall down?" My unbelief was about to change.

We were at a church in Toronto; Todd was calling people up for healing. There was a young lady sitting about six rows back who kept waving at me to come to her. After awhile I asked Ivan, who was Todd's disciple at the time, what I should do. He told me to go to her. She said that God told her if I helped her to the front and prayed for her she would walk. She had been in a wheelchair for 10 years. I laughed and went back to my seat. I told Ivan I thought she was crazy. I stayed in my seat but she kept waving. I went back to her and tried to explain that she couldn't walk because she was in a wheelchair. She insisted on me taking her up front and praying for her.

I sat back down and Ivan told me to do what she wanted. With not one ounce of belief I gave her my arm and kind of dragged her up front. She went down on the floor and took me with her. It appeared to me that she had fallen asleep, but she said, "Pray for me." I still didn't know how to pray for someone so I said the same sort of prayer I used when Barbie was sick. The woman said she "felt something," so would I please help her up. I did and she went back down, holding on to me even tighter than before.

After about 20 minutes she said she wanted to walk around the church. My thought was, "Yea, right. I bet you do." She asked if I would hold her hand, boyfriend and girlfriend style, and walk with her. We started to walk and WOW she was walking, slowly, but we actually walked around the church twice. Then she wanted to go up stairs. She did it! When we got to the top Todd and the whole congregation started to clap. This woman left the church walking and someone else was pushing her wheelchair. Praise the Lord! That was the first time the Lord used me.

The next night, at the same church, everyone was praying for people. Ivan told me to pray. I went to pray for a woman who had white blotches in both eyes. I watched every one else pray, they seemed to be touching the person they were praying for so I put my hands on her eyes. Then for some reason I thought I shouldn't do this. I took my hands away and looked at her. "Excuse me but did your contacts fall out?" The white was gone. She said she could see well. I thought she was joking but her friend said she had cataracts for 3 years and was almost totally blind. Well, I'll tell you, that experience sure helped boost my faith that God really does heal and that he can use anyone to do it.

I have been traveling with Todd for eight months now and have been saved for 18 months. Together we have been all over the world: India, Africa, South America, Mexico, Europe, and many other places. I have seen all kinds of healings and miracles, from headaches to limbs growing as well as the blind seeing, the deaf hearing, and the cripples walking. The only thing I haven't seen yet is the dead raised. But I know we will also soon see this because we ask people to bring the dead to our meetings.

If you're hungry for these experiences, come with Fresh Fire on an overseas crusade and you will see these things too. God bless you. I hope my testimony helps you to believe, even more, that God is the same today, and He does the same miracles as He did in the Bible. Let's go out and obey Jesus' command to His disciples: "Preach the Gospel, heal the sick, cleanse the lepers, raise the dead, cast out demons…" (Matthew 10:8).

Dave Bentley

CHAPTER 21

GET READY!

Let's talk about the incredible future that lies before us. God is getting ready to do amazing things. Get ready for supernatural visitation and open heavens—the supernatural is about to become natural. There's coming a release of an apostolic anointing, which I call the popcorn release into ministry, where men and women are going to be thrust into worldwide ministry overnight. Tomorrow you're going to go to work and the next day your city is going to be in revival. Can a nation be born in a day? "Can a country be born in a day or a nation be brought forth in a moment?" (see Isa. 66:8). Yes!

Get ready. There are things that are about to happen in the church that eye has not seen and ear has not heard and you can be part of it. Even if I told you, you wouldn't believe it. "For the earth will be filled with the knowledge of the glory of the Lord, as the waters cover the sea" (Hab. 2:14).

I want to share with you in more detail than I did in the opening chapter, the four aspects of what I believe will happen in our future and the future of the church.

1. HEALING REVIVAL

"And the inhabitant of the land shall not say I am sick" (Isa. 33:24). I believe that this verse is speaking of a time in the church where there will be such a level of healing anointing that no sickness or disease will touch God's people, just like when Israel came up out of Egypt. "He also brought them out with silver and gold, and there was none feeble among His tribes" (Psalm 105:37). Not one feeble or weak? Think about that, more than 3 million people healed after 400 years in oppression and bondage!

Kathryn Kuhlman prophesied that there would be a day when the church would say, "I am not sick!" and in some meetings every single person would be healed. Many others have prophesied a great healing revival in the end times, including John G. Lake. There will be a renewed focus on the message of repentance. Sickness and disease started with sin. In the beginning the Garden of Eden was paradise without sickness, disease, poverty or death. That was always God's plan for us! When sin entered the world then came sickness, disease, and death. "Therefore, just as through one man sin entered the world, and death through sin, and thus death spread to all men, because all sinned" (Rom. 5:12).

But with the resurrection of Jesus came a new law. Romans 8:1-2 states, "There is therefore now no condemnation to those who are in Christ Jesus, who do not walk according to the flesh, but according to the Spirit. For the law of the Spirit of life in Christ Jesus has made me free from the law of sin and death."

A new force is in motion today to empower us to live holy and be made righteousness. All the angels of Heaven are prepared to back up that law. "For the law of the Spirit of life in

Christ Jesus has made me free from the law of sin and death" (Romans 8:2).

We are redeemed from the curse of the law. "Christ has redeemed us from the curse of the law, having become a curse for us (for it is written, 'Cursed is everyone who hangs on a tree') that the blessing of Abraham might come upon the Gentiles in Christ Jesus, that we might receive the promise of the Spirit through faith" (Gal. 3:13-14).

Today God's will is Third John 1:2, "Beloved, I pray that you may prosper in all things and be in health, just as your soul prospers."

Most of the world's sickness and disease stems from turning away from God to other idols and false religions. Whole nations are under curses (see Deut. 28) because they have turned to other gods. When we examine the beliefs of countries in Africa, India, and South America, many are rooted in witchcraft or idol worship. In India alone, they worship over three million gods. I have been in many nations and have seen innocent children affected by poverty, famine, hunger, war, and sickness. I have grieved as I've driven down some streets and seen a temple on every corner. The innocent suffer because of the unrighteousness of governments and leaders.

In order for us to see a greater wave of healing in the church today there needs to be a renewed focus on repentance and personal holiness because many times our own sins of bitterness, envy, jealousy, unforgiveness, sexual sins, etc. are not only the roots but the hindrances to healings. In the coming healing outpouring, as people repent of their wilful sin and make a fresh commitment to holiness, then when healing is preached we will see more miracles.

James 5:15-16 says, "And the prayer of faith will save the sick, and the Lord will raise him up. And if he has committed sins, he will be forgiven. Confess your trespasses to one another, and pray for one another, that you may be healed."

The Lord has also showed me that as the Church and as nations repent of corruption and worldly ways and turn back to God, He will bring a mighty healing revival. Hosea 6:1-2 implores: "Come, and let us return to the Lord; For He has torn, but He will heal us; He has stricken, but He will bind us up. After two days He will revive us; on the third day He will raise us up, that we may live in His sight."

As repentance and the revival of righteousness sweeps through the church, so will more healings and miracles. Healing will take place supernaturally without the laying on of hands. In Jesus' ministry He healed every sickness and disease among the people. "When evening had come, they brought to Him many who were demon-possessed. And He cast out the spirits with a word, and healed all who were sick." (Matt. 8:16).

2. SAINT'S REVIVAL

Another thing we'll see in the future will be a saint's revival. God is going to do away with a clergy/layman mentality and raise up the saints—the Body of Christ—to do the work of the ministry. I strongly believe in the local church and godly leaders, the five-fold ministry and apostolic relationships built on trust and friendship. But, it will not be just the pastors or evangelists, but the saints released by God who will begin to preach the Gospel and heal the sick. It has always been God's plan that every believer gets involved in the ministry of Jesus. John 14:12 says, "He who believes in me, the works that I do he will do also; and greater works than these he will do, because I go to my Father."

I believe that when the early church was birthed, many ordinary people moved in signs and wonders. "The Apostles called out seven men full of good reputation and the Holy Spirit. They laid their hands on them. The number of the disciples increased greatly" (Acts 6:1-7). We all know Stephen, full of faith and power, was doing signs and wonders, but who were the rest in verse five? We never hear of them again or their works of power. But, I believe they flowed in an anointing just like Stephen. God is going to use the church deacons, business-men, cashiers, housewives, and children to work His great power—"nobodies," as it were, a nameless faceless generation. People we don't know, just like those chosen by the apostles, will flow in this anointing.

Through the Church God will show signs and wonders in the heavens and the earth. The Church will have the same power as Jesus over the natural elements—the winds and the sea obeyed Him. We will move into a ministry of wonders, fulfilling Joel 2:30-31. We will speak to limbs like Jesus did in Luke 6:10, when He said, "Stretch forth your hand." and it will happen.

The wonders we will perform will be like in the day of Elijah or Moses. We will walk in authority like Joshua who spoke, and the sun stood still. I don't just see healings and miracles, but signs and wonders of great proportion, which will jolt people from their busy lifestyles—the world will stop and see the glory cloud literally come down upon the Church just like it did with Moses. In some cities we will witness signs of the Lord's glory for days that will even capture the media's attention.

"These have power to shut heaven, so that no rain falls in the days of their prophecy; and they have power over waters to turn them to blood, and to strike the earth with all plagues, as often as they desire" (Rev. 11:6). This Scripture says, concerning the two witnesses, that they could do their signs as often as they desired. Now that's power! Pray it in. Let's believe God to confirm His word and trust us with the last days' anointing we'll need for the last days' harvest. The God of Abraham, Isaac, Jacob, and Moses will once again begin to show up in the Church just like He vis-ited His people in Old Testament times.

3. CHILDREN'S MINISTRY

I have seen a great move of healings and miracles by the hands of children. I had a vision of an eight-year-old boy with a Bible in his hand preaching with fire and boldness to thousands. He preached the word of the Lord, and the sick recovered in their seats. I see children being used to grow limbs working creative miracles by the spoken word and faith. Some children will become part of the prophetic Samuel generation as young as eleven or twelve years old.

We know that the Kingdom isn't in word only but in power. Children are going to move in the power of the Kingdom, drive out spirits, and heal the sick because the Kingdom is theirs. Jesus said in Matthew 19:14: "Let the little children come to me do not forbid them, for of such is the Kingdom of heaven."

4. LAST DAYS' ANOINTING OF POWER

I have seen a glimpse of the anointing that will be on the last days' church. We think the Book of Acts was glorious, but the glory of the latter house will be greater than the former. We are going out with a bigger bang than we came in with.

The end-time anointing is the Elijah anointing! The Elijah anointing turns the hearts of the nations to God like it did in First Kings 18, where Elijah called down fire on Mt. Carmel in a confrontation with the prophets of Baal. In these last days, it won't be Elijah as one man, but it will be the Spirit and anointing of Elijah working through the Church that will get the job done. We'll do miracles and signs like Elijah did. Some thought John the Baptist was Elijah the man, but they were actually seeing the Elijah-anointing on his life.

In Matthew 17 on the Mount of Transfiguration, the Father sent Moses and Elijah as a prophetic fulfillment and to show that Jesus was who He said He was. I believe as we near the second coming of Christ, God will again confirm the Church as His voice in the land. He will do this by bringing the spirit and power of Moses and Elijah upon His end-time army to release forerunners to prepare the way of the Lord and to prepare the nations for God.

> *"Behold, I will send you Elijah the prophet before the coming of the great and dreadful day of the Lord. And he will turn the hearts of the fathers to the children, and the hearts of the children to their fathers, lest I come and strike the earth with a curse"* (Malachi 4:5-6).

It will be a movement of the prophetic, power evangelism and healing that will turn nations to God—some in a day! I'll develop this is more detail in the next vision.

That hour is at hand and you need to reach out for this. The supernatural needs to be natural. It shouldn't be rare in the Body of Christ. I believe that those who are hungry to have an encounter with the Holy Spirit will be filled.

It's not about who you are, or your righteousness, it's not about your ability, it's about your availability. It's about the time we live in and a mighty God who has chosen to work through weak human vessels. The Spirit and the anointing have the power and the wisdom. "Not by might, norby power, but by my Spirit says the Lord of hosts" (Zechariah 4:6).

HOUSES OF PRAYER FACILITATE THE GREAT HARVEST

Recently I was in Latvia, a small Baltic state in Eastern Europe, formerly under Soviet rule. While traveling to an evening crusade I was caught up in an interactive vision. I saw the great harvest field already white. The angels were working in this field.

Then Jesus came to me. I knew in my spirit He was the Lord of the Harvest but He came to me dressed as the Good Shepherd (see John 10) and holding a staff. I wondered why the Lord of Psalm 23 was the Lord of the Harvest. Then I understood that this is not just about winning souls but also about discipling these same souls. Jesus doesn't want to just be Savior, but He also wants to be the great overseer of their souls and He wants to lead them into the depth of Psalm 23. He desires to restore their souls and to lead them beside the still waters.

Immediately these Scriptures came to my mind:

- Psalm 24:1, "The earth is the Lord's, and all its fullness, the world and those who dwell therein."

- Revelation 11:15, "The kingdoms of this world have become the kingdoms of our Lord and of His Christ, and He shall reign forever and ever!"

- Isaiah 40:15, "Behold, the nations are as a drop in a bucket, and are counted as the small dust on the scales; Look, He lifts up the isles as a very little thing."

- Psalm 2:8, "Ask of Me, and I will give you the nations for your inheritance, and the ends of the earth for Your possession."

This was a faith level where whole cities and nations can be saved in a day. The Lord said to me, "Todd, enter into My harvest power! It's the Harvest of Amos 9:13: "'Behold, the days are coming,' says the Lord, 'When the plowman shall overtake the reaper, and the treader of grapes him who sows seed; the mountains shall drip with sweet wine, and all the hills shall flow with it.'"

There is coming an acceleration of the laws of sowing and reaping. The seed will be planted and as soon as the seed is sown it will be reaped. There will be harvest until the days of sowing and sowing until the days of harvest—a holy overlapping of continual sowing and reaping. When this acceleration happens, men and women will cry out, "What must I do to be saved?"

As I continued to walk in the harvest, I noticed a tent in the field and asked, "Lord, what is that tent doing in the harvest and why does it look so old and ragged? It's not as glorious and golden as these fields." The Lord responded, "Todd, this is the tabernacle of David and it looks that way because, for many, prayer is so uninviting. It is a matter of perspective and priority. To many, prayer is tedious work but to others it is the glory. Most importantly the tabernacle releases the Amos 9:13 harvest."

In the Book of Acts, Paul, Barnabas, Peter, and their ministry teams are seeing tremendous harvest in cities. Churches are being planted and the Holy Ghost is falling on the Gentile believers as well as the Jews. In Acts 15 they meet for the Jerusalem council and give reports of the harvest and discuss whether Gentile believers need to be circumcised. In the midst of this, James quotes Amos 9:11-12:

> *After this I will return And will rebuild the tabernacle of David, which has fallen down; I will rebuild its ruins, and I will set it up; so that the rest of mankind may seek the Lord, even all the Gentiles who are called by My name, says the Lord who does all these things* (Acts 15:16-17).

I said, "God there it is again—the great harvest and the house of David." Night and day prayer, 24 hours a day, seven days a week is already taking place in the church. These houses of prayer are essential to the releasing of an end-time signs and wonders movement, healing revival, and the geographic healing centers.

THE HEALING CENTERS

I've already spoken about the many healing pools of Bethesda (like in John 5) that I've seen throughout North America and different countries. The grace of God will give us an outpouring of the rains of healing and miracles, until the power of God increases and we have a flood of miracle rain and many pools of healing. Once again great multitudes will come from all over the world to geographical healing centers just like God did in Spokane in the early 1900's with John Lake's ministry. This coming healing outpouring will be the forerunner to the great harvest.

ELIJAH ANOINTING

God has promised the spirit and power of Elijah in these last days. With the spirit and power of Elijah we also have a promised healing revival in Malachi 4:2: "But to you who fear My name The Son of Righteousness shall arise with healing in His wings; and you shall go out and grow fat like stall-fed calves."

The great prayer movement is the key to the release of the great healing revival that comes in the day of the Elijah spirit. But, before God releases the power to the church spoken of in Revelation 11:3, ("And I will give power to my two witnesses, and they will prophesy one thousand two hundred and sixty days, clothed in sackcloth") the Lord conducts an evaluation of the church in Revelation 11:1: "Then I was given a reed like a measuring rod. And the angel stood, saying, 'Rise and measure the temple of God, the altar, and those who worship there.'" The angel was to measure three things: the temple of God, the altar, and those who worship there. The temple can represent the believer's lives or the church, local, citywide or national. When the levels of worship, prayer, and intercession are right in the church, God will release His end-time power and the promise of the spirit of Elijah. Only when the bowls of Revelation 8:3-5 are full will God release His power:

> Then another angel, having a golden censer, came and stood at the altar. He was given much incense, that he should offer it with the prayers of all the saints upon the golden altar which was before the throne. And the smoke of the incense, with the prayers of the saints, ascended before God from the angel's hand. Then the angel took the censer, filled it with fire from the altar, and threw it to the earth.

And there were noises, thunderings, lightnings, and an earthquake.

God is checking the levels of intercession, worship, and prayer in the believer's life, in churches, in cities, and in nations. And when the levels are right, then He will give power to the two witnesses. The House of David model (24 hours, seven days a week, day and night prayer, worship, intercession, and intimacy with Jesus) are key to releasing power to prophesy and witness with signs following to the last days' generation.

Now here is the part of the vision that should encourage us, but also make us tremble. When I asked the Lord which cities would have these healing centers He replied, "Which cities want them? I am checking the levels of worship, intercession, and prayer. Their hunger will be the deciding factor. Every city has equal opportunity."

If there was ever a time to press in and go for it, now is that time. I repeat the question I asked at the beginning of the book. If not now, when? If not you, who?

BE ENCOURAGED

My life has been marked by the supernatural: my conversion; three-month visitation; move to Abbotsford; marriage; three months of soaking and God launching me into an international ministry with supernatural miracles, signs, and wonders.

Maybe you are reading this and getting discouraged or feeling jealous. You're asking the Lord why things like this haven't happened to you. I want to say, I'm a sovereign vessel in a sovereign time. God will use and anoint anyone, but He has a timetable and makes sovereign choices. God is God and we are not.

I encourage you who have been serving the Lord and waiting for the prophetic promises that haven't come true yet, to keep your eyes on Jesus and hold on to God's word. Jesus loves you as much as he loves me. I am only where I am because of faithful laborers who have come before me. Some of you were praying for this move of God while I was getting high on drugs! I'm the first fruit of your labor. It's the time in which we live, certainly not because of my righteousness. I'm looking forward to the day when Jesus will do greater things than He's done with me. That's my prayer for faithful pioneers and intercessors.

Don't forget the parable of the laborers in the vineyard (Matt. 20:1-16) who worked for one hour and got paid the same as those who labored all day. It's not what track you run on it's that you finish the track the Lord put you on. Fight the good fight of faith.

DARE TO ASK!

I wrote this book to help you understand what God is doing in our time and to encourage you to take steps of faith in areas where you may have been holding back. I want your heart to be inflamed with passion for Him and your vision to soar. I'm boasting in a big God. I'm excited about what He's done, but I'm more excited about what He's going to do. He wants the supernatural to be natural. In Daniel 11:32 the Lord says, "…the people who know their God shall be strong, and carry out great exploits." That refers to you too, not just me.

I encourage you to believe in a big God and dare to ask Him to fulfill big dreams. This has become a key verse for me: "Ask of Me, and I will give You the nations for Your inheritance, and the ends of the earth for Your possession" (Psalm 2:8).

God will do amazing things with ordinary people who totally yield their lives to Him.

MY PRAYER FOR YOU

After receiving several e-mail requests asking for the transfer of the healing anointing through the internet, I felt God prompt me to also release that anointing through this book for those who would come into agreement with a prophetic proclamation calling for the release of God's miraculous power.

First, let's establish a biblical precedent for this. We know that Jesus didn't have a laptop, and they weren't "online" in Jerusalem. But consider the story of the centurion who said to Jesus, "Just say the word, and my servant will be healed" (see Matt. 8:5-13, Luke 7:1-10). Jesus marveled at the centurion's faith, not because he believed Jesus could heal, but because he believed Jesus could heal even though He was far from the sick person physically. Jesus lavished praise on the centurion, saying he had more faith than anyone He had met in all of Israel! How would you like to have Jesus say that about you?

> *When Jesus heard it, He marveled, and said to those who followed, "Assuredly, I say to you, I have not found such great faith, not even in Israel...Then Jesus said to the centurion, "Go your way; and as you have believed, so let it be done for you." And his servant was healed that same hour* (Matthew 8:10, 13).

There are other New Testament examples of people getting healed "from a distance." The use of prayer cloths is one example. "Now God worked unusual miracles by the hands of Paul, so that even handkerchiefs or aprons were brought from his body to the sick, and the diseases left them and the evil spirits went out of them" (Acts 19:11-12). It's funny that people think it's an awesome miracle when they read about Paul using prayer cloths, but when we try the same thing, or a variation of it today, the same people think it's weird or "New Age-y."

In my ministry I've seen the healing anointing transferred through prayer cloths and over cell phones. People are regularly healed, even of AIDS, when listening to my crusades over the radio. One of my favorite stories about this comes from Cal Pierce at the Spokane Healing rooms. He tells how a woman in

Africa was healed when someone made a Xerox copy of a prayer cloth and faxed the copy of the cloth to Africa. What great faith! What great use of technology!

Can this transference really happen through a book? Well, if God can heal through cloths, over telephone lines and through radio waves, it's safe to assume He can also work through the printed page. In fact, He's done it before because people used to get healed when they would read John G. Lake's newsletters.

All these examples indicate what we really already know—God is not limited by time and space. If you believe that the anointing is transferable and you want to agree with me that a greater release of His healing virtue is going to come into your life, ministry and church, I want you to align yourself in simple faith with this prayer.

Here's the prayer I've prayed for you: "Father I ask You right now in the name of Jesus to begin to release Your transferable, tangible healing anointing for those asking for more of Your power on their life and ministry. I release healing virtue in Jesus' name! Let an explosion of miracles and healing come to them now. I pray that they would be forerunners; that they would lead the way into the coming healing revival. I pray that the spirit of Elijah would fall on them and that they would evangelize in the marketplace with signs and wonders confirming their message. Lord let them enter into the night and day prayers of the tabernacle of David. Father, pour out Your power and grace. I ask, that those agreeing with this prayer will receive a fresh anointing now in Jesus' name."

Now, I want you to pray out loud:

Father, I want more of the anointing transferred into my life. I believe now for the healing power to fill me. Give me a greater release of miracles, signs, and wonders from this day forward. Come now, Holy Spirit. I receive. I exercise my faith and declare that, "The same spirit that raised

Jesus from the dead lives in me." I will take this healing gift to the sick in Jesus' name.

From this day forward, I want you to believe God, to preach the Gospel, and to heal the sick! Go lay hands on them and see them recover. Start where you live, one person at a time. Now if you need a healing miracle get ready! If you are believing God for a healing right now I want you to put your hand on the part of your body that needs to be healed. Or, if there is someone in your house that needs healing, lay hands on them and pray this prayer of faith with me: "Come Holy Spirit; heal me now in Jesus' name. Father I command this sickness to go; I command my infirmity to go. Satan loose me now in Jesus' name. Touch me Jesus. I receive my healing!"

I stand in agreement with your prayer, "Lord, I pray that you would let Your healing touch every infirmity of those reading this book, right now." Rise up in Jesus' name and do something you couldn't do before. Move your body; thank God now for healing you.

Let's not stop. He's got an unlimited storehouse and He loves you—continue asking for more: "Father, I want to cooperate with what You are doing in heaven, so I pray for the Spirit of wisdom, revelation, council, and might. Please give me eyes to see and ears to hear so that I can understand eternal things. I earnestly desire spiritual gifts, especially that I would prophesy. Let it come right now, Lord—let the Holy Spirit fall with that prophetic mantle. Holy Spirit come! I want a download of the Spirit of prophecy.

"Lord give me the word of knowledge for my workplace and for my school. Let me go into the marketplace with Your anointing, authority, and mantle. Let me hear Your word, wherever I am, whenever the lost and hurting need

Your loving touch. Oh God, let your mantle fall on me for healing and for prophetic evangelism.

"Lord, thank you for the coming power, miracles, healings, signs, and wonders. According to Your word Father, as I speak words of faith, I can see supernatural manifestations. Let the authority and spirit of Elijah come again— let it come into my life. Surprise me Lord, it's not by my might or power but it's through Your Spirit.

"Let me produce 100-fold fruit that remains for your Kingdom. Help me to do exceedingly, abundantly above all I can ask or think for Your glory. Lord, draw me into night and day intercession too. I want to help fill those golden bowls to hasten Your coming. Let me not grow weary; open my eyes to see the power and impact of my simple prayers on the lives of others.

"Thank you, Father for answering this cry of my heart."

PRAYERS

Now, here's a tear-out sheet of prayers. Place it on your mirror, refrigerator, or any place you think you'll see it often! Pray these prayers every day and see what the Lord dos in your life over the next year!

1. *I want more of the anointing transferred into my life. Father, I believe now for the healing power to fill me. Give me a greater release of miracles, signs and wonders from this day forward. Come now Holy Spirit, I receive. I exercise my faith and declare that, "The same spirit that raised Jesus from the dead lives in me." I will take this healing gift to the sick in Jesus' name. Thank You Lord.*

2. *Come Holy Spirit, heal me now in Jesus' name. Father, I command this sickness to go; I command my infirmity to go. Satan loose me now in Jesus' name. Touch me Jesus. I receive my healing!*

3. *Father, I want to cooperate with what You are doing in heaven, so I pray for the Spirit of wisdom, revelation, council, and might. Please give me eyes to see and ears to hear so that I can understand eternal things. I earnestly desire spiritual gifts, especially that I would prophesy. Let it come right now Lord—let the Holy Spirit fall with that prophetic mantle. Holy Spirit come! I want a download of the Spirit of prophecy.*

4. *Lord, give me the word of knowledge for my workplace and for my school. Let me go into the marketplace with Your anointing, authority, and mantle. Let me hear Your word, wherever I am, whenever the lost and hurting need Your loving touch. Oh God, let your mantle fall on me for healing and for prophetic evangelism.*

5. *Lord, thank You for the coming power, miracles, healings, signs, and wonders. According to Your word Father, as I speak words of faith, I can see supernatural manifestations. Let the authority and spirit of Elijah come again—let it come into my life. Surprise me Lord, it's not by my might or power but it's through Your Spirit.*

6 *Let me produce 100-fold fruit that remains for your Kingdom. Help me to do exceedingly, abundantly above all I can ask or think for Your glory.*

7. *Draw me into night and day intercession. I want to help fill those golden bowls to hasten Your coming. Let me not grow weary, open my eyes to see the power and impact my simple prayers have on the lives of others.*

INDIVIDUAL TESTIMONIES

Here are more testimonies from people of all ages that have been on a Fresh Fire Mission's trip. The first testimony is from a self-proclaimed, "grandma type" and the others are from young people, men, and women of various ages and backgrounds. There's a place for everyone in the harvest!

Patricia Mason (Spring Hill, Kansas)

I am a woman who is a "grandma" type. But I told God I wanted to re-fire and not retire, and He met me at that season of my life. It was totally awesome what I saw in Malawi and South Africa. God used just little nobody people like me to open blind eyes and bring deliverance to people who had been deep into witchcraft. I was used a lot in ministering deliverance especially to young people and children, just pouring out motherly love to them and seeing them change in the spirit. Mothers lined up for me to just bless their infants and I believe the Lord released destiny to them as we laid hands on the future of Africa these young ones represented. I will never be the same seeing God perform miracles of all kinds through Todd, his family, and us, his team—it was amazing and over the top. I think I was one of the oldest ones on the team and I loved every minute of it. No one discriminated against me because I was a senior citizen—they just loved me.

Lindsay Larson (Portland, Oregon)

Hey, I went to Mexico with Todd and a bunch of other youth in July. That mission trip changed my life. Before I went I never felt comfortable worshiping God or talking about God around my parents even though they were Christians themselves. After I got back from Mexico I realized I was totally free. I worship God in church, at home, and I talk about him with my parents all the time. I even spend more time praying and seeking God. I love it. I would go on another mission trip with Todd in a heartbeat. God bless you to the fullest!

Kevin Basconi (Infirmity Prayer Service, Bluefield, WV)

I could write a book about how Todd's ministry changed my life! However, I will put together a couple of short paragraphs. I first met Todd Bentley in a very small church in Newfoundland, Canada, November 2001. During those meetings I was healed of near deafness, a ruptured disc in my spine, and heart and lung disease. Today I have perfect hearing, (had it tested), and have not suffered any back pain for nearly three years. On the night of November 26th, 2001, at 10:37 P.M., after Todd prayed for me and released the healing anointing, I received a visitation of the Lord Jesus which lasted for nearly five hours. Since that night, I have walked in "the Book of Acts" on a daily basis and been released into ministry. I see Jesus heal all types of infirmity in my ministry including around 22 people healed of total blindness, cataracts dissolved, several deaf ears opened, mutes speaking, and documented cases of AIDS and cancer healed. I have seen Jesus touch paralytics and raise them up, I have witnessed legs grow more than two inches in length, spines straighten, fingers and toes grow, withered hands restored, and, recently, I saw a blind man, who had no orb, grow an eyeball and have his vision restored. However, the greatest miracle of all is that the Lord has allowed me to lead about 1,380 people to Him.

The only miracle I have not witnessed is the dead raised, and I believe God for that this year. The Lord has supernaturally opened doors for me to minister all over North America, and beyond, confirming his word with signs following. Todd imparted the word of knowledge, and I receive detailed downloads from the Holy Spirit on a daily basis including types of illness, how injuries occurred, many times with dates and names, as well as accurate prophetic words of encouragement. I have never had someone who responded to a word of knowledge that Jesus did not touch and heal. I give God all glory for these things. I believe that Todd is a forerunner of the coming move of God in the younger generation. He is called to release this generation into such miracles, signs, and wonders that the four walls of our churches will not be able to contain them! I consider Todd to be my mentor and spiritual father even though I am 44 years old.

Jim Drown (Atlanta, Georgia)

I was at Todd's meeting in Atlanta, Georgia about 3 1/2 years ago. I had a growth on my inner thigh that really hurt badly, especially when I walked. I didn't get specific prayer from Todd, just the general prayer for everyone. When I woke up the next morning the growth was gone.

I'd been reading books about John G. Lake and had been asking for a powerful experience with the Holy Spirit, wanting that healing anointing. Todd was the closest thing I'd seen. I started listening to all his tapes and going to more of his meetings and he's right, the anointing is transferable and tangible.

Now I have confidence to do what God has called me to do. We've been doing crusades or meetings about once a month either on our own or with Fresh Fire. We've done several crusades in South

America this year and have seen miraculous healings with thousands coming to the Lord.

Ardena Shipp (Canada)

I had been really seeking God's direction in my life. God directed me to take this trip. He provided finances for me that I didn't have which was a miracle. I went on the trip thinking, I know that this is a God-directed thing because I would not just decide to go to Mexico without my friends, and I would not just decide to go on a trip like that out of the blue. I am not that adventurous and I am not usually a risk-taker. But God is changing me. I prayed that God would teach me about healing and that He would use me to bless others. Praying for others on my own was an easy thing for me, but when I would go to pray in groups I would feel bound up. The first night we were in Mexico Todd called us to go and pray with the sick. I remember praying "God help I can't do this without you." We went and prayed for a young girl with a lump in her breast. The lump got smaller as we prayed. We kept praying for her, and I felt like I should pray for emotional healing. I was like, "God I don't even know this girl, if this is You, You have to confirm it." The translator suddenly says, "She needs emotional healing." It was so cool—that was all it took to release me to trust that what I was hearing was the direction of the Holy Spirit. It gave me a confidence to pray with boldness for people all week, and it has continued since I returned home. I am walking in an incredible knowledge that my God is a God who heals and one that I can place my hope in. We will see the captives set free and people healed.

Jessica Maldonado (Gardena, California)

I've traveled with FFM to Tanzania, Malawi, and South Africa in the summers of 2002 and 2003. Traveling with Todd Bentley has changed my life drastically. The spiritual covering that we ministered under allowed me to move in supernatural ways I had never experienced before. I prayed for the blind, deaf, and crippled and they were healed. My faith grew by leaps and bounds in a matter of seconds and *increased rapidly over the following two weeks that we ministered to-gether. It was out of this world!*

I always believed that we served the God of the impossible. However, I had never seen Him do the impossible through me. I was blown away and loved every minute of it. I preached at a church of approximately 60 members on a Sunday morning. The Lord used me to prophesy over people. It was like a chain reaction, one after the other non-stop. I didn't know what hit! It had to have been the Holy Spirit because it certainly wasn't me.

Traveling with Todd and the Fresh Fire team has changed my life, expanded my faith, and built life-long relationships. I've enjoyed being part of a ministry that truly moves in the full Gospel of Jesus Christ and I can't wait to do it again.

Judy Desjardins (Springfield, Massachusetts)

I went to Goma, DRC, Africa with Fresh Fire in March 2003. Afterward, I wrote a 16- page report. I was so moved I spent months weeping over Africa, trying to understand all I experienced. I hear the children's voices in my mind's ear still. I see their eyes looking at me. I have never seen such desperation and at the same time so much faith as I saw in those eyes.

The anointing that is on Todd is transferable. My husband and I prayed and God moved with power, healing blind eyes, tumors, fevers, and every sort of sickness. I have faith I never knew I had. We prayed for rain to stop and it did, convincing many that the witch doctors were not as powerful as our God. Many miracles happened.

The last person I prayed for was a believer in Rwanda named Peter. He asked us to pray for his daughter, Glory. This man spoke perfect English. He said a man with AIDS had raped his daughter, and his wife was fasting and praying for the test results to come out negative. When I asked how old his daughter was, he said 2 years old.

This wrecked me. I knew that I could never go back to life as usual. The call of God on my life compelled me to change. I am planning another trip to Africa now. I am going on missions trips until Jesus comes. It was the best choice I made in my life. My husband agrees.

Cliff Pash (Lawrence, Kansas)

When I traveled with Todd Bentley, I saw God work in the same way that He did in the Bible. I believe that every believer should accompany somebody such as Todd on a ministry trip. Being a part of a large Crusade is exciting enough, but to see the miracles, the healings, and the manifestations of the power of God as He moves through a crowd is an experience that every Christian must have. Then, to pray for people under the anointing that God has put upon Todd Bentley, and see our God move and break into lives and change them causes the whole Bible to come alive in ways my 30 years of being a Christian never really prepared me for.

For the most part, we are a people who are filled with such doubt and fear and unbelief. While we believe that God exists and that He has the power, most of us have never experienced that power, nor do we believe God would ever manifest Himself through us. To watch tumors disappear, to pray for a woman who was blind for 30 years and see her receive her sight back, and to watch as a whole deaf school receives prayer and 28 out of 32 get healed. Well, all doubt, fear and unbelief have just melted away and I am now filled with an awe of God that just continues to grow.

My wife and I have been in business for ourselves for over 20 years. Our world is being rapidly changed as we find God working through us in ways we had only talked about or dreamed about before. We are being called to ministry work in Uganda and Kenya—that could have never happened years ago. The purpose for which we were created and the works we have been called to are finally being fulfilled.

Debbie Lenz (Columbia, Missouri)

Thirty-three years ago I took three years of high school Spanish hoping to travel to Mexico on a mission trip. My 12 year old daughter and I both saw the "Youth Outreach to Mexico" on Todd's website and God quickened it in our hearts. Although I was no longer a youth at 50 years old, and my daughter was only 12, we began to pray about it.

Neither one of us will ever be the same again! Todd has an amazing heart for God and freely imparts everything that God has given him—so we got to do "the stuff!" We saw miracles, healings, deliverances, and salvations as we watched deaf ears open, tumors leave, lung conditions healed, cancer healed, gang members saved, people receive the baptism of the Holy Spirit, and demons cast out!

While we were in Reynosa, I realized I did not really have a heart for the lost, but I wanted one. The Holy Spirit did that for me. I began to weep uncontrollably as I looked over the homes in the village and realized there were precious people that did not know the saving power of Jesus Christ. I have an intense longing to return and minister in the streets of Reynosa, but now I also have a longing to go into the streets of my own city and see the same things!

I came away with a larger vision of the IMMENSITY and the POWER of God's love. God's heart is that the Holy Spirit would be released in power, that Jesus would be exalted in the earth and that all people would come to know the Father's love. Todd asked me if the trip had met my expectations, and I had to be truthful and tell him, "No, it did not." Then I continued, "It so far exceeded anything I could have ever imagined, or hoped for, or even dreamed about that I can hardly contain *what He has done in me!" Would I do it again? Absolutely! In fact, we are already praying about when the Lord will have us return to Mexico with Todd.*

COME SEE THE WORLD WITH US!

Fresh Fire Ministries is an international ministry called to global harvest. Todd Bentley and his team take God's saving, healing, delivering power to the nations. Todd and his team conduct healing crusades throughout Africa, India, South America, Europe, and beyond. Thousands have been saved, healed, and delivered.

Todd preaches the word of God with the power and demonstration of the Spirit—God confirms His word with signs and wonders following. God has released an increase of the healing anointing into Todd's life and the blind see, the deaf hear, and growths dissolve as Jesus heals sickness and disease.

The harvest has never been so ripe, and we are praying for laborers to go on these crusades to help bring in souls for the Kingdom of God. Literally, dozens of nations have been calling us, and urging us to come and hold pastors' and leaders' conferences in the mornings, and crusades in the evenings.

Whether you're a housewife, student, or pastor, there's room for everyone. It seems wherever Fresh Fire Ministries goes, and whatever nation we are in, Matthew 10:7-8 is fulfilled. The sick are healed, the spiritually dead are raised (and we are believing for the physically dead to be raised as well!), devils are cast out, the lame are walking, and the blind are seeing. Without a doubt, we are fulfilling Acts chapter 29, experiencing the very same miracles as the early disciples did!

We have great anticipation, believing the Holy Spirit is going to double our efforts in the area of miracles, signs, and wonders, and in the giving of prayer and financial partners.

Todd has been impressed by the Holy Spirit to include humanitarian aid in many of their overseas crusades. We believe it is important to minister to the whole man—spirit, soul and body.

The many partners and friends of FFM are shaking the kingdoms of darkness because of their passionate praying and giving. I guarantee your spiritual life will never be the same after coming on a crusade with Todd and the FFM staff. Your life will be absolutely "wrecked" for Jesus! We trust that you'll impart that fire and passion back to your local churches.

We at FFM desire to work in close association with the pastors and their local congregations. If you have any questions about us, or are considering sending those from your church, (i.e., youth groups, college and career groups, etc.), please don't hesitate to contact us. If we can be of any service to you, it would be an honor and a privilege. Together, let's reap a worldwide harvest for the King of kings and the Lord of lords!

Pastor Ken Greter
Missions Director-FFM

If God is touching your heart to be a part a FFM crusade you can call for information at our

U.S. office, 816-761-0033 or
Canadians call 604-853-9041.
E-mail missions@freshfire.ca or ken@freshfire.ca.

FRESH FIRE 🔥 MINISTRIES

Fresh Fire Ministries is an international ministry called to global harvest. Todd Bentley and the FFM team take God's saving, healing, and delivering power to the nations of the world, sparking revival fires and equipping the body of Christ in power evangelism and healing ministry. FFM conducts healing crusades throughout Africa, India, South America, Mexico, Europe and beyond. Hundreds of thousands have been saved, delivered and miraculously healed. Each year, Fresh Fire also hosts several conferences, teaching schools, and anointing services, accommodating the training and equipping of thousands.

Fresh Fire is also active in humanitarian and mercy ministry, communicating the gospel of Jesus Christ, not only in word and power, but also in compassionate action. This practical ministry includes the building of orphanages and homes, feeding outreaches, providing medical supplies and treatment, and clothing distribution.

Our vision is to see people revived in a new passion for Jesus, burning with the fire of evangelism to reach the lost. We achieve this goal through conferences and training schools, the Jesus Road School Intern Program, the Supernatural Training Center seven-month equipping program, and short term missions trips to the nations.

For more information about:
Todd Bentley and Fresh Fire,
FFM missions trips, ministry partnership, and all of our
resource products, please visit our website.

Fresh Fire Ministries
P.O. Box 2525 Abbotsford, BC, Canada V2T 6R3
Phone: (604) 853-9041 Fax: (604) 853-5077 Email: info@freshfire.ca
www.freshfire.ca

TODD BENTLEY RESOURCES
FROM
FRESH FIRE MINISTRIES

CHRIST'S HEALING TOUCH - VOL. I
Understanding How To Take God's Healing Power To The World
BOOK ~ by Todd Bentley

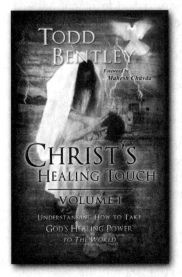

Christ's Healing Touch is written as a complete war manual on the healing ministry, so you, like Jesus, can heal all who are "oppressed by the devil" (Acts 10:38), and with God's power, "destroy the works of the enemy" (1 Jn. 3:8). Together Volumes I & II will help give you a complete theological understanding of healing and will impart a new passion and anointing for doing the supernatural works of Jesus.

"Todd Bentley is a man from outside the camp, who God is using to actually embarrass many who have been in the ministry for a long time (and many who have much training). May Todd's life, ministry, and books provoke us to a holy jealousy and stir in us a desire to see and experience more of the biblical promises in our lives. I recommend this book as one which will increase your faith and understanding regarding the ministry of healing and the miraculous. I am going to add it to the reading list for my interns."

~RANDY CLARK, Founder and President of Global Awakening
Mechanicsburg, PA, USA

"Todd's book, Christ's Healing Touch, is dynamic, informative and powerful. I highly recommend it."

~DR. CHE AHN, Senior Pastor, Harvest Rock Church, Pasadena, CA, USA

TODD BENTLEY RESOURCES
FROM
FRESH FIRE MINISTRIES

DEVELOPING YOUR SEER GIFT
How to See in the Spirit
6 CD TEACHING SERIES ~ by Todd Bentley

In this dynamic new series about seeing in the spirit, Todd will teach you how to grow in your prophetic giftings, and how to develop a keen spiritual sensitivity so that you'll reach the lost with the gospel in an effective way that will make them hungry to know God.

SUPERNATURAL REALMS OF HEAVEN
19 CD or DVD TEACHING SCHOOL ~ by Todd Bentley
*Comes with a 110 page student manual

This exciting school by Todd Bentley and Fresh Fire Ministries combines teaching on prophetic ministry with instruction on how to engage the revelatory realm of Heaven. This tape series consists of 18 hours of teaching in which Todd shares and imparts everything he has learned and experienced in the area of prophecy and revelation. Todd shares many of his prophetic experiences and teaches how to activate spiritual senses.

The manual will help you follow the lessons and study many of the related scriptures. Saints, get ready to fly like an eagle into the supernatural realm! This tape series will help launch you there.

TODD BENTLEY RESOURCES
FROM
Sound of Fire

MARINATING ... *Pickling in God's Presence*
SOAKING CD ~ by Todd Bentley

This CD is sure to take you into the glory and presence of God. You will hear Todd speaking powerful soaking prayers over inspiring instrumental sounds and sweet female vocals. This CD is for those who want to be saturated with the presence of the Holy Spirit and whose hearts long for deep intimacy with Jesus. During recording, Todd experienced visions and visitations of heaven. Todd and others present in the recording studio felt the tangible presence and anointing of the Lord in a new and exciting way. This anointing is transferable and is definitely captured on this very special recording.

SOAKING IN THE SECRET PLACE
SOAKING CD ~ by Todd Bentley

If you have ever heard Todd's teaching on the Secret Place (Soaking), or as he puts it, pickling in the presence, then this prayer CD will help you come into the Father's House and sit at the feet of Jesus. Join Todd on a journey into the Presence of God with prayers from the bible and prayers that come from a deep passion and longing for Him. This is a meditative, contemplative CD that combines piano style music and numerous sounds such as: rain, flute, trumpet, shofar, and more, for a deep prayer experience.

*Both of the CD's above are also available in **instrumental versions** which do not contain any prayers or vocals on them, only the music.*

FOR ORDERS:
PHONE: (250) 245–7003   EMAIL: soundoffire@shaw.ca
www.soundoffire.com